HICK

HICK

THE TRAILBLAZING JOURNALIST
WHO CAPTURED
ELEANOR ROOSEVELT'S HEART

by **SARAH MILLER**

RANDOM HOUSE **STUDIO** NEW YORK

A note on language:
In Lorena Hickok's time, words to describe sexual orientation and gender identity were limited, as well as taboo. If Hick ever described or defined these aspects of her identity, that information has yet to come to light. The meaning of the words she did have at her disposal have also evolved significantly in recent years, and will no doubt continue to evolve. These facts have led me to choose the present-day umbrella term *queer* to describe Hick and the other women in these pages who had same-sex relationships. Once a slur, *queer* has metamorphosed into an inclusive term for any and all members of the LGBTQIA+ community willing to embrace it.

Text copyright © 2025 by Sarah Miller
Jacket photograph copyright © 2025 by Fotosearch/Getty Images

All rights reserved. Published in the United States by Random House Studio, an imprint of Random House Children's Books, a division of Penguin Random House LLC, New York. Random House Studio with colophon is a registered trademark of Penguin Random House LLC.

Visit us on the Web! rhcbooks.com

Educators and librarians, for a variety of teaching tools, visit us at RHTeachersLibrarians.com

Library of Congress Cataloging-in-Publication Data is available upon request.
ISBN 978-0-593-64909-1 (trade)—ISBN 978-0-593-64910-7 (lib. bdg.)—ISBN 978-0-593-64911-4 (ebook)

The text of this book is set in 11.8-point Dante MT Pro.
Interior design by Cathy Bobak

Printed in the United States of America
1st Printing

The authorized representative in the EU for product safety and compliance is
Penguin Random House Ireland, Morrison Chambers, 32 Nassau Street, Dublin D02 YH68, Ireland,
https://eu-contact.penguin.ie.

I love you & you've made of me so much more of a person
just to be worthy of you.

—Eleanor Roosevelt to Lorena Hickok

CONTENTS

PROLOGUE

March 3, 1933
Mayflower Hotel, Washington, DC

ASSOCIATED PRESS STAR REPORTER LORENA HICKOK—HICK, AS she liked to be called—was just thinking about getting herself some dinner when the telephone in her hotel room rang.

"Franklin is tied up," Eleanor Roosevelt's voice said. An endless stream of people were flowing in and out of the president-elect's room in a flurry of last-minute inauguration preparations, the first-lady-to-be explained. To her surprise, she was alone. "Would you mind coming over and having dinner with me?" Eleanor asked.

Hick didn't have to think twice. There was no one she'd rather be with, no one in the world she loved more, and chances to be alone with Eleanor Roosevelt—already scarce—would become rarer yet the minute Eleanor's husband, Franklin Delano Roosevelt, took the oath of office the following day. Everything about their relationship might be about to change, but here, like a gift, was one more moment to share.

Hick sailed through the swarm of reporters in the Mayflower's lobby and out to the side entrance, where the Secret Service stood guard. Unlike the other reporters, she slipped past the agents with hardly a murmur. Not only was Hick's face familiar to the Secret Service by now, but they knew Mrs. Roosevelt was expecting her.

Lorena Hickok was perched at the apex of her career. She had interviewed queens, governors, starlets, explorers, and divas. Her name had appeared above the fold in the *New York Times,* and her articles were hailed as some of the best in the nation. She had covered every kind of beat, from sports to politics, in an era when most of her female colleagues had been relegated to writing columns on tea parties and wedding gowns. The next day, she would interview the first lady of the United States, in the White House itself—a feat no journalist of any sex had ever pulled off. "I was just about the top gal reporter in the country," Hick later said of her standing that night. "I was good, I knew it." It had taken her twenty years to get there.

Outside the Mayflower, the country roiled on the edge of financial hysteria. The crash of the stock market in 1929 had wiped out fortunes of investors and businesses alike, and the intervening three years had only strengthened the crash's calamitous reverberations. On the eve of Franklin Delano Roosevelt's inauguration, one-quarter of the nation's workforce was unemployed. Cities like New York and Chicago did not have the funds to pay their workers. Frantic citizens rushed to the banks to empty their accounts, desperate to get enough cash to see them through whatever hardships were still to come. The banks, in turn, had panicked and snapped their doors shut, trapping people's savings inside. Outgoing president Herbert Hoover had all but begged Franklin Roosevelt to join him in implementing bipartisan actions to stop the downward spiral.

FDR had refused. Any decisions he made to quell the crisis would be his, and his alone. Roosevelt wanted no taint of his predecessor's disastrous administration upon his own policies, even if it meant subjecting the American people to a few more days of unbearable uncertainty. The risk and the menace of the people's mounting fear were enormous.

The nation's mood hung heavily over the presidential suite that night, clouding any hopes Hick had of soaking herself in the companionship and intimacy she and Eleanor had so often shared before.

Dinner arrived and sat mostly uneaten on the table between them.

Both women were fidgety and inclined to pace. Neither of them could focus. Even Hick's feeble attempt to outline their interview for the next day failed. "Anything could happen," Eleanor said more than once. "How much can people take without blowing up?"

Advisors came and went from Franklin's sitting room next door, keeping him apprised of the escalating crisis. Hours after Hick arrived, FDR sent his inaugural address in for his wife to preview. Eleanor read it aloud, including the line that would ring down through history: *Let me assert my firm belief that the only thing we have to fear is fear itself.*

"It's a good speech, a courageous speech," Eleanor said to Hick when she'd finished. "It has hope in it. But will the people accept it? Will they believe in him?"

At that moment, Lorena Hickok stood at a crossroads. "There I was," she recalled long afterward, "a newspaper reporter, right in the middle of what, that night, was the biggest story in the world." Hick could have leaked the highlights of the inaugural address to the Associated Press, informed papers from coast to coast who the president was conferring with and what plans they were preparing to shore the nation up. No reporter in American history had ever had such an opportunity.

The thought never crossed her mind.

All Hick could think about was Eleanor, and the magnitude of what lay before this woman she loved above all others. The weight of Eleanor's worry, not only for her husband, but for the people of the United States, occupied every atom of Hick's concern, rendering Hick oblivious to the professional dilemma staring her in the face.

☙

It was sometime close to three or four o'clock in the morning when Eleanor's son Jimmy came in. "They've all left," he said. "Pa's going to bed." Eleanor excused herself to say good night to her husband. Even then, with no one in the room to hinder her, Hick did not tiptoe to the telephone to report all she'd heard. Instead, she slipped off her dress and shoes, put on the dressing gown Eleanor had lent her, and lay down on one of the twin beds. By the time Eleanor returned, Hick was asleep.

"That night," Hick later reflected of herself, "Lorena Hickok ceased to be a newspaper reporter."

PART ONE
LORENA

CHAPTER 1

NO HEADLINES PROCLAIMED HER BIRTH ON MARCH 7, 1893. Alice Lorena Hickok was one of a thousand or so babies born in the United States that day and attracted no particular notice outside her own family. There was not one single reason to suspect that this baby girl—born over a creamery in East Troy, Wisconsin, to a butter maker and his wife—would one day reside at the White House.

❧

From the very first, Lorena proved herself a keen and quiet observer. Even as an infant, she watched and listened, slowly, carefully absorbing the sights and sounds that orbited her. As she thought of it years later, she was acclimating herself to the world, learning how things felt, moved, smelled, tasted, the way babies of every species must. But Lorena seemed to do it more deliberately—so deliberately, in fact, that she managed to hold on to some of her earliest babyhood experiences tightly enough to keep them from fading away entirely.

Light was her first memory, "warm and yellow." Light, and then music. It had no form or melody. Just a vague and gentle humming, accompanied by the soft sway of the rocking chair where Anna Hickok often tucked her baby daughter into a nest of pillows while attending to the household chores.

Perhaps Lorena's mother hummed as she worked. Or perhaps the music came from the baby herself. "Ever since I can remember, through almost every waking hour," she would muse as a grown woman, "music has run through me, somewhere in the back of my throat." The sounds were like a current, as constant as the movement of blood through her veins.

She took her time learning to talk—so long that her mother's family began to whisper their worries among themselves. Here was a child who would rather have inaudible conversations with cows than talk with people, a child who secretly believed the animals could converse among themselves just as humans did. She seemed more intent on deciphering the language the hens spoke than on bothering with English, and snuck about the chicken yard, trying to surprise the birds into divulging their gossip.

Human companionship offered little to Lorena, compared to the raptures of the natural world. "In the memory pictures of my very early life there seem to be no people at all," she recalled. "No real people—only here and there a shadowy figure." The earth, the grass, the tiny insects crawling through it—these she would remember vividly. She regarded trees with the same fondness that most children reserved for a beloved parent, "wide-spreading trees that sang to a child and might sometimes reach down and pick her up in their strong, rough arms."

It required a near cataclysm to make Lorena take notice of the living, breathing people around her. One day she stood in the kitchen doorway during a thunderstorm as her grandfather navigated the wooden walkway that led to the barn. The narrow planks were slick with rainwater and shone faintly blue each time the sky flared. Suddenly, her grandfather slipped. At the same instant, "a sizzling flash" and a ground-shaking crack of thunder rattled out of the sky as the old man hit the ground.

Then and there, Lorena said, "I first knew terror."

"I do not remember what my grandfather looked like, except that he had bushy white whiskers, but I can still see his shadowy form, so gigantic to a three-year-old, as he collapsed in the blinding light." Loud noises or sudden flashes of light sent bolts of terror through her forevermore, whether it was Fourth of July fireworks or the flashbulb of a camera.

The arrival of her sisters, first Ruby and then Myrtle, went largely un-noticed in Lorena's realm. Cows and horses, dogs and cats, and even her uncle's pigs were the living things whose company she sought. "When I was hardly more than a baby I sensed the truth that an animal's estimate of you is based on something deeper than what you look like, how you are dressed, or how you rate with your fellow humans," she explained. Unlike other children, she did not feed her doll with a bottle, instead preferring to leave it in the pig trough to dine with the pink and squeal-ing piglets. Dolls that were made to look like people were dull playthings anyway, as far as Lorena was concerned. "A doll was just a doll," she scoffed. "You couldn't pretend it was anything else."

CHAPTER 2

AROUND THE AGE OF FIVE, LORENA BEGAN RELUCTANTLY TO part the curtains of her small internal paradise and move into what she called "the other world—the world in which I was actually going to have to live."

This world bore little resemblance to her private reality, for her father, Addison Hickok, was a man whose presence could darken the air in a room. Flashes of temper sizzled out of him as suddenly as the terrifying lightning strike that had felled her grandfather.

The first true human contact Lorena could remember was not a mother's embrace, a grandparent's lap, or a game of patty-cake with her little sisters. It was her father cramming her fingertips into her mouth and wrapping his own big hands around her head, forcing her jaws to clamp down over them until her cheeks were streaked with tears. She had been biting her fingernails; this was Addison Hickok's way of breaking the toddler's habit.

"There must have been times when he was not angry—times when he was gay, affectionate, even indulgent with us children," she mused as an adult. "But I do not remember them." Instead, she remembered the sounds of Addison's horsewhip whistling through the air and cracking over the back of her collie pup. The dog had been chasing bicycles, and Lorena's father had no more tolerance for a fun-seeking puppy than for a nail-biting child. That day, as she sat clutched in her mother's lap listening to the little collie's yelps and her mother's sobs, was the first time in her four years on earth that Lorena knew anger.

Lorena's fury toward her father would never fade. He was the sort of man who'd whip his daughters as readily as he'd whip a horse, or throw a chair after his wife as she fled the room, weeping. He fought with his employers, too, fights that often cost him his job. Judging by the number of times the Hickok family moved, Addison's temper was notorious enough to blackball him in one town after another. "My childhood was a confusing, kaleidoscopic series of strange neighborhoods, different schools, new teachers to get acquainted with, playmates whom I never got to know very well," Lorena recalled. By the time she was ten years old, she'd lived in ten different places across southern Wisconsin and northern Illinois.

No protection existed in the Hickok home when Addison was present. Lorena's mother, Anna, rarely stood up to her husband. Anna's meekness baffled her daughter. "I kept wondering, all through those childhood years, why my mother, who was a grown-up, too, and just as big as my father, let him do the things he did."

Toward her mother, Lorena felt "a kind of resentful bewilderment." Addison was forever beating Lorena and her sisters black and blue, whipping the pets Anna loved until they ran away, getting himself fired, and causing friction between his relatives and Anna's. Yet anytime he went off to hunt for another job, a mission that could take days, weeks, or months, loneliness drove Anna to tears. The older Lorena got, the sorrier she felt for her mother. Even a child could see that Anna Hickok was a bitterly unhappy woman.

At the same time, an unspoken contempt tarnished Lorena's feelings toward Anna. Lorena's clashes with her father were more likely to trigger a scolding from her mother than sympathy. For Anna, it was simpler to blame Lorena for the beatings than to hold Addison accountable for his violence. The scoldings, with their implication that she was at fault, were worse for Lorena than the crack of a butter stave striking her legs and back. All her life, she would hate the sound of harsh voices.

Her sisters offered little solace or solidarity, either. They were so different, so cheerful and outgoing. Ruby in particular knew how to "get along," to "play up" to the elders and somehow dance just out of reach of Addison's discipline. She'd seemed to learn the knack of it without effort or guidance. Lorena's inability to perform the same simple maneuvers was beyond Ruby's understanding, and made Ruby resentful of having to witness Lorena's increasingly harsh punishments. "Sometimes it would make me sick, and I couldn't eat!" Ruby complained.

Perhaps even worse, Ruby and Myrtle were both as winsome as cherubs. "Nobody ever called me pretty or cunning, adjectives I was always hearing applied to my sisters," Lorena mourned. In an era when daintiness was prized, she was tall and broad, with a face inclined to break out in a red rash at the slightest irritation. One night as her mother washed the supper dishes, Lorena overheard Anna speaking with pride about Ruby's looks. Ruby had lovely golden curls, the precise opposite of Lorena's straight reddish-brown hair.

"Crouching behind the kitchen door, I decided that the trouble with me must be that I was not a pretty child. What I needed, to get on in the world, was curly hair." Lorena knew how to get it, too. She'd heard plenty of stories of victims of typhoid fever who'd had to have their hair cropped to keep it from falling out altogether. Often it grew back curly. So Lorena filched her mother's sewing shears and carved out great chunks of her long, thick hair. Disaster ensued. Instead of transforming herself into a curly-haired angel, she succeeded only in looking like a boy. Then came the inevitable teasing.

"After a while I ceased being miserable about my lack of beauty, simply accepted the fact that I was homely, and did not expect admiration or compliments," she said.

In a house where she bore the brunt of her father's rages, where everyone but she was worthy of admiration and praise, Lorena came to the only conclusion that her young mind could piece together: something must be wrong with her, something that made her deserve such treatment.

Once more, Lorena drew into herself, crafting an armor of the materials she had at hand—introversion and imagination. She craved "a kind of hiding place," she said, "where I could relax and feel happy and contented, away from the frictions."

Books formed the foundation of that refuge. Once she learned to read, Lorena's world "became thickly populated and richly furnished." Now she counted among her friends Ben-Hur, George Washington, the outlaws Frank and Jesse James, Black Beauty, the knights of King Arthur's Round Table, and all the deities of Greece and Rome.

In her jungles and savannas, upon the ramparts of Troy and the battlefields of old Quebec, Lorena could be "happy and contented enough." It wasn't that she wanted to be apart from everyone else. Quite the contrary. "I desperately wanted to be liked, but I simply did not know how," she said. "I was always in trouble. So I remained aloof, inarticulate, defiant, and, for the most part I daresay, thoroughly disagreeable." The adults regarded her as "a queer, surly, unpromising youngster."

Only one person had the power to coax Lorena into unlocking her imaginary gates and stepping into the world beyond: Aunt Ella. Ella Ellis was not an aunt at all, but rather Lorena's mother's cousin. Still, in terms of affection, Anna and Ella were more like sisters, and the children were told to call her Aunt Ella.

The sound of Ella's voice, soft and blessedly free of reprimands, enraptured Lorena the same way music did, embedding itself forever in Lorena's memory. "Everything about her was exquisite" in Lorena's eyes— her gentleness, her understanding, her daintiness. It was thanks to Aunt Ella that the Hickok girls were always well dressed enough to inspire envy in their neighbors. Every year a box arrived from Chicago, filled with the lovely clothes her daughter had outgrown.

Yet the dresses paled in comparison to the intangible gifts Aunt Ella bestowed upon Lorena. Around her, Lorena felt free and easy. Aunt Ella listened, and was interested in what the child had to say. "She was the first person who ever made me feel she loved me, who managed to get inside the guards I started throwing up before I was really out of baby-hood, who gave me confidence in myself.

"Through those sullen, resentful, inarticulate years, she was the only steadying influence I knew, the only person I really trusted."

❧

At eight years old, Lorena got her first taste of how it felt to break a news story.

Playing out in the street one September afternoon, she heard a report straight from a telegraph operator, the likes of which hadn't crackled across the wires since 1865—President McKinley had been shot. Addison Hickok was gone, off on one of his incessant job-hunting expeditions, so Lorena did not hesitate to run into the house, shouting the news. The reaction was not what she had hoped. The grown-ups promptly hushed her and hustled her back out the door. Inside, her grandmother was dying.

Nevertheless, whether Lorena knew it or not, that incident was her first tentative step on the path that would lead her to the White House.

CHAPTER 3

ADDISON HICKOK UPROOTED HIS FAMILY ONCE AGAIN IN 1903, not to a new neighborhood or town, but to a place where his reputation would not so easily shadow his efforts to find a job. Lorena was ten years old when she stepped from a train into South Dakota, one of a half dozen newly minted states the federal government had recently wrested from its Indigenous inhabitants.

South Dakota, in Lorena's eyes, was "round and flat, like an empty plate." The sky was cloudless, the winds relentless. Horizons stretched eternally in every direction.

Lorena loved it. The vast open spaces represented "infinite and intoxicating freedom" to a child who had always retreated inward to find sanctuary and safety. "You could run all the way to the rim of the world if you wanted to!" she marveled.

~

Addison had not left his temper behind, and so for the next three years, the Hickoks would drift westward, inhabiting what Lorena called "a succession of dusty little prairie towns, each a little more forlorn than the last," as Addison hopscotched from one job to another.

Anna Hickok was miserable in every one of them. For a woman accustomed to the glades and lakes of Wisconsin, Lorena figured that South Dakota "must have fitted to perfection my mother's idea of hell."

The landscape made Anna feel small, lost, and isolated. She thirsted for the sight of trees, hills, and, most of all, lakes. There wasn't an inch of shade in South Dakota, except in the shadow of the squat one-story buildings that "huddled together" to form towns.

When Anna heard tell of a lake in the vicinity, where locals gathered for Sunday school picnics, she persuaded Addison to hire a team of horses and drive out to its shore. What she saw when they arrived cracked her in two. The so-called lake was hardly more than a ring of rushes with a muddy hole at its center. "Sitting there in the surrey, with the reins in her hands, she broke down and cried as though her heart were breaking," Lorena remembered.

⁓

The Hickoks reached Bowdle in 1905, a place Lorena called "the dustiest and dreariest of the little Dakota towns my mother was to know." Cowboys tortured stray dogs and cats to death in the alleyways behind Bowdle's saloons for sport. The hotel, generally full of traveling salesmen, occasionally bred a scandal. Lorena once watched, "frozen in horror," as the coffin of an unwed woman who had drunk carbolic acid after finding herself pregnant by one of those married salesmen was carried out of the town hall. Lorena and her schoolmates treated the hotel like a haunted house after that, running past on the opposite side of the street. The town had its requisite drunkard, too, but he posed no real menace. The greatest dangers to Lorena remained where they always had—at home.

By the time she reached adolescence, Lorena's dislike of her father had matured into "a bitter hatred." And as Lorena grew, so did the whippings. At least once Addison struck her hard enough to knock her down— hard enough to provoke one of Anna's rare protests. "Do you want to kill the child?" she pleaded, stepping between her husband and her daughter.

Anna's objection had no effect. Addison Hickok had taken a notion to break his daughter's temper, oblivious to the fact that rather than beating the anger out of Lorena, he was beating it into her.

"Never once did he whip me—and the whippings grew progressively more severe as I grew older—when I didn't mutter, inaudibly behind my gritted teeth: 'You wouldn't dare do this to me if I were as big as you are,'" Lorena would write.

The man's temper knew no sense of proportion. Catching Lorena and her sisters playing with their kitten, Tweezer, when they should have been getting dressed, Addison swooped in, snatched Tweezer by the hind paws, and strode out to the barn, where he dashed the kitten's brains out upon the wall. The Hickok girls never had another dog or cat after that.

Addison committed other, more painful abuses, too, ones that Lorena would not consign to paper. She would not even speak of them for decades. At least once, under circumstances Lorena did not describe to the few friends she confided in, her father had not only beaten her, but raped her.

～

There was only one thing Lorena could do to earn herself any praise, and it was something she hated to do: sing for an audience.

The child who had taken so long to talk had an unexpected gift—a voice rich and low and resonant. Unfortunately for Lorena, those warm alto tones were perfectly suited for funeral solos. Standing up in front of a roomful of people at Addison's insistence was torture enough. Lorena thought herself abominably tall and "hopelessly ugly"; the heat of her self-consciousness ought to have been enough to burn a hole through the floor. Singing for church and school programs constituted "a terrible ordeal." The prospect of experiencing that same mortification while standing beside an open coffin filled her with so much dread that she was willing to risk her father's wrath by refusing.

All of this is reason enough to suspect that the week leading up to Sunday, September 16, 1906, was an unpleasant one in the Hickok household.

According to the *Bowdle Pioneer,* Lorena was scheduled to perform a recital at the Christian Endeavor Society meeting that Sunday evening. All the elements for another of her violent sieges with Addison were in place.

But the suffering that beset Lorena that Saturday and Sunday came at her from a wholly different direction.

Shortly after seven o'clock on the evening of Saturday, September 15, Anna Hickok was taken "violently ill." It was a stroke, severe enough that she could not speak. Six hours later, Anna was dead. Lorena was thirteen years old.

Within a few weeks of Anna's burial, a housekeeper moved in with the Hickoks. She was a familiar face, a friend of the family who'd given Lorena lessons on the pump organ.

At first, there was little in the new arrangement for Lorena to complain of. The woman (Lorena never referred to her as anything but "the housekeeper") kept the house reasonably clean, if not as well scrubbed as Anna had. Meals once again arrived on the table at appointed hours. The housekeeper even prevailed upon Addison to give up butter making and take a position as a traveling salesman for a livestock feed company instead. Off he went, looking pinched in a new tan suit and white shirt that were too small and stiff on him. His absences gave Lorena space to breathe more freely, as always.

Those outside the household had their own opinions about the Hickoks' housekeeper, however. Eyebrows began to rise as folks contemplated exactly what kind of relationship had already developed between this woman and Addison. The fact that she had been divorced was enough to cause a stir in Bowdle, and Lorena—as both the oldest and the most observant of her sisters—quickly sensed a shift in attitude toward her family. The neighbors stopped coming by to visit. The way people looked at Lorena and Ruby and Myrtle changed. Now teachers and friends' mothers regarded them "in a peculiarly sympathetic way" and lavished them with kindness that struck Lorena as unusual, even in the face of their mother's sudden death. The mood on the playground turned conspiratorial, too. Schoolchildren huddled together, whispering and giggling while Lorena watched from outside their ranks. She knew without being told that those whispers and giggles were about her family.

"One Sunday," Lorena remembered, "my sister and I were told that we could no longer see our playmates or go to their houses." The talk in town had finally reached a pitch that ignited Addison's temper, and the Hickok girls would not be permitted to get within earshot of the gossip.

Whether that gossip matched the reality is impossible to say, but circumstances in the Hickok home were indeed deteriorating. When Addison was away, Lorena, Myrtle, and Ruby frequently came home after school to find no one there at all. Nor did the housekeeper return at suppertime to feed the three youngsters in her care. Lorena and her sisters foraged what they could from the pantry, then went out to amuse themselves in the streets.

With no one at home to enforce her father's edict forbidding her from mingling with other children, Lorena congregated with her schoolmates under the corner streetlamps. The boys engaged in "boasting and strutting" while the young ladies in the crowd teased and swapped secrets. "We were at the age when we were beginning to get interested in boys—the other girls more than I," Lorena remembered, "for I was inclined to judge the opposite sex by my father." It was more than that, though. Lorena might not have known it yet, but neither boys nor men would ever hold her in the same thrall that captivated other girls and women.

CHAPTER 4

who had filled her place calmly informed Lorena that her father was "breaking up housekeeping." Put more bluntly, Addison and the housekeeper were to be married, and his children would not be part of their new household. One of Lorena's younger sisters would have to live with the housekeeper's sister in a neighboring town. The other they packed off on a train to Wisconsin, to Anna's people. For fourteen-year-old Lorena, they made no arrangements. She would have to find somewhere else to live herself.

"You'd better see about it today," Lorena's stepmother-to-be said.

"Perhaps I should have been dismayed," Lorena remembered. "But I wasn't. I was actually relieved, exhilarated." The prospect of leaving the violence and shrill lectures behind far outweighed the drawbacks of being evicted from her own home.

A girl Lorena's age had one option for employment in Bowdle: as a servant. Full-time servants who got paid a weekly wage were called hired girls. In a town like Bowdle, positions for hired girls were scarce. Most folks were only willing or able to pay their $4-a-week wage temporarily, to help with the extra chores that arose after a birth or a death. Much more common were the plain "girls" who traded their before- and after-school hours for meals and a bed, easing the workload in the household and helping mind the babies.

Lorena immediately set her sights on a position as a girl.

"Feeling grown up and important," Lorena stood in the schoolyard that morning and informed her chum, Lottie McCafferty, of what had transpired at her house. At recess Lottie trotted straight home to speak with her mother about Lorena's predicament. Class had begun again before she returned, "red and puffing," from her errand. The instant the teacher turned away, Lottie passed Lorena a note. Mrs. McCafferty thought that a lady named Mrs. O'Reilly might have use for a girl. The O'Reillys had two young children, and Lorena had a reputation for kindness toward animals and babies.

When the lunch bell rang, Lorena went to see Mrs. O'Reilly, whose house happened to be right across the street from the school. Mrs. O'Reilly greeted her with cookies and milk. "She showed no surprise, asked no questions," Lorena recalled. When Lorena went back to class that afternoon, she had a job. The possibility that Lottie's mother had conspired with Mrs. O'Reilly to ensure her a safe place to live never crossed Lorena's mind. She went home, packed her belongings into a canvas bag, and bade her sister goodbye.

⁓

The O'Reillys were so unlike her own family, they might have been characters in a book rather than living people.

The fact that they were Catholics preoccupied Lorena at first. Among her mother's side of the family, Catholics were regarded with "a suspicion that amounted to obsession." Mentioning the name of an Irish schoolmate at the dinner table was enough to make the grown-ups whisper darkly, "Catholic." Such scorn had struck Lorena as absurd.

Now she discovered that the O'Reillys did indeed do things that Protestants did not, though none of it seemed worthy of disdain. That first night she watched with shy curiosity as Mr. and Mrs. O'Reilly's hands moved in "some sort of fluttering gesture" before they ate their dinner. When she went up to her room, she noticed that a small color print of the Madonna and Child hung on the wall over her bed. Lorena considered it a long time before deciding she liked having it there. In the O'Reillys' bedroom a stubby white candle burned day and night in a red glass holder, which Lorena found "rather cheerful and cozy." And, wonder of wonders, Mr. O'Reilly accompanied his wife to church every single Sunday. Lorena's mother had always attended services alone. Methodist men in Bowdle only bothered with church if their children were reciting in holiday programs.

More than anything else, it was the O'Reillys' good humor that made Lorena feel as though she'd stepped into another realm. The brightness and gaiety of the whole family bore no resemblance to her former circumstances. The man of the house laughed and sang. Mrs. O'Reilly never scolded—not her husband, her children, or even Lorena.

Lorena was profoundly grateful to be in such a place, among such people, and was equally unable to express it. "What they got in return for their generosity was an over-grown, sleepy adolescent, inclined to be sullen and suspicious, too inarticulate even to thank them or let them know how much she liked them," she admitted. Only with the babies, both of whom were under three, could she "be natural."

The affection Lorena craved still eluded her. At school, no one but Lottie seemed to like her. Lottie was popular, with an easy grin, freckles, and red braids. "In her warm, careless way, she carried me along with her, and I adored her." Any other time Lorena tried to make friends, her eagerness came off as bombastic insincerity. She tried too hard, showed off too much, laughed too loudly. The stories she told on the playground, realistic at first, soon grew to outlandish proportions more likely to prompt eye rolls than admiration. "Everyone in our small circle was perfectly aware of the fact that I was the direct descendent of a noble European family," she remembered, "that my youngest sister had fallen downstairs when a baby and that a skillful surgeon 'back East' had mended her broken neck with plaster; they had already heard many times about my hereditary fits of insanity which alone were causing my father's hair to turn gray." Dismissal and ridicule were her rewards; she answered to "Fatty."

In one ill-fated attempt to impress, Lorena composed a few lines of disparaging doggerel about the teacher, Professor Johnson:

His eyes are green, his hair is white,
His nose is crooked, he's a fright!

Her classmates awarded her with appreciative sniggers as the paper passed from one desk to the next, then abandoned her when the poem fell into the schoolmaster's hands. Whether by accident or by design, Professor Johnson meted out a punishment guaranteed to mortify Lorena Hickok. "One bleak afternoon, he made me stand up before the whole room and apologize." The whippings she'd endured at Addison's hands did not sting half so badly as the shame Lorena felt stammering out her apology to the classmates she so longed to win over.

Once again, Lorena immersed herself in books—any kind of books at all. From the "sugary scenes" of *Little Lord Fauntleroy* to epic clashes of battle, she inhabited every plot and character. She could stand before a kitchen sink, lost in a reverie, while the wet plate in her hand dripped all over her shoes. In those moments, Lorena was not in a kitchen at all. "The plate might be a shield, the dish towel a sword" while she defended a mountain pass in ancient Greece, or contemplated how exactly it would feel to be devoured by a lion (headfirst? feetfirst?) in a Roman Circus.

CHAPTER 5

BY CHRISTMAS, THE "BRIGHT INTERLUDE" WITH THE O'REILLYS was over. Addison and the housekeeper were married and moved sixty miles east, to Aberdeen. For reasons that made sense only to the newly-weds, Addison yanked Lorena out of her position at the O'Reillys and deposited his daughter in a new job at a boardinghouse in Aberdeen.

"I lived at the kitchen sink," Lorena remembered, "with mountains of dirty dishes, oceans of greasy, scummy dishwater, and an endless succession of dish towels that were always grey and damp and smelly." If she was not at the sink, she was waiting tables, making up beds, or lending a hand with the innumerable other chores.

Within a month or so, Lorena was out on the street yet again. An old oak sideboard in the dining room had proven to be her undoing. After each meal, the landlady collected the uneaten crusts and scraps of bread and tossed them into the bottom of the sideboard. When enough leftovers accumulated, she made them into dressing and served it back to her boarders. That wasn't the only thing that made it unappetizing. "House cleaning in the institution was most casual," Lorena recalled, "and there were mice." The dish was as likely to be seasoned with mouse droppings as with sage and onion. For a nickel, Lorena would warn the boarders if dressing was on the evening's menu so they could be sure to get their supper elsewhere that night. When the landlady discovered Lorena's treachery, out she went.

A want ad brought Lorena to her next job in the spick-and-span home of a "kindly and courteous" couple with a picture-perfect baby. Unlike the proprietor of the boardinghouse, the mistress of this house made it her duty to see that Lorena attended school every day.

Lorena had never been to a school that boasted a different classroom for each grade. That novelty lost some of its luster when instead of the high school class she expected to attend, she was put back with the eighth graders. Education in Bowdle had not been as rigorous as in Aberdeen.

Clothes occupied Lorena more than lessons as she sat through the eighth-grade curriculum for a second time. Years ago she had deemed herself permanently unlovely, and the idea of comparing her appearance to her classmates' had not crossed her mind since. Suddenly, the contrast became unavoidable. Lorena was, in her own words, "an exceedingly shabby, grimy spectacle."

All the dishwashing had left her hands red and chapped, and she still bit her nails. She didn't know the first thing about arranging her hair, or even how to properly wash it. Well over a year had passed since she'd had any new clothes, and her dresses were growing shorter and more threadbare by the day. Her shoes were so thin, she had to stuff paper into them to keep out the snow and pebbles.

Sitting in a classroom with girls like Elizabeth Ward, the hotel owner's daughter, awakened a new sense of inferiority. Elizabeth captivated Lorena. Her hair bows hovered "like great, crisp, silken butterflies" over her matching dresses—a different dress for every day of the week. She had her own pocket money and would treat her classmates to jelly doughnuts and candy, once rewarding a euphoric Lorena with sweets in exchange for help with arithmetic.

Elizabeth Ward became "the first living person ever to become an inmate of the world into which I retired with my imagination," Lorena recalled. She stared at Elizabeth every chance she got, so that she could pretend to be her idol, "looking like her, dressed like her, graciously accepting the homage of the other children, the favorite of the teacher."

As far as Lorena could tell, she herself was a "surly, sloppy savage" who didn't fit in at school, or in the household where she had been hired. As if to confirm her suspicions, her mistress dismissed her with utmost gentleness after only a month.

~

This time the want ads sent Lorena to the rooming house of Mrs. Hagedorn, down by the railroad tracks. The "sooty premises" catered to the men who ran the trains and built the rail lines. Mrs. Hagedorn, "scrawny and dirty, with stringy grey hair, bad teeth, and a horrible breath," paid Lorena $3 a week, though she was a full-time maid in name only. The railroad men slept in rooms that were never swept or dusted, on linens that never saw the inside of a laundry tub. The kitchen floor boasted a coat of grease thick enough to skate on. Once in a while Mrs. Hagedorn assigned Lorena some unfathomable task, like washing the kitchen ceiling. Her primary duty, however, was fetching Mrs. Hagedorn's "medicine" from the druggist. Whatever the powders were, she took them incessantly.

Mostly, the landlady sat by the window, waving at the train crews. Her other favorite pastime was regaling Lorena with stories of what went on at "the houses"—a bungalow and a two-story frame building just outside the town limits where railroad men and construction workers went to exchange their pay for an evening of female companionship. Lorena never could figure out if Mrs. Hagedorn had ever set foot in the fabled red-light district herself. "Whether by imagination or experience, she was fascinated by them," Lorena remembered. "Over and over again, until I knew the whole routine by heart—although a lot of it I did not understand—she would tell me what happened at night."

Looking back, Lorena realized that Mrs. Hagedorn might have been dropping hints about how Lorena might earn a living. "What Mrs. Hagedorn did not know, of course, was that my hatred of my father made me dislike and distrust all men."

One of Mrs. Hagedorn's roomers affirmed Lorena's opinion of the opposite sex when he came stumbling into the little kitchen closet the fifteen-year-old used as a bedroom. "Wakened out of a sound sleep, I let out a good resounding yell, and he backed out." After that, Lorena did not go to bed without wedging a chair up against her doorknob.

⁓

Lorena's days "flowed along in this pattern" until Mrs. Hagedorn suggested she answer an advertisement placed by the *Dakota Farmer*, an agricultural magazine that was looking for girls to staff its printing plant.

Off she went, and promptly landed herself a position at the bindery— her fourth job in six months. Mrs. Hagedorn even promised to let her stay at the rooming house until she found another place to live. Lorena's triumph lasted only a few days. The workings of the machine she had been assigned to were beyond her comprehension. But a single moment at the bindery stayed with her for the rest of her life. "The forelady, trying once more to show me how to operate the machine, addressed me as 'my dear.'" That tiny dab of affection nearly melted Lorena on the spot. "I can still feel the warm glow that suffused my lonely, adolescent heart," she recalled over forty years afterward. The woman's kindness only went so far, however. At quitting time that night, that same lady dismissed Lorena.

One misfortune piled upon another. Walking home from work at the bindery one night, Lorena had crossed paths with her father for the first time in weeks. Shortly after that unwelcome meeting, Addison showed up at Mrs. Hagedorn's door. Addison removed Lorena from Mrs. Hagedorn's establishment, bought her just enough new dresses to make her look respectable, and installed her in the home of his new wife's cousin, Mr. Searles, where a baby was expected.

Lorena called the place "the house of discord." She, who had known little but discord in her own home, still managed to be appalled by what she encountered with the Searleses. "In all my life I have never known a more poorly adjusted, completely wretched family."

It was perfectly plain to Lorena that Mrs. Searles never should have gotten married. This was a woman who'd wanted a singing career, not a husband and babies. "I never heard her sing," Lorena said, "but in her beratings of her husband, her small daughter, and me, she certainly demonstrated that her voice had power and range." Day in and day out, Mrs. Searles seethed with frustration. Her daughter was just learning to walk, and already Mrs. Searles was expecting another child. She wanted neither of them, and when rage overtook her, she'd scream the fact to anyone within earshot, loud enough for the neighbors to hear it. If men had to bear the children, Mrs. Searles railed, "there wouldn't be so many brats in the world."

Every last thing in the house immediately became Lorena's responsibility. Cooking, cleaning, washing, ironing—Mrs. Searles abdicated all of it. Lorena had to look after the toddler, "a pallid, nervous, fretful little thing," as well as wait on Mrs. Searles.

Lorena tried, "really tried," to keep up, but it was a task fit for a giant. To top it off, "I was slow," she acknowledged. "I have never been able to do anything rapidly." The work beat Lorena down, both physically and emotionally. Even her wages provided no satisfaction, for they were not her own. Every week, she turned over her $3 to Addison to repay him for her new clothes. "I drudged along, hopeless, weary, and more lonely than I had ever been in my life before."

Lorena had one small solace: her letters to Lottie McCafferty. How she found the time to write them at all is a bafflement, but write them she did. Long letters, apparently full of woe, for what else did she have to share?

Then came a letter in return. Lottie told of a woman named Mrs. Dodd, a widow raising her three-month-old granddaughter. The infant's mother had died in childbirth, and Mrs. Dodd needed help. She lived just south of Aberdeen, in a town called Gettysburg. Mrs. McCafferty would recommend Lorena if she wanted the job.

Did she! Lorena wrote to Mrs. Dodd, never breathing a word of it to Addison or the Searleses. When an envelope came from Gettysburg with money for railroad fare, Lorena quietly packed her canvas bag and hid it in the barn while Mrs. Searles napped. Lorena tidied up, cooked supper, and washed the dishes as usual that night. After everyone was asleep, out she snuck.

CHAPTER 6

SERENITY WASHED OVER LORENA THE MINUTE SHE WALKED INTO Mrs. Dodd's house. The cleanliness and the calm were an antidote like no other. Mrs. Dodd was an echo of Aunt Ella—gentle, patient, and kind. Polished spectacles and a touch of gray at her temples lent her a warm, bright demeanor.

Ever so tactfully, Mrs. Dodd took it upon herself to smarten up Lorena's appearance. Gifts of scented soap and talcum powder melted away the dingy aura that had stubbornly clung to Lorena since her mother's death. Mrs. Dodd taught her how to shampoo her hair, and how to soothe and protect her sore dishpan hands. Next came her wardrobe. With Mrs. Dodd's advice, Lorena carefully spent her wages on more becoming garments. Mrs. Dodd even honored Lorena with some of her daughter's clothes, altering them to fit her properly.

Mrs. Dodd eased the burdens of Lorena's work, too, showing her how to complete household tasks more efficiently. "She even praised me when I did things right!" Lorena said, awestruck by such a fundamental kindness. "I think I might have stayed on with Mrs. Dodd forever and might even have become an outstanding success as a housemaid."

But one day a letter arrived from Wisconsin for Mrs. Dodd. Her son-in-law, the father of her granddaughter, wanted her to bring the baby and live with him. Mrs. Dodd had grown fond enough of Lorena that she considered taking the teenager with her. A more devoted maid did not exist in the state of South Dakota. Ultimately, the expense was too great, and Mrs. Dodd and her grandchild set off for Wisconsin alone.

"So one day in August, with my clean, neat wardrobe packed in a new wicker suitcase Mrs. Dodd had given me, I landed back in Bowdle to look for another job."

⤫

Before long, Lorena got wind that the county school superintendent wanted to hire a girl to live with his widowed mother, "a fussy old woman" stubbornly operating a wheat farm a good way from Bowdle. The thought of his mother out there all alone worried him. Lorena's presence would provide peace of mind. "It would be a good home for the right girl," the superintendent assured her.

The road never curved, and the sun struck them like a blow as they drove over the "vast, round, golden plate" that was South Dakota's wheat country. Out on the open plains, the lady's homestead was visible for miles before they reached it—"a forlorn muddle of shabby little buildings."

No welcome awaited Lorena. The widow had not expected her, and furthermore, had no desire for a hired girl. "Through faded, near-sighted eyes she peered at me over a smoking lamp, muttered a curt greeting for her son," Lorena recalled. She consented to let the girl stay only because threshers were coming the next day to harvest the wheat crop and she could use the help in the kitchen. Feeding threshers taxed even the most capable farm woman's abilities.

⤫

As the sun set the following day, in came the threshing team with their thunderous machines and legendary appetites. "The old lady, who had hardly spoken to me all day, handed me an alarm clock set for 3 a.m.," Lorena recalled. The threshers expected to sit down to their breakfast at five o'clock the next morning.

Stars still winked in the blue-black sky when the alarm clock jangled a groggy Lorena out of bed. First on her list of chores was getting the stove going. Lorena followed the instructions she'd been given the night before, but the coal refused to burn. She pushed in some paper to encourage the flames. "The paper burned, and the flames licked the kerosene off the surface of the coal," she remembered. "That was all."

Lorena fought valiantly with the stove until daybreak, when one of the hungry threshers came in and forced the stubborn coals to burn.

Over the next three days, Lorena battled every minute to keep ahead of the threshers' appetites. For a girl no good at hurrying, it was a task doomed to failure.

"I was a squirrel in a sweltering cage, running frantically round and round in a wheel, never getting anywhere," she remembered. Working in that kitchen was like standing in the mouth of hell. "Dripping perspiration, in clouds of steam and smoke and soot that caked on my skin and smarted in my eyes and nostrils, I struggled along, losing ground all the time, through an agonizing routine of boiling, baking, frying, through bushels of grimy potato peelings, through sliding avalanches of greasy dishes."

When the threshers left, Lorena followed. Bright and early on the fourth morning, she climbed onto the seat of the widow's lumber wagon to sit beside the hired man as he drove toward town. There, she bought a train ticket back to Bowdle.

Just as Lorena was about to step into one of the cars, she spotted her father. His tan salesman's suit and brown derby weren't new anymore, but he looked just as awkward and uncomfortable in them as he always had. Lorena ducked into another car and took a seat. Addison followed. He sat down behind her, and a cloud of fury began to billow out of him, burning at the back of Lorena's neck as he fumed at her.

Lorena was "an ungrateful daughter," he seethed, who ought to be thrown in jail for running out on the Searleses. "No good end" would come to her, he predicted, vowing to wash his hands of her.

For the first time, Lorena did not find herself beaten down as the lash of Addison's tongue fell against her back. Instead, "I felt myself lifted up in a new and wonderful exhilaration." There was something unfamiliar in Addison's manner she had never sensed before, something that she could only later identify as impotence.

"That change in his attitude gave tacit recognition that I was no longer a child, to be cuffed about and beaten," Lorena realized. She had defied him by walking out on that job with the Searleses, and there was nothing he could do about it. With that understanding, Addison's power over his daughter evaporated on the spot. Lorena knew then and there that he would never lay a hand on her again.

When the train pulled into the depot at Bowdle, Lorena stepped off. Addison remained aboard. Lorena did not know it, but she had just seen her father for the last time.

CHAPTER 7

ONCE AGAIN HOMELESS AND UNEMPLOYED, FIFTEEN-YEAR-OLD Lorena Hickok took stock of herself.

Thanks to Mrs. Dodd's kindness, the seed of a change had begun to germinate within her—a sense that she could be more than a speck of dust swept about on hostile winds. Her life could have purpose and direction. Only, she did not know what direction. Nor did she dare hope for any kind of love or affection. Years of abuse and indifference had trained her heart to protect itself. Still, Lorena wanted *something* to strive for.

Her sense of purpose might have been vague, but Lorena knew perfectly well what she did *not* want. No more of the many kinds of violence her father had perpetrated upon her. No more women nagging and shrieking like Mrs. Searles and her stepmother. "I could not have put it into words at that time," Lorena would recall, "but I think now that what I really wanted was self-respect."

"What I needed, I decided, was a better education." An educated girl could at least earn a living as a teacher, or perhaps even go to business college, as Lottie McCafferty's older sister had.

It took this newly determined Lorena only a week to find a position in the home of the Bickerts. Wealthy by Bowdle standards, the Bickerts had a manicured lawn and flower beds, drove a team of beautifully matched bay horses, and took trips to Minneapolis to see the newest shows and purchase the latest fashions.

On the first day of the fall term, Lorena presented herself at Bowdle's pink frame school building to enroll. To her dismay, she found herself reassigned to the ninth grade under the tutelage of the principal, Professor

Johnson—the selfsame Professor Johnson she'd lampooned in rhyme as an eighth grader.

Hating the teacher helped Lorena fit in just a little. The whole town looked with a mixture of suspicion and irritation upon Professor Johnson's attempts to educate his pupils. What use were such "daring innovations" as Latin, algebra, botany, and geology in a place like Bowdle? the taxpayers grumbled. All their children needed to know was how to "read, write, 'n' figger."

Professor Johnson's earnest reverence for scholarly pursuits, paired with his tactlessness, impatience, and temper, made him resoundingly unpopular in the classroom. Fortunately for Lorena, he possessed an unfathomable stubbornness. Despite his neighbors' derision, this man who looked like a Scandinavian version of Ichabod Crane persisted in holding his meager handful of high school students to loftier standards than they would otherwise aspire to. It was Professor Johnson, Lorena later acknowledged, "who gave me my first glimpses into a world of the mind and the eye and the ear." Only in retrospect would her teacher take on "the stature of a hero" in an adult Lorena's eyes.

Outside school, the situation was much as it always had been for Lorena. "After resolving that I was no longer going to be an under-dog," she lamented, "I found myself right back in the old rut, which kept grinding deeper and deeper." Drudgery dominated her waking hours, for the Bickerts were not so wealthy as they seemed. Though there were chores enough for a full-time maid, the budget wouldn't stretch. It fell to Lorena to keep everything looking as though the Bickerts had servants galore.

Any minute Lorena was not inside the schoolhouse "belonged" to Mrs. Bickert. There wasn't a moment for homework in between the washing and ironing and hauling coal. Mrs. Bickert demanded that Lorena work every available instant in the mornings, often forcing her to run all the way to school if she did not want to be marked tardy.

Worse was Mrs. Bickert's attitude, which crumpled the few scraps of confidence Lorena had managed to accumulate. "She would say things to me, insulting personal remarks, that no human being ought to have to take from another without answering back."

Lorena was willing to tolerate the workload. She was used to that. But the way Mrs. Bickert talked to her was another thing entirely. Somewhere along the line, Lorena had gotten her fill of mistreatment. Kindness like Mrs. Dodd's might still have seemed like a luxury, but by now Lorena had come to understand that she was in fact entitled to basic human decency.

Only her resolve to finish the school year kept her from marching out of the Bickert house once and for all that winter. Each time she found herself teetering on the edge of giving up, some happening at school tugged her back. In February, it was an essay contest on Abraham Lincoln. Lorena labored over her paper late into the night, stealing from the hours Mrs. Bickert allocated for sleep as she hunched over a base burner coal stove. And she won. Close behind that accolade came another— a declamatory competition to be held in Aberdeen in the spring. Professor Johnson chose Lorena as Bowdle's contestant.

The very thought of reciting in front of a crowd "appalled" her. Lorena had proven time and again that she'd rather take a beating than perform before an audience. Besides, Mrs. Bickert would never let her take a whole day off from her chores to make the trip to Aberdeen. But Professor Johnson and the county superintendent would not let up. Both insisted it was an honor she could not refuse. The two men even promised they would handle Mrs. Bickert.

Lorena gave in.

The piece they assigned her, a patriotic poem about Union and Confederate soldiers swapping songs across the Rappahannock before the Battle of Fredericksburg, "seemed like awful drivel" to Lorena. Worse, there were parts she had to sing. Nevertheless, she dutifully gave up her recesses to practice reciting. Lorena knew Mrs. Bickert would spare her no time for such frivolity. That worked well enough until the afternoon

Professor Johnson's wife arrived after school to play the piano so Lorena could practice the singing portions. The rehearsal took almost two hours.

By the time Lorena got home, Mrs. Bickert was livid. Lorena had never bothered to mention the contest to her, and with the trip to Aberdeen still two months away, neither had Professor Johnson nor the superintendent. Nothing Lorena had listened to before compared with the tirade Mrs. Bickert let loose this time. The mistress of the house decreed that for punishment Lorena had to scrub the kitchen and the pantry before school the next morning, no matter how long it took. If she was late for class, that was just too bad.

Lorena lay awake long into the night, pondering how to untangle herself from this awful muddle. Once she decided, she had to summon all her nerve. Morning came and Lorena scrubbed, just as Mrs. Bickert had ordered. The school day was half over by the time she finished. And then, with the kitchen and pantry shining, Lorena quit. She did not slink away quietly as she'd done so many times before, but snapped right back at Mrs. Bickert and walked out in broad daylight.

CHAPTER 8

LORENA'S MOMENT OF TRIUMPH CAME WITH ITS OWN SNAGS, however. For the umpteenth time in two years, she had no place to sleep, nothing to eat, and no money with which to buy either one.

Desperation led her to the doorstep of the O'Malleys. Simply ringing their bell was a kind of rebellion, for, as Lorena well knew, "the 'nice' women of Bowdle did not call on Mrs. O'Malley."

It was bad enough that Mrs. O'Malley was the wife of a saloonkeeper. To the horror of the women of Bowdle, she also strutted about in ostentatious "costumes," wore a wig, and "painted her face" with cosmetics. Rumor had it that she drank and, on one occasion of drunkenness, "gave utterance to profane remarks."

If the "good women of Bowdle" hoped to shame her into compliance, they failed. As she cursed and laughed at her detractors, Mrs. O'Malley looked to Lorena like "an elderly and somewhat frayed bird of paradise stalking defiantly about a barnyard populated by little brown hens."

Lorena knew perfectly well that her own mother would not have invited Mrs. O'Malley into their home. Yet Lorena also recalled how Mrs. O'Malley had stopped her in the street one day after her mother's death, taking the time to speak to her with rare gentleness and sympathy.

Fortunately for Lorena, Mrs. O'Malley was as generous as she was defiant. She took Lorena on—not as an unpaid "girl," but as a servant with real wages.

The O'Malleys' little yellow house was the very picture of everything Mrs. Bickert detested. Unkempt trees and shrubbery shielded the interior from prying eyes and sunlight alike. The perpetual dimness only partially disguised the dust that rested softly on all the clutter. Mold, damp, and a poorly housebroken pug gave the place an odor perhaps best described as distinctive.

Lorena had few household duties to speak of. Sweeping, dusting, and the like were of no great consequence to Mrs. O'Malley. She and Lorena got by on bacon and fried potatoes most days, for cooking anything else was deemed more bother than it was worth. Two- and three-day slumps regularly overtook Mrs. O'Malley, leaving Lorena alone with the little pug while the mistress of the house slept her doldrums away. Once in a great while, the elusive Mr. O'Malley stumbled in after dark singing an old Irish song about a field of daisies. Mostly, though, the two women had the place to themselves.

When she was awake and feeling lively, Mrs. O'Malley cared only for ferreting out a cache of money she'd convinced herself that her husband had hidden in the barn after selling off his saloon. "Hunting for Tom's money" occupied her waking hours more than any other pastime.

Into the barn she and Lorena delved, sifting through decades of accumulation: "boxes of letters, old books, old bits of finery, discarded furniture, hay and straw." Nearly everything they unearthed had a memory attached to it, and Mrs. O'Malley regaled Lorena with endless tales of her sordid youth, "smacking her wicked old lips over each lewd detail."

Yet for all her eccentricities, Mrs. O'Malley knew how to treat a hired girl with decency. If she wasn't as openly nurturing as Mrs. Dodd had been, the saloonkeeper's wife had her own unorthodox ways of showing Lorena that she mattered. Mrs. O'Malley insisted, right from the start, that the girl wear rouge and powder to brighten her plain and somber face. Despite earning full-time wages, Lorena was free to attend school. The hours she needed to practice her recitation for the contest caused no fuss, either. Only one thing about Lorena seemed to perturb Mrs. O'Malley. "My wardrobe distressed her," Lorena remembered, and before long Mrs. O'Malley was buying fabric to sew the young lady new dresses with hats trimmed to match, smothering them in the ribbons and lace she was just a little too fond of. "Even I knew I looked funny,"

Lorena later confessed of the gaudy clothing Mrs. O'Malley lavished upon her.

~

Bedecked in one of Mrs. O'Malley's frilled concoctions, Lorena traveled to Aberdeen on May 14, 1909, filled with a dread so heavy it ought to have slowed the train. Of the seven students scheduled to perform at the declamatory contest that evening, Lorena was to speak last of all. Silent panic poisoned any chance she had to enjoy the other recitations as she sat waiting for her turn to do the thing she hated most in the world.

"It was a nightmare," Lorena recalled of her few minutes onstage. "I managed to get through it without breaking down, but that was about all."

Probably it wasn't as bad as all that, at least if the Aberdeen newspaper reports are to be believed. One called her performance "a very delightful reading," while another noted that the musical accompaniment "was cleverly done and won her much applause."

But Lorena's roaring sense of failure deafened her to the applause. "I returned to Bowdle convinced that I had disgraced myself and my school forever. I wanted to crawl away and hide." So she did. Lorena never showed her face at Bowdle High again. In the heat of her embarrassment, the urge for an education that had sustained her through a winter of Mrs. Bickert's tirades went up in smoke. "The year was nearly over anyway," she reasoned.

Lorena slumped into Mrs. O'Malley's routine, sleeping when she slept and trailing behind her as she rifled through the barn on her endless hunt for cash. For a change of scene, they'd wander out to the depot to see who was coming and going on the trains. For weeks, Lorena did little else.

CHAPTER 9

"SOMETHING OUGHT TO BE DONE," MRS. O'MALLEY SUDDENLY decided. For reasons no one could discern, that summer the usually listless Mrs. O'Malley appointed herself in charge of Lorena's future. All the "knocking about" Lorena had done for the last two years just couldn't go on, she declared.

Marriage was the simplest solution, Mrs. O'Malley figured. Bowdle practically swarmed with young men working the rail lines, outnumbering women so sharply that girls Lorena's age could take their pick of a vast array of potential husbands. Lorena didn't care for male company any more than she ever had, but she let Mrs. O'Malley play Cupid and select a "stocky, sandy-haired" fellow one day at the train station.

After an evening of moving pictures and ice cream with Nabisco Wafers, her beau tried to steal a kiss. "Whereupon I slapped him, with all my might." That was the end of railway romance for Lorena Hickok, no matter how Mrs. O'Malley prodded.

"Of Mrs. O'Malley's next move I took a dim view," Lorena remembered. "She asked me about my mother's people." Lorena knew what that could lead to—busybody relatives swooping in to take care of her—and that was something she wanted no part of. In spite of all the bumps in the road, Lorena liked being on her own. "I had a horror of family authority—of being bossed," as she put it. If a place didn't suit her, she could just pack up and leave, with no one to answer to but herself. All that would end if she let herself be taken in by far-flung aunts, uncles, or cousins. "The chances are I'd have been sent away somewhere to be trained to be a good servant," she remembered with disdain.

But Mrs. O'Malley wheedled, and Lorena told her about Aunt Ella.

Write her, Mrs. O'Malley urged. Lorena balked. Three years had passed since she'd seen her mother's cousin. Lorena had hardly been more than a child the last time Ella had come to visit.

"I still thought of Aunt Ella as the loveliest person I had ever known," Lorena said, "but I doubted if she could take me to live with her." There had even been letters from Aunt Ella in the meanwhile, but she'd never answered them. A vague reluctance had held Lorena back then, just as it did now. Perhaps deep down she dreaded the possibility of being turned away as much as she dreaded the thought of relinquishing her hard-earned independence.

Mrs. O'Malley wheedled some more, until Lorena grudgingly divulged Ella's address. Mrs. O'Malley promptly scribbled out the letter that Lorena refused to write—"one of the worst spelled, funniest letters" Ella Ellis would ever receive.

Aunt Ella's reply came back so fast, she might have fired it from a cannon. And not only a letter, but train fare for Lorena to Chicago.

Mrs. O'Malley wore her success like fresh plumage. She had a mission now—to send Lorena Hickok off to the big city in style—and she abandoned her pocketbook and sewing machine to the cause with "joyous enthusiasm." More lace, more frills, more hats! Shining patent leather oxfords tied with inch-wide ribbons!

A light blue suit that Mrs. O'Malley had made for Lorena was deemed travel-worthy, once it was paired with a hat and blouse lacy enough to make a peacock feel plain. Mrs. O'Malley washed the suit up fresh, starching the skirt until it could stand by itself.

Lorena's long braids, which she always coiled "Gretchen style" about her head, would never do. Mrs. O'Malley unwound them and proceeded to rat, wave, puff, twist, and sweep Lorena's hair into a valiant pompadour, complete with a roll dipping down over the forehead. Then powder and rouge, of course.

So it was that in the heat of an August afternoon, Lorena Hickok found herself standing at the depot with a suitcase dangling from one arm and a shoebox heavily laden with provisions tucked under the other. The trim on her hat guaranteed she'd be noticed by one and all, and her starched blue suit would see to it that she stood straight and tall, no matter how much she might wish to shrink away.

"With what I took to be perspiration cutting furrows down through the cosmetics on her cheeks, Mrs. O'Malley kissed me goodbye." Blessed by Mrs. O'Malley's tears, Lorena stepped onto the train that would carry her from one life to another.

CHAPTER 10

SEVEN HUNDRED AND FIFTY SOOT-CHOKED MILES STOOD BE-
tween Lorena and Chicago. The August heat demanded open windows
in the cars—windows that allowed every speck of the locomotive's endless stream of smoke and cinders to fly inside. Lorena quietly perspired
all afternoon and into the night as the train doggedly chugged its way to
Minneapolis.

Following a long wait the next morning, she changed to the Chicago-
bound train and repeated the whole sooty, sweaty experience. Lorena's lunch box was not faring any better than she was in the heat. Mrs.
O'Malley had crammed it full of an array of food as motley as her wardrobe, including an entire freshly fried chicken and some rapidly blacken-
ing bananas. By noon of that second day, the smell from the shoebox was
enough to draw unhappy glares from passengers in neighboring seats.

With a pang of regret, Lorena pitched the whole box out the window. For the rest of that long afternoon, she ate Cracker Jack, bought
from the news butcher who walked the aisles selling candy and newspapers.

Dusk had fallen by the time Lorena's train eased itself into Chicago.
Out of the coach she tumbled, into the roiling confusion of the biggest
hubbub she'd ever seen in her life. The place boiled with activity, as busy
and as crowded as an anthill. And then, there was Aunt Ella, looking
tinier than ever in contrast to the vast station. "Immaculate in a grey
ensemble," she limped toward her cousin's daughter.

Lorena could not speak. Faced by this delicate little woman who
seemed to gleam with neatness, she suddenly felt conscious of every inch
of her height, every wrinkle and soot smudge on her suit. The weight

of her drooping hair, her powder, rouge, and sweat made it impossible to smile.

Aunt Ella did not seem troubled in the least by Lorena's bedraggled appearance and outlandish attire. Everything about her radiated welcome. "The hands she held out in greeting were encased in spotless chamois gloves," Lorena remembered with awe. "It was the first time I had ever seen a pair of real chamois gloves."

~~

Lorena had been right about one thing all along: Aunt Ella could not take her in. Now a widow, Aunt Ella had moved into her elderly parents' home, which they also shared with an unmarried daughter, as well as a grandson and his wife. The household's sole breadwinner was Ella's nephew, a young doctor. The house, the budget, or both could not accommodate one more person.

Within weeks, if not days, Lorena had another train ticket in her hand, this one to Battle Creek, Michigan, where she would board with the family of William and Anna Fish, of 52 South Avenue. Like Ella, "Aunt" Anna was a cousin of Lorena's mother. Her husband and two sons were proprietors of the OK Laundry on Jefferson Avenue.

~~

Lorena arrived in Michigan just in time to enroll as a sophomore at Battle Creek High School—a school like none she'd ever seen. Newly opened that year, the domed steel-and-stone structure was the pride of the city.

Marble stairs and double glass doors led into a corridor that would soon be adorned with murals of Michigan history. At its center sat a 386-seat auditorium, complete with a choir balcony at the rear. The basement gymnasium included an elevated rubber running track, accessible by a spiral staircase.

Sparkling new laboratories for chemistry and physical science occupied one wing; a domestic science department furnished with two kitchens and five sewing machines dominated the other. A museum of cabinets stocked with specimens of birds, rocks, corals, moths, and butterflies filled the end of one corridor, complementing the five-hundred-volume library.

The fifth-floor dome topped off the building in every sense. Not simply decorative, it rotated to serve as an observatory for astronomy students.

Battle Creek itself was just as dazzling to a girl from "bare, bright, windy Dakota." Thanks to its early history with the Underground Railroad, a thriving community of Seventh-day Adventists, and the San—more properly known as the Battle Creek Sanitarium, a thirty-acre health resort renowned throughout the country—Battle Creek was a bustling city of nearly twenty-five thousand. The Kellogg brothers and C. W. Post had also founded cereal empires there, built on Corn Flakes and Grape-Nuts, inspiring the nickname Cereal City.

In Battle Creek, no threat of violence hung over Lorena. No worries about food or shelter nagged at her. For the first time, she could simply be a schoolgirl with the freedom to indulge in all the things other young people enjoyed.

Lorena's student transcript shows a schedule of classes that would have made Professor Johnson back in Bowdle dance a gleeful jig: algebra, geometry, English, physics, German, Latin, Greek, history, drawing, physiology, and commercial geography. She excelled in her studies, earning As in every class but drawing and physics. Just as important, she began making friends.

First and foremost was Leta Browning. The two were in the German club together and took part in its Christmas party, sleigh ride, oyster supper, and Mother Goose masquerade party. Lorena and another friend, Ruth Kelsey, went to the masquerade as Tweedledum and Tweedledee.

Ruth was a Glee Club member, and before long Lorena was singing alongside her at rehearsals. There, among two dozen other altos and sopranos, Lorena could let her voice take wing without drawing the individual scrutiny she so detested.

Lorena was also a perfect candidate for the Girls Amateur Literary Society (the GALS, they called themselves), a group of straight-A students who gathered to read and discuss books. But Lorena never joined. Refreshments were vital to GALS meetings, just as they are to today's book clubs, and Lorena couldn't impose upon the Fish family to host one of the GALS' monthly feeds—a generous spread that might include meat loaf, potato salad, fruit salad, sandwiches, olives, nuts, candy, ice cream, and cake for a crowd of thirty-five young ladies. Yet the idea of her membership in that flock of bookish girls was so natural that at least one friend would unconsciously imagine Lorena into her memories of GALS meetings decades later.

Lorena was so cautious about intruding on her foster family that she never even invited Leta or Ruth to the Fishes' house. Still, both the girls valued her friendship and would remember her fondly to the end of their days. They especially recalled how she laughed—almost crying at the same time, so that tears rolled down her cheeks until she had to shove them away with her sleeve or the back of her hand. To her friends, she was also "sensitive," "a clever, lovely girl," and "awfully funny." You couldn't quite call her carefree, though. Something keen and earnest simmered quietly beneath her surface, awaiting the chance to boil over. A curious combination of self-deprecation and drive—ambition without ego—that was Lorena Hickok. "We always admired Lorena, that's for sure," Ruth Kelsey said.

And then there was Miss Alicent Holt, Lorena's Latin teacher. As an adult, Lorena would shower her with superlatives—"The most gifted teacher I ever knew," she insisted, though Miss Holt was fresh out of college and only a handful of years older than her students. "The best teacher I ever had, who taught me Latin, Greek, and manners." Lorena never did say just what made her Latin instructor so special, but it's clear from her reverent tone that Miss Holt had a profound impact that resonated well beyond her school years. That reference to "manners" is the only clue, for Miss Holt did not teach etiquette—not formally, anyway. Perhaps, as old Mrs. Dodd had, she sensed the gaps in Lorena's upbringing and found a way to gently shepherd her toward the self-assurance she craved. Something about Miss Holt captivated Lorena, and something in Alicent Holt responded. An affinity blossomed between teacher and student that would last a lifetime.

As Lorena's intellect expanded, so, too, did her confidence. Somehow, the girl who hated to speak in public got herself roped into yet another oratory contest during her junior year and took home second prize. Though the text does not survive, her "remarkable" piece, called "Educational Monopoly," sounds very much as though it grew out of her own struggle to balance the necessity of earning food and shelter against her desire for an education. "She spoke of the need for a fund to help high school students graduate," the yearbook related, "and so true were her arguments that they made a deep impression on everyone."

The next year, there she was onstage again with a new oration. Ruth Kelsey remembered that contest, and the pity she felt for her friend as she watched Lorena perform. "She had the build for an opera singer," Ruth recalled, and Hick's face still flushed as it always had when she was flustered, nearly matching a "most unbecoming" red dress that might have been a relic from her days with Mrs. O'Malley.

Physically awkward though she was, Lorena also had an undeniable eloquence. She captured first place and a $20 prize for her oration entitled "The Cry of the Children." "Last night she gave one of the most fluent and interesting orations that the students have ever had the opportunity of hearing," the *Battle Creek Daily Moon* reported of Lorena's plea for the children of the slums.

By her senior year, everyone knew that Lorena Hickok had a knack for putting words together. She'd earned a top spot alongside Leta Browning on the yearbook staff, and another as the literary editor of the school magazine, *The Key*. A senior class satire in the yearbook characterized her as a girl so buzzing with plans that she exclaimed, "I've got so many ideas that my head itches!"

CHAPTER 11

WITH HER COVETED DIPLOMA FINALLY IN HAND, LORENA HAD decisions to make.

Not long after Lorena's graduation, the Fishes' twenty-nine-year-old son died suddenly. That spring, according to Lorena, Anna Fish "went sort of crazy." The time had come for Lorena to move on. But where, and to what?

Marriage was already luring scores of her classmates into domesticity, but Lorena was not among them. Despite the haziness of the path before her, she once again knew perfectly well what she did *not* want, and matrimony was near the top of the list. That resolution came with drawbacks. "The 'unfortunate' women who had not found husbands taught school, clerked in stores, became dressmakers or milliners or nurses, went into domestic service, or lived with relatives," she recalled. "A few hardy sisters had invaded the professions, but they were still regarded as freaks." Although by now Lorena had an inkling that her desires didn't align with her peers', she wasn't quite ready to commit herself to the role of a "freak" just yet.

Lorena moved in with the Browning family during the summer of 1912 and found herself a job that allowed her to pay her board with enough left over to quietly amass a small savings. One afternoon, Leta Browning remembered, Lorena walked into the house and announced to Mrs. Browning, "Well, I've decided to go away to college."

"Oh my goodness, Lorena!" Mrs. Browning exclaimed. "Do you think you can afford it?"

"Well, I've got sixty dollars," Lorena said.

As usual, Lorena had been reading. Among other things, she'd read

Dawn O'Hara: The Girl Who Laughed, Edna Ferber's popular novel about a female journalist making her way in a man's world. Ferber, who'd filled the pages of *Dawn O'Hara* with snatches of her own life, was something of a local hero. Born in Kalamazoo, just twenty-five miles west of Battle Creek, she'd attended Lawrence College, in Appleton, Wisconsin, then supported herself as a newspaper reporter (just like her fictional Miss O'Hara) before launching a celebrated career as a novelist.

If a girl from west Michigan had begun her path to success at Lawrence, Lorena reasoned, why couldn't she? So she set her sights on Ferber's alma mater. The college catalog said that a year's expenses would run $75, and she already had $60. If she could get a position in a professor's house as a maid, that would make up the rest.

⁂

College was not much more hospitable to Lorena than grade school had been. In her later years she grimly summed up her difficulty at Lawrence in two words: "sorority trouble." Lorena didn't spell out the details, but it's easy enough to imagine how she felt when the Lawrence girls didn't welcome her into their circles.

Nothing she did to ingratiate herself with her classmates worked. Lorena knew as well as anyone that she wasn't pretty, but she was smart, ambitious, funny. Nevertheless, whatever elusive something the other girls required of a sorority sister, or even just a plain old chum, Lorena didn't have it.

Lorena ended up as lonely as she'd ever been—more so, maybe, after the friends she'd made and the clubs she'd joined in high school. She so dreaded eating in the dormitory that she found a job at a local grocery store and got her meals there instead. While her classmates socialized, she burrowed into the library and placated herself with volumes of Kipling.

Her grades sank along with her mood. Shoddy attendance progressed into ditching some classes altogether. When the chapel bell rang for daily services, and when the girls swapped their skirts for bloomers for the compulsory weekly sessions of physical education, Lorena wasn't among them.

⁓

Is it any wonder, then, that the earliest surviving piece of Lorena's writing reflected her woes? That winter she published a cautionary tale called "The Reward of Stuffing"—a recollection of the comeuppance she'd received for trying to impress her grade school classmates back in Dakota with pure braggadocio—in the university's literary magazine.

"At first my extravagant tales had been received with respect and admiration," Lorena's story began. But soon she'd crammed her fibs with "stuffing" until nobody believed her blatant exaggerations anymore. "But, filled with egotism, I had utterly refused to realize the fact." One day, after Lorena had regaled a group of girls with "a wonderful masterpiece of fiction" about all the tricks she could do on horseback, a sly classmate named Kate invited her to go riding. Cornered by her own embellishments, Lorena had no choice but to agree.

"My heart utterly refused to beat," she recalled of the moment she saw the horse Kate had chosen for her—the first Lorena had ridden since her grandfather plopped her aboard his old plow horse for a turn around the yard.

Quivering with fear and determination, she approached, chanting, "Pretty May! Sweet May!" May parted her lips to show Lorena an ominous mouth full of yellowed teeth.

Slapstick ensued as Lorena tried to mount, but she stubbornly refused to acknowledge her ignorance as she stumbled and fumbled with May's saddle and reins. No one who had so recently exclaimed "It is so exhilarating to feel oneself borne over hill and plain upon the back of a spirited steed!" could admit defeat so quickly.

First to her relief and then to her chagrin, May turned out to be anything but spirited. No matter how Lorena urged the tall gray mare along the road, May grazed dispassionately among the grass and weeds lining the ditches.

"I gently tapped her on the flank using about half the force of a sick mosquito," Lorena recounted. May was not impressed.

Kate volunteered to help, swatting May with a piece of lath.

"I have always been convinced there was a nail in that stick," Lorena wrote ruefully, "for the fanciful May bolted down the road as though chased by a whole army of demons."

"Perhaps," Kate called out grandly as Lorena flailed for her life, "when you are a little more accustomed to the saddle, you can do some of your stunts for me, I'm so anxious to see them."

Stunts aplenty had transpired, though nothing like those Lorena had bragged about. "Every time [May's] hoofs would touch the ground I would bound up fully two feet into the air," Lorena wrote, "only to come down again with the force of a thousand bricks." Lorena held on for what seemed like six miles before jerking the reins and pleading, "Whoa!"

Contrary May obeyed instantaneously.

Next thing she knew, Lorena was splayed on the ground with Kate wailing from above, "Fatty, Fatty, are you killed?"

The only thing more bruised than her backside was her pride. "For weeks I was subjected to all the torture which youthful minds can invent," Lorena concluded her cautionary tale. "It will suffice to say here that I never told any more yarns to that crowd."

"The Reward of Stuffing" could have been a gloomy account of adolescent humiliation. Instead, Lorena had bent her memories as if passing her foibles through a prism until they refracted into comedy.

~~~

However late she might have been about turning in her assignments, her professors could not overlook the fact that, like "The Reward of Stuffing," Lorena Hickok's papers were *good*.

One day, Dr. Spencer called her into his office. Dr. Spencer was not just a rhetoric professor. He also worked as a reporter and a copyreader for the *Milwaukee Journal*. Something in Lorena's assignments had stood out to his newspaperman's eye. He suggested that Lorena consider pursuing a career in journalism instead of teaching.

But Lorena's grades did not match her abilities. The reports that reached Chicago by the end of that year alarmed Aunt Ella enough that she wrote to the university's administration, asking what, "other than sickness," could be the "cause of deficiency."

"Miss Hickok is a very bright girl and could stand among the very best in college," the president of Lawrence assured Aunt Ella. "It is simply a question of her dev[i]ling habits of regularity and faithfulness." Even with her absences and late assignments, Lorena's marks never slid below a 73. If she would just show up, just turn in the work, her success was practically assured.

Ella knew better than to scold. Instead, she encouraged. "Now my dear girlie you know my faith in you," she wrote to Lorena in June. "I do sincerely believe that next year you will rank among the very best in college. Oh how proud I would be of you."

Aunt Ella's words could only go so far. Lorena had worn herself out trying to contort into the shape of a Lawrence College girl. A year of that had been plenty. Back to Battle Creek she went, with no intention of returning to Appleton.

CHAPTER 12

ONCE MORE, LORENA SET OUT TO SUPPORT HERSELF. FIRST she found a place to board at 4 Fairview Avenue. The Brownings wouldn't stand for that, especially with Leta heading to college in Ohio, leaving room for Lorena in their home. Soon Lorena was part of the Browning household again, with Leta's parents as foster mother and father, and Leta's sister, Edna, as her sister.

Lorena wouldn't stay without paying her way, though. Nor would she hire herself out to cook and scrub. Those days were behind her. For all her indifference to college, she'd taken hold of Dr. Spencer's advice about journalism. Shortly after her arrival in Battle Creek, she presented herself at the office of the *Evening News* in search of employment.

Doing so took a certain amount of courage, a willingness to buck stereotypes, for newspaper reporting stood firmly outside the realm of feminine respectability.

In 1901, *Ladies' Home Journal* had published an article asking: "Is the Newspaper Office the Place for a Girl?" Nearly every newspaper editor who replied did so in tones of abject horror. "I would rather see my daughter starve than that she should ever have heard or seen what the women on my staff have been compelled to hear and see," one proclaimed. Another counseled: "In my eighteen years of experience in this office I have never yet seen a girl enter the newspaper field but that I have noticed a steady decline in that innate sense of refinement, gentleness, and womanliness with which she entered it . . . they lose something— what, I cannot say in words."

All that supposed concern was largely a sham. What newspapermen truly dreaded was the thought of changing their own workplace to accommodate the presence of a lady. She'd be "regarded as a threat to the peace, honor, and coziness of that sound haunt of masculinity—the city room."

Male editors and reporters wanted to be able to take off their suit coats and roll up their sleeves. They wanted to keep right on smoking, spitting, and swearing at their desks and swapping bawdy jokes over their coffee and cigarettes. None of that was possible if a lady was anywhere in sight.

"A woman—never!" cried one editor at the prospect of hiring a female reporter. "Why, you can't say d[amn it] to a woman!"

Even the few women in the newspaper business cautioned their prospective sisters against the job's demands. "In order to make any progress in her work, she must break over the barriers raised against [her]," reporter Anne Eliot wrote in 1909. "This means that she must be aggressive instead of gentle, pushing herself where she is not wanted. That she must be rude, if necessary, persistent, impertinent, callous—anything to gain her point. In short, she must forget that she is a woman."

One of the warnings was true—it was strenuous work for both mind and body. As Anne Eliot described it, "The editor calls out: 'Rush copy—just twenty minutes, Miss H—; hurry!' And she bends to her task with every nerve strained to make the next edition. All about there is commotion—typewriters rattling, telegraph instruments clicking, copy boys running hither and thither, editors giving commands.

"But this is not the worst. At each elbow stands a copy boy ready to snatch the story from her page by page or paragraph by paragraph. Her thoughts are practically pulled from her brain before they are written." The strain, thought most minds of the day, was simply too much for a creature as frail as a woman to endure.

But Lorena had no one to discourage her. On the contrary, Aunt Ella thought trying her luck with the local papers would be preferable to the physical strain that would come with a job at the Fish family's laundry. Working at a newspaper office "would be *fine*," she wrote, emphasizing her approval. "Laundry would be very hot work in the summer."

Unlike her hapless foray into domestic service, Lorena had some genuine qualifications for this kind of work. She'd held editorships on the school newspaper, as well as the yearbook. Thanks to those oratory contests, her ability to express herself clearly and effectively was well documented. She had Dr. Spencer's endorsement. Ruth Kelsey's father, business manager of the *Battle Creek Journal,* also spoke up in her favor. The *Evening News* took her on.

Lo and behold, Lorena liked it. Better yet, she was good at it.

Her assignments were the most mundane "news" in town. Weddings, engagements, club meetings, dances, tea parties, ice cream socials, and so forth were the realm conceded to women reporters. Hard news—which included everything from politics, finance, and sports to murders, fires, accidents, natural disasters, and scandal—remained very much a man's domain.

Mostly, Lorena's duties consisted of loitering at the train station, waiting to see if any prominent personages were arriving or departing—"collecting 'personals,'" they called it. She also poked her nose into shops and offices, foraging for whiffs of news and dreaming of the day when she might earn the chance to interview someone of real fame—someone like the actresses and singers she'd read about, or the hero of her child-hood, President Theodore Roosevelt.

The tidbits she collected weren't much more than gossip, but for her efforts Lorena earned $7 every week. Within months, she abandoned the *Evening News* for the *Battle Creek Journal,* where she made $8 a week for the same work. When she heard that papers in larger cities were easing editors' workloads by employing copyreaders—someone to read the reporters' stories and catch errors of fact and grammar, perhaps smooth out any awkward passages, and compose headlines—she convinced her editor that she could do the job, and her weekly salary increased to $10. Every afternoon, when the seasoned reporters saw what this twenty-year-old rookie had done to their copy, they "promptly raised hell." That didn't deter Lorena. Being "cordially disliked" by reporters was all part of a copyreader's territory.

CHAPTER 13

AFTER TROOPING AROUND ALL DAY GATHERING THE INFINI-
tesimal details of other people's social lives, Lorena generally preferred to cozy up in her bedroom with a library book. "People who knew her thought a great deal of her," Edna Browning recalled, "but she just seemed to want to be by herself a lot." On Sunday mornings before church, Lorena would say with an almost cheerful sort of resignation, "Come on, Edna, let's go upstairs and get ready to appear before the public." She stuck to the newspaper, the library, and church, and not much else.

As Edna saw it, Lorena was someone who "loved fun but couldn't make fun," so when girls and boys came to the Browning house, Edna always ensured that Lorena was invited to join the group. But Edna knew that Lorena wanted something bigger from life than neighborhood taffy pulls could offer. "I'm going out and make a name for myself in this world," she'd informed the Brownings with striking conviction, and she kept herself resolutely pointed in that direction. Edna couldn't remember Lorena ever having a beau or even attending a party.

❧

Something more than her powerful amalgam of ambition and introversion might have been compelling Lorena to keep to herself, however. Young men and women her age were mixing at those parties and taffy pulls, giddily pairing up and forming couples. Sure, she'd always been the introspective sort who loved to lose herself in a good story, but the fact of the matter is that Lorena just wasn't entranced by the opposite sex the way so many of her peers were. Quite the contrary.

All her life she'd admired and idolized other girls and women. Lottie McCafferty, Elizabeth Ward, Alicent Holt. Whether she knew it already, whether the knowledge hit her all at once or crept up gradually, is anyone's guess, but this might have been when Lorena Hickok began to fully understand that what she felt toward women amounted to something much more significant than admiration.

What she thought of these feelings can only be imagined. In the Midwest of the 1910s, shame and disgust are the most likely candidates. Because of the intense taboos surrounding queer relationships in the late nineteenth and early twentieth centuries, Lorena very likely had no opportunity to learn that women who were in love with each other, who had formed fulfilling lifelong partnerships, did indeed exist. The magnitude of that silence would have been enough to make her understand that her ardor for women had to be kept secret at all costs. For all Lorena knew, she might be the only girl in history who had ever felt the way she did when she looked at another young lady.

But Lorena couldn't completely mask herself. Hints that she was different insisted on leaking out. When they did, the humiliation was almost more than she could bear.

"What in the world?" Mrs. Browning exclaimed when Lorena came home on the verge of tears one day. Witnessing Lorena upset was a shock in itself. Little things got under her skin so infrequently that she hardly bothered to complain. With her sights so firmly set on the future, it was usually easy for her to brush off petty annoyances. Not this time, though.

As she walked home, she confessed, some boys on the street had hollered out at her, "Look at the woman in man's clothing!"

The taunt made no sense. She had on a long skirt and shirtwaist, like any other woman. True, her clothes weren't fancy or cut in the latest style, but they were unequivocally women's clothes. Nevertheless, the boys' words stung something deep in her, and all the worse for the truth buried in them.

No matter how she tried, she'd never been able to make herself look the way a woman was supposed to look. Lorena could have rattled off a whole list of feminine attributes no one had ever applied to her: cute, pretty, beautiful, dainty, graceful, elegant, ladylike. None of the girls she knew seemed to have to try at all to receive those compliments. So far as Lorena could see, there was exactly one way to be a woman, and she was the only girl on earth who could not decipher the formula.

It came in part from her lifelong habit of hunching over, of trying to minimize the features she was eternally self-conscious of: her build and her size. Even Edna Browning had noticed something similar to what the jeering boys had seen in the way Lorena moved through the world. "Kind of a slovenly walk," Edna called it, "more like a man's walk." Despite her efforts, something about Lorena betrayed the truth she so desperately needed to keep hidden from the world—that she felt things only men were supposed to feel.

Lorena had always hated being conspicuous, but this was another matter. It had been one thing to stick out because of superficial circumstances—to hear schoolmates whispering about the housekeeper, or to have to answer to "Fatty." Now she inspired ridicule because of who she was deep down within herself.

CHAPTER 14

WAR ERUPTED IN EUROPE IN THE SUMMER OF 1914. BATTLEFIELD tales had captivated Lorena since childhood, whether they were set in ancient Troy or the American West, and United Press reporter Karl von Wiegand's breathless, gory coverage of the German front sparked in Lorena a desire to become a war correspondent. For that, she needed formal schooling in journalism.

And so on Valentine's Day of 1915, Lorena set off once more for Lawrence College. This time, she would not solely be a student. She also managed to wrangle herself a part-time job as a correspondent for the *Milwaukee Sentinel*.

The coursework was no more an obstacle than it had ever been. Yet once again Lorena hungered more for acceptance than for good grades. Without one, she had no use for the other. It wasn't enough that she secured a place on the staffs of both the yearbook and the literary magazine. Lorena still perceived herself as a "complete misfit" on Lawrence's campus. That feeling of not belonging proved intolerable. Lorena dropped out after a single semester.

~~~

As she so often had back in South Dakota, Lorena landed on her feet, securing a $15-a-week position at the *Milwaukee Sentinel*. The previous society editor had let an important story slip through her fingers, so Lorena got the job.

Most of the details of Lorena's time on the *Sentinel* have blurred in the hundred years since she was hired. "I was young then and full of hope and bright dreams. No money," she recalled fondly years later. "I lived at the YWCA, sometimes mostly on beans. But those were brave days!" Lorena found a fine German coffeehouse and treated herself regularly to rich cups of hot chocolate and Bavarian pastries, just like the ones she'd read about in Edna Ferber's *Dawn O'Hara*. She became a suffragist, and cultivated friendships with Germans.

German friends were practically a requirement in Milwaukee for anybody who did not want to dedicate their leisure hours to solitude. Milwaukee during the early twentieth century "was as German as Germany." German often drowned out the sounds of English on the streets, and restaurant menus featured Wiener schnitzel and Apfel Pfannkuchen. Beer-brewing empires funded the luxurious homes on Grand Avenue, where families named Pabst, Schlitz, Uihlein, and Schandein ruled the upper echelons of capital-S Society.

Those Milwaukee socialites looked down from a loftier peak than any Lorena had covered for Battle Creek's papers. Perhaps it was inevitable that a young woman from a "fly-specked" prairie town offended one of them. How exactly Lorena managed to infuriate a grande dame of the Uihlein family is lost to history—likely some unforgivable breach of high-society etiquette. Mrs. Uihlein demanded Lorena be fired.

But Lorena had been making herself useful at the *Sentinel*. Edna Ferber's books had taught her the benefits of lingering at the newspaper office after turning in her own bland articles about rich ladies' club meetings and engagement parties. There was no better way to learn the ropes, and no better way to ingratiate herself with the city editor, than by volunteering for night assignments. Lorena's diligence paid off. Instead of firing her, Lorena's boss transferred her to the city staff, which handled the daily local news stories.

She could not have been more pleased if she had deliberately engineered the switch. Now, at last, she might get the chance to cover breaking news rather than relaying the carefully planned details of formal events. That is, if her editor would send her out on the kinds of assignments she longed for.

Though she'd escaped the society department, sexism still barred Lorena from the most coveted stories. Ishbel Ross, a *Toronto Daily News* reporter who faced the same obstacles, later explained: "The city editor—chivalrous soul—keeps her down for two reasons: he doubts her capacity, and he hates to throw her to the wolves in the rough and tumble of big news events. He handles her with kid gloves when she wouldn't object to brass knuckles."

But in the city room, with all its rattle and clamor, Lorena found for the first time in her life that so much of what she had cursed about herself suddenly became a kind of asset. The "womanliness" that she'd tried for so many years to emulate didn't do her any good in a crowd of men pounding on typewriters with pipes clenched in their teeth. On the contrary, the lack of many of those so-called feminine attributes helped her fit in.

The stereotypical and much-disdained "girl reporter" used her looks and her tears to manipulate sources and always got emotionally tangled up in her stories. Her opposite, the hardened male reporter, witnessed the news by peering out of a cloud of cigar smoke with a dispassionate glare. Lorena fell smack in the middle.

She wasn't inured to the world, but she wasn't fragile in mind or body, either. Though starved for affection, she was no flirt. She'd survived both physical and sexual assaults and heard true tales lewder than any of the reporters' off-color jokes. After all the time she'd spent serving meals to railroad workers and farmhands, a roomful of men didn't necessarily intimidate her. None of that was anything Lorena would talk about outright, but it made a difference. Concealing that tender heart of hers was an unusually sturdy, levelheaded mien that gave her an edge.

To this day, only eight *Milwaukee Sentinel* articles by Lorena Hickok have been found, making her development as a reporter tough to trace. The earliest, from her stint as a Lawrence College correspondent, featured an interview with a classmate, Fredrika Brown, also known as Princess Klabado of Liberia's Grebo people, who had been sent to the United States to be educated. The next saw Lorena investigating the conditions of Milwaukee's reform school for girls. In college, Lorena had signed her own name to her interview with her Liberian classmate. After leaving school, she took on the pen name Lorena Lawrence for the next three years or so.

Lorena had a decided knack for crafting a lede—the opening sentence or paragraph of a newspaper article. Most leads are straightforward summaries, but Lorena's articles often opened in ways that quirked an eyebrow, arousing curiosity even as they informed. "Wisconsin has within her borders a real, live, sure enough princess," her interview with Miss Brown began. In her reform school feature, her lead declared that the life of an inmate "does not differ in many respects from that of their more fortunate sisters in colleges and boarding schools throughout the country," a claim sure to draw her readers in to learn more.

Those first two articles were competent, if otherwise unextraordinary. The third, an interview with a local orchestra leader, took a mischievous tone. "Girls! Here's Your Chance to Get a Husband! Cupid Points the Way, Provided You Qualify," the headline announced. Apparently deprived of any substantial information about the man or his profession, Lorena nonetheless managed to turn out several inches of column space with a tongue-in-cheek discussion of the musician's qualifications for a wife. "I won't do," she declared of herself in the lead. "I'm too tall, and too radical a suffragist." Even when an article had almost nothing to say, Lorena could lure readers in at the start and hold them captive until the end.

CHAPTER 15

cess for women reporters in the 1910s. "Fundamentally, there is no better outlet for the newspaper woman's skill," Ishbel Ross wrote in her history of women journalists, *Ladies of the Press.* "It is the one job that the city editor does not necessarily think a man can do better."

"The most difficult assignment that can be given to a women reporter, or to any reporter, in fact, is that of securing interviews with the socially prominent and exclusive," agreed Anne Eliot in a *Collier's* magazine article in 1909. "The editor prizes as fine gold a genuine conversation with a real leader of society on some timely topic, or even a personal chat."

That November of 1915 brought just such a figure to Milwaukee: Geraldine Farrar, diva of operatic stages from Monte Carlo to New York City. Only a month before, she had starred in a silent film, making her one of the first multimedia celebrities. An interview with Geraldine Farrar was all but guaranteed to boost circulation.

Twenty-two-year-old Lorena got the assignment.

Lorena fairly reeled with excitement at the thought of speaking with Geraldine Farrar, her "heroine of heroines," the very next day. No loitering around the office that night—back to her room at the YWCA she scurried to wash her only spare blouse, the best one she owned.

Next morning, she buttoned her Sunday suit over the blouse. The suit, which had been with her since her freshman year at Lawrence, tended to shrink if it got wet. To disguise that flaw, she'd bought some cheap silver fur and sewn it around the cuffs and hem of the jacket. Lorena added her finest shoes and topped it all off with "a $4.98 hat with wings never worn by any bird."

Miss Farrar did not arrive that day, or the next. Each night Lorena descended to the YWCA's basement laundry room and rewashed and reironed her blouse, scorching a sleeve in her anxiety.

By the third day—the day before Farrar's concert—Lorena was a solid mass of jitters. Geraldine Farrar still had not reached Milwaukee when the clock struck noon. At one o'clock, the city editor told Lorena to call the rail yards. She did, and called five more times as the hours ticked by. Finally, at four-thirty, the rail manager rang in to confirm that Miss Farrar's private railcar had at last arrived.

Lorena flung herself toward the elevator. Two male colleagues—a drama critic and a court reporter—bolted after her, shouting, "Wait a minute! You don't want to chase down there alone—it's getting dark!"

Rain drizzled, cold and gray, as Lorena and her escorts sloshed their way to the train station, all of them sharing a single umbrella. Lorena could not speak. Something like stage fright had overcome her. At the lakefront rail yard, the manager pointed out where Miss Farrar's private car sat on a siding half a mile away.

Lorena could hear her heart thumping as it had never thumped before as she waded down the muddy track. In mere minutes she'd be standing face to face with Geraldine Farrar.

"Good luck," the court reporter said as she skittered up the steps of the prima donna's railcar. "Don't get scared," the drama critic advised with a squeeze of her trembling hand.

Lorena entered a vestibule that faced the car's inner door. Presently a maid came out. Lorena asked for Miss Farrar. The maid disappeared back inside. Ten minutes passed, then twenty, then thirty. The flush that always crept up Lorena's neck and onto her face when she got excited burned higher and higher. Lorena alternately pressed her palms to the cold window glass and to her cheeks to cool them. In between, she peered at her skirt for any signs of shrinkage. The fabric was already so wrinkled and mussed, it was impossible to tell.

After who knows how long, the two soggy *Sentinel* men convinced Lorena to come out and get some supper. By eight o'clock Lorena was back in that vestibule, waiting with grim determination. Her *Sentinel* colleagues had left with the umbrella to finish their own assignments, promising to send someone back to fetch her. The clock ticked, and an unidentifiable smell slowly filled the little compartment. Unbeknownst to Lorena, the glue that held the so-called wings on her hat was disintegrating into a feathery goo.

At long last, a sound came from the other side of the door—a scratching sound. Out came not Geraldine Farrar, but a Boston bulldog named Wiggles. Wagging his stumpy tail, Wiggles took a lick at Lorena's fur cuff, and then a bite. By the time the door opened again, he'd munched his way through half of one cuff and was starting in on the other.

Only a hairdresser emerged into the vestibule this time. The man shook his head "doubtfully" when he heard Lorena's mission and went on his way. Next came "an Ethiopian gentleman," who admitted her to the railcar's living room while he went in search of Miss Farrar's manager, Mr. Ellis. Lorena idly surveyed the piano, the photographs, the music and flowers . . . and waited.

Sometime after nine o'clock Mr. Ellis arrived, gushing with sympathy. An interview on the night before a concert would be "absolutely impossible," he apologized. Miss Farrar needed her rest. Besides, reporters never made any inquiries of consequence. "They ask so many impudent and personal questions about her private affairs," he complained.

Perhaps a meeting the next morning? Lorena suggested.

"What, on the day when she is to sing?" Mr. Ellis exclaimed. "O, never!"

Mr. Ellis placated her with a signed photograph of Miss Farrar and turned her out into the deluge.

Every head in the city room swiveled to see Lorena when she returned to the *Sentinel* office.

Her suit had shrunk a full size, its fur in tatters thanks to Wiggles. The trimmings on her hat had drowned in a sticky soup of glue, and her best shoes were goopy with mud.

Someone laughed.

Lorena's temper sparked, then blazed. "Angry doesn't describe it at all," she remembered. She was plain mad, spitting, stinging mad—not at the laughter, but at the prima donna who had caused it.

Anyone could tell what kind of an article Lorena Hickok was writing as she worked. You didn't even have to know her. If it was a sob story, tears sluiced down her cheeks. When it was funny, her whole body "rippled with merriment."

That night, the *Sentinel* staff watched as Lorena "pounded a scorcher," taking out all her frustration on her typewriter. It was a story crafted to shame the mighty diva for her hauteur, for lacking the common courtesy to speak to a reporter who had slogged through half a mile of mud and rain and waited hours, only to be turned away. Also, there was the matter of the ruined suit.

In the absence of any real news to report, Lorena did what a whole generation of newspaperwomen before her had done: she put herself smack in the center of the story. "After splashing through exactly 163 puddles of water and plowing through an acre or so of nice, rich mud, most of which clung to my best shoes," she wrote, "I arrived at the private car of the peerless Geraldine, only to learn first that she was indisposed; second, that she was 'too tired to see reporters tonight,' and lastly that she had become annoyed at the impudent questions which gentlemen and ladies of the press had been asking her and therefore would submit to no more newspaper interviews.

"I find consolation in the fact that all those nice interviews which will be published about Miss Farrar for the next few weeks will be fakes. Her manager told me so, and who on earth would know if not he?"

Denied even a glimpse of the prima donna to share with her readers, Lorena detailed her "interview" with Wiggles instead. "He also kissed me—oh, the thrill of it! To be kissed by Geraldine Farrar's dog!"

As she battered the keys, Lorena imagined a far-off day when *she* would be more famous than Geraldine Farrar, a day when Geraldine Farrar would beg to see *her*. Oh, the things she would relish saying to the prima donna on that glorious, glorious day.

Her fury spent, Lorena turned in the story, then flopped at her desk to sulk over the women's club items she hadn't finished that afternoon.

Not five minutes later, a gale of laughter gusted through the newsroom. Out of his office came the night city editor, exclaiming, "Say, that's great stuff! Why didn't you tell us you could write funny yarns?" What she'd meant as a spiteful "stinger" read to him as "a crackerjack" piece of comedy. He'd print it, and without a single change.

The next morning Lorena's story ran, adorned with a two-column-wide photo of Geraldine Farrar. That same afternoon a telephone call came for Lorena. She picked up the receiver to find Mr. Ellis on the line. Miss Farrar had been delighted by the story, he said, so delighted that Miss Hickok was invited to visit the famous soprano at the opera that evening between acts.

Everyone in the city room heard Lorena's retort. "You tell Miss Farrar for me to go to hell!" she barked, and slammed down the phone.

CHAPTER 16

NOW THAT THE CITY EDITOR HAD GOTTEN A GLIMPSE OF HER talent, Lorena started getting the kinds of assignments she'd lusted after.

When the legendary Australian soprano Nellie Melba performed in Milwaukee, Lorena had not only a seat in the auditorium, but a pass to the diva's dressing room. For a young woman who had cherished music since infancy, it was an experience to rival the divine. Melba's rendition of a popular lullaby brought Lorena to tears, reviving one of the precious few good memories she had of her own mother. "What I have to say to you won't mean much," Lorena quavered like a twenty-first-century fangirl, "but I just want to tell you that never before in my whole life have I enjoyed anything more than your 'Songs My Mother Taught Me.'"

"'God bless the girl!' boomed out the diva's rich, vibrant voice," Lorena recounted for the *Sentinel*'s readers. And then Melba kissed her.

Lorena's article read more like a rapturous diary entry than an interview, but the newspaper printed it nonetheless, and sent her out on even more high-profile assignments.

∾

When President Wilson and his wife visited Milwaukee in January 1916, Lorena was there. "I clasped the hand of the president of the United States, but—I was afraid to shake hands with his wife," Lorena's article began. "Beautiful, smiling Edith Bolling Wilson inspired me with more awe and shyness than did her distinguished husband."

The article detailed the "gone feeling" and every mounting twinge of panic that overtook Lorena at each footstep of the first lady's approach.

"My heart gave a sudden bound as I gazed at her exquisite features, and as her wonderful gray eyes rested on me for a moment I felt like kneeling," she rhapsodized.

It was the same formula she'd followed with the Melba story, only this time it hit an odd note, coming from a reporter who aspired to the kinds of assignments her male colleagues received. Anyone who read it couldn't help but conclude that Lorena Lawrence was just another fawning girl reporter whose constitution was too fragile for the excitement of real news.

The stories were right there in front of her, with no need for any fluttering. All she had to do was gather the information and report it without theatrics.

※

Or maybe, just maybe, Lorena knew what she was doing all along and was playing a role—crafting another of those "funny yarns" the night city editor had praised when she'd lampooned Geraldine Farrar. How else is it possible to explain the drastic shift in tone that occurred less than a week later, when she interviewed famed actress Lillian Russell?

Every bit of fluff about trembling at the sight of a woman renowned the world over suddenly vanished. Lorena herself was entirely absent from the article. Lillian Russell, and only Lillian Russell, spoke to the *Sentinel*'s readers, offering her opinions on how a woman should secure her independence before marriage.

That interview landed on the *Sentinel*'s front page—not because it was a good laugh, but because it was good news. With that article, Lorena Hickok showed the first signs of what she was truly capable of.

CHAPTER 17

JUST ABOUT THE TIME LORENA WAS GETTING A GOOD STRONG foothold in Milwaukee, something in her started "itching" for more. By-lines in the *Sentinel* had become "a matter of course," but that wasn't enough to satisfy her now. Real journalistic fame, the sort of fame that put your byline in papers from coast to coast, seemed only to happen to reporters in bigger cities than Milwaukee—cities like New York.

The thought of New York was "dazzling"—too dazzling, perhaps. Chicago, though, felt within reach. Lorena pulled up stakes and made badgering Chicago editors for a job her pastime. When she couldn't talk her way onto the *Chicago Tribune,* she settled for a stint as a press agent for a Belgian actress, writing publicity material and traveling ahead to see that it appeared in the papers before performances. Somehow that went awry as fast as her jobs in South Dakota had. Lorena's twenty-fourth birthday, March 7, 1917, found her in a bedbug-infested Minneapolis rooming house without a dime to her name.

～

What happened next? The same thing that always happened to Lorena Hickok. Within days she nabbed herself a $20-a-week job at the *Minneapolis Tribune.*

The situation for women reporters at the *Tribune* was about the same as it was at most any other newspaper. "Whenever possible, they are steered into the quieter by-waters of the newspaper plant, away from the main current of life, news, excitement, curses and ticker machines," Ishbel Ross recalled. "They are segregated where their voices will not be heard too audibly in the clatter. They get tucked away on the upper floors where the departments flourish."

Lorena wanted nothing to do with the "departments"—society, fashion, beauty, recipes, club reporting, homemaking. "Women's page stuff," she called it. Lucky for her, the United States joined World War I in April. Suddenly, men became a rare commodity as troopships filled with American soldiers set off for France.

"Women began getting into all kinds of things," Lorena recalled. "We ran trolley cars, collected fares on trains, became policewomen, took men's jobs in the factories, and suddenly the newspaper offices were filled with us. There were women police reporters, women sports writers, even women city editors."

There were still the older fellows to contend with—the editors and seasoned reporters who'd been at it for decades—but a great many of the young men who normally would have elbowed their way past her were now headed to basic training instead.

Lorena plunged in to fill the gaps in the *Tribune* office left by those newly minted soldiers. The leaps and bounds of her progress that year are nearly invisible now. No bylined articles by Lorena Lawrence or Lorena Hickok for all of 1917 have been unearthed. Yet there are clues.

One July feature, a first-person report of the Barnum & Bailey Circus's arrival in Minneapolis, includes four photographs of a broadly grinning Lorena as she rides horseback in the parade, poses in front of a rearing elephant named Alfred, and models a performer's costume. The half-page article bears the printed signature "Yours truly, THE GIRL REPORTER." Three other "Girl Reporter" features, strikingly similar in tone and turn of phrase, were likely written by Lorena as well.

Of course she did more than write four articles that year. The *Tribune* wouldn't have paid her $20 a week for such a paltry output. Her wages and her apparent invisibility suggest that Lorena was working much more closely to the beating heart of the newspaper office than she had before. There's no doubt that she did everything asked of her, and paid attention to everyone else's tasks as well, studying the ins and outs of the newspaper business just as she had in Milwaukee. Within months, she'd become "an experienced and trusted" member of the staff.

Lorena was earning more than money now. She also earned esteem, both from herself and from her colleagues. As one fellow recalled, every man on the *Tribune*, from the editors and reporters to the typesetters and printers, paid her "the well deserved tribute" of "complete respect with never a deviation into impudence, sexy insinuation [or] anything of that kind." Lorena was an asset to the paper, "a thoroughly comfortable and intelligent colleague" everyone felt lucky to work with.

～～

Somewhere in the clatter and clamor of the city room, Lorena Hickok faded into the clouds of tobacco smoke and profanity. In her place emerged a reporter known simply as Hick.

She'd always hated her name, and now she openly corrected anyone who tried to use it. "Not, I *beg* of you, *Lorena*," she once griped to a colleague. "It sounds like a patent medicine ad."

Hick she was, and Hick she would be for the rest of her life. Only a handful of adored folks who'd known her as a child—folks like Aunt Ella, the Brownings, or Miss Alicent Holt—could get away with calling her Lorena, Rena, or anything else but Hick.

Before long, Hick could drink, play poker, and swear as well as any of the men, "alternat[ing] 'hell' and 'damn' as punctuation marks," one reporter noted of her. She smoked a pipe and put her feet up on her desk.

"Many pecksniffs judged her by her pipe," another of her male colleagues sneered. "Her associates judged her by her competence."

Her competence had grown mighty.

PART TWO

HICK

CHAPTER 18

RIGHT IN THE MIDST OF THE STEADIEST PERIOD OF SUCCESS she'd ever known, Hick broke out in a brand-new itch. News of the Battalion of Death, a Russian combat unit composed solely of women, captivated Hick's imagination. She burned to cross the ocean and enlist. "Not from any altruistic motives," she later clarified, "but for the experience and news value of it."

So she quit.

It was a rasher move than any she'd made. She had a job in a field she enjoyed, earning higher wages than ever before. Colleagues and readers alike valued her contribution to the *Tribune*. She'd even been elected to an honorary journalistic sorority, Zeta Pi, by the staff of Lawrence College's literary magazine. By all measures, she was well on her way to making a name for herself, just as she'd vowed.

Hick had also made a friend, a young woman from the *Tribune*'s society department named Ellie Morse. But Hick wouldn't have to leave Ellie behind. In ten months' time, the two had become so devoted to each other that Ellie was willing to follow her—at least as far as New York, where Hick would have to pause awhile to earn enough to get to Russia.

And so in January of 1918, twenty-four colleagues treated Hick and Ellie to a farewell dinner at the Hotel Radisson, toasting them with songs specially written for the occasion.

❧

"Overwhelmed."

"Appalled."

That's how Hick remembered her first crack at New York City. Standing before the buildings of Park Row (also nicknamed Newspaper Row), Hick came face to face with the realization that she'd entered a city capable of making nearly anyone feel as if they'd shrunk, not only in stature, but in importance.

The *New York Times, New York Herald,* and *New York World* all had their headquarters in Newspaper Row skyscrapers, and the nearby Potter Building housed the Associated Press and the *New York Observer.* Hick had banked her future on the conviction that a reporter with her skill and experience would be able to find a job at one of these towering institutions of American journalism.

That's where Hick was wrong. Nobody wanted her. She even found the benches outside the newspaper offices to be "inhospitable." Finally, the editor of the *New York Tribune,* a paper just a block off Newspaper Row, took a chance on her.

For six weeks Hick bumbled along, too "bewildered, shy, and worn-out" to do the job she'd been so capable of in Minnesota. Then she was fired. Hick "felt as if the sky had fallen." She didn't have the journalistic chops to make it in Manhattan, much less on a Russian battlefront.

Hick bounced from one failure to another. Trolley car conductor. Secretary. She tried to enlist in the Naval Coast Defense Reserve as a yeomanette. The last straw was a stint as a policewoman for the Commission on Training Camp Activities, a military organization dedicated to hindering drunkenness and debauchery in the neighborhoods surrounding army bases. Up and down Riverside Drive she tramped, doing what the CTCA liked to call a "moral survey" of the parks on New York's Upper West Side. In plainer terms, Hick's job consisted of "separating girls from sailors." (Where Ellie was during all of this is a riddle. In recounting her ill-fated jaunt to New York, Hick told the story as though she'd set out from Minnesota all on her own.)

Four or five months of that was more than enough. By July, she'd had it with New York.

~≈~

Once again, Hick's path spiraled backward. Back to Minneapolis and the *Tribune,* and back to college—this time at the University of Minnesota. Hick couldn't shake the "uncontrollable habit of going after higher education." What else but lack of schooling could be keeping her from bigger and better things?

The *Minneapolis Tribune* welcomed Hick back with open arms, simultaneously rewarding and insulting her. On one hand was her $5-a-week raise. On the other was the publisher who refused to grant Hick the position she wanted and deserved: night city editor. The fact that she was female rendered her ample experience and qualifications null and void, for he "did not think that the post should go to a woman."

Every morning starting at eight o'clock, Hick attended five hours of class, then went home to sleep until her seven o'clock shift at the *Tribune* began. On slow nights, she could usually squeeze in some studying between midnight and three a.m.

Owing to her school schedule, Hick's specialty became the night rewrite. When the telephone rang in the wee hours, Hick was there to answer it and take down the facts from the reporter on the other end of the line. Fragments of information barked into Hick's ear surged through her fingers and came out of her typewriter transformed into smoothly flowing sentences and paragraphs in time to make the morning edition. It wasn't byline material—it couldn't be, since she hadn't done the newsgathering herself—but it was honest-to-goodness news. A good deal of it was front-page news.

Meanwhile, echoes of the same old troubles dogged her at the university. No sororities welcomed her, leaving Hick "deeply hurt." The dean of women insisted that she should live in the dormitory, which was just about the last thing on earth Hick wanted to do after all the sorority fuss she'd put herself through. Hick refused, and apparently got away with it, perhaps because her coursework was as good as it had always been. "You write well," her rhetoric instructor complimented her one day. "I thought you might be interested in knowing that the *Tribune* wants to get some campus reporters on space." Space was freelance work that only paid a flat rate for every column inch. All Hick could do was laugh. Half the news on the *Tribune's* front page was already coming straight from her typewriter.

~∿~

On October 10, 1918, a train passing through the village of Cloquet loosed an ember into the surrounding brush. Northern Minnesota's logging country had not seen such a dry summer and fall in nearly fifty years. What with nearby camping fires, peat-bog fires, and farmers burning off brush to clear fields, the smoke attracted no particular notice. Then a stiff southwest wind came gusting through. One by one, the small fires began first to spread and then to unite. By the late afternoon of October 12, a sixty-mile-an-hour wind was propelling two walls of flame east toward Duluth, and southeast to Moose Lake.

Telegraph lines—the lines that had not been engulfed—vibrated with the news. Every reporter south of Duluth scrambled for the assignment.

Of course the *Tribune* sent a man to cover the story. They wouldn't send a woman into that inferno, no matter how she begged. Hick had never known a disappointment so keen.

As Hick sat in the office waiting for the telephone to ring, her heart bubbled over with "black murder." But when their reporter in Duluth called with news, Hick did her job as she'd never done it before. While the reporter on the other end of the line clung to the top of a telephone pole and shouted the facts, Hick spewed out column after column of "brilliant" rewrites. It was the kind of story that had to fly from the typewriter straight to the Linotype machine, likely with a copyboy ripping off each paragraph the moment Hick banged the return key.

"Hundreds of people are reported missing, cities and towns have been wiped out, scores after scores of farms have been fire-swept and the fate of the people in a large area of Northeastern Minnesota is unknown as a result of restless, gale-fanned forest fires which carried everything before them last night," the *Tribune* announced the next morning under a bold "EXTRA" headline.

For three solid days, Hick's fire rewrites dominated the front page. It was probably the best and most important work she'd done in her life, and yet she couldn't help mourning "the greater excitement of being on the spot" instead of sitting behind a desk.

⁕

A year passed, a year in which the slaughter of the Great War came to an end and the influenza pandemic claimed millions of lives. Hick worked through it all, juggling her double life as reporter and student. When she telephoned the president of the University of Minnesota seeking news of how the pandemic was affecting the student body, President Burton had no idea he was chatting with one of his own freshmen.

As the university closed at the end of the 1919 summer term, the *Tribune* appointed Hick the Sunday editor. It was an undeniable promotion, and it was also almost exclusively desk work.

Each weekend, Hick was effectively in charge of the *Minnesota Tribune*. She decided which leads to pursue, which stories to feature, what angles the reporters should take, and whether a news item warranted seventy-five or eight hundred words of coverage. She decided what belonged on Sunday's front page and in what size type the headline should be set. She also learned the art of makeup—not the application of rouge and lipstick, but the layout of headlines, photographs, and columns that prompts a reader's eye to move effortlessly from article to article and page to page.

All of that put an end, once and for all, to her college career. The fact that no diploma hung on her wall was clearly not hindering her rise through the ranks of the *Tribune*. Pausing for three more years to get a degree in journalism would only slow her climb.

CHAPTER 19

ANOTHER YEAR OF DESK WORK WENT BY, BRINGING WITH IT A new editor to run the *Tribune*. Tom Dillon looked like he belonged on a football field instead of in a newspaper office—from the neck down, at least. With hair the color of swan's down and a complexion like a radish, he also looked a great deal older than his forty-two years. Behind his back, his reporters referred to him as "the old man."

He was the kind of fellow who disguised his colossally sentimental heart behind a curtain of bellow and bluster that rendered him "at once the terror—and the idol—of the newsroom."

"Writing is just like laying bricks," Dillon declared. "You take the bricks one at a time and place them on top of each other." Anything less than perfection in that simple process earned a bawling-out.

Once, in his early days as a reporter, he'd picked up his own city editor and dumped the man into a wastebasket. Yet he was too soft to fire anyone on his staff himself—he'd duck out and foist the task on someone else.

Hick adored him.

Tom Dillon, she recalled, "taught me the newspaper business, how to drink, and how to live." He also knew talent when he saw it. A writer of Hick's caliber, male or female, had no business being stuck behind a desk all day long.

If Dillon sent Hick out into the city or up into the north woods, Hick came back with news. There wasn't a thing she couldn't cover, from politics and murder trials to million-dollar fashion shows.

Under Dillon's management, Hick quickly became known as "the cleverest interviewer in this section of the country." Her roster included murderers, athletes, musicians, authors, politicians, hypnotists, explorers, dancers, and human carnival exhibits. Ferdinand Foch, commander in chief of Allied forces in the First World War, made Hick's heart thunder as it hadn't thundered since she'd trooped through the mud toward Geraldine Farrar's private railcar. The queen of Romania, on the other hand, she dubbed "rather frowsy."

As an interviewer, she could be hard-nosed, as she was with the self-absorbed musician who informed her that "it was a great bore to submit to press interviews."

"Look, Mister," she retorted, "I have no greater regard for you than you have for me. But I have a job to do, so let's sit down and get the job done." Whereupon the fellow "submitted with the meekness of a lamb" and answered every question she posed.

Empathy, however, was her greatest strength, both in gathering the news and in reporting it. When Elsie Salisbury, a thirty-year-old stenographer for the Milwaukee Railroad, was charged with shooting her sweetheart dead in the railroad's office, Hick earned the woman's trust and became her confidante. Hick witnessed Salisbury's collapse in court while her victim's deathbed statement was read into the record. And as Salisbury awaited the jury's verdict in a Montevideo hotel, Hick sat by her side and listened to her reminisce. The resulting series of news articles, with their combination of close proximity to the accused and straight courtroom reporting, read like true crime—a genre of literature that hadn't yet been invented.

But Hick interviewed more than just the famous and the infamous. One Christmas she undertook a series on the plights of six of the poorest families in Minneapolis. Her Christmas Eve finale featured a widower with five children ranging from eight years to six weeks old, who had recently given up his farm and placed his youngest daughter with an adoptive family. "The baby—I hated to see her go," the man confided to Hick. "She was a fine baby. Never was sick. Never cried. But I didn't think she ought to have to suffer, when she could have a good home."

Hick had honed the skill not only of letting people speak for themselves, but also of distilling their circumstances and feelings to their very essence. Often she did it in the final line or two, leaving her readers with a lingering emotional impression. "And in the meantime," she concluded the widower's story, "one 8-year-old girl, one pair of twins, boy and girl, aged 6, and one 4-year-old boy are wondering what Santa Claus is going to bring them—tomorrow. Is there a Santa Claus?" The series so moved an inmate serving a life sentence at Stillwater Correctional Facility that he offered $20 to one of the featured families.

Journalism, Hick was seeing firsthand, could make a real impact on people's lives.

≈

All the while, Hick was also turning out "Girl Cub Reporter" features in which she chronicled herself dashing about town in search of inane bits of news, or starring in minor capers like working a lunch-hour shift as a Santa Claus in a local department store. "May I be boiled in oil, inch by inch, and never get another Christmas present as long as I live, if I ever deny [Santa Claus] again!" she proclaimed after trying to persuade the skeptical youngsters who crowded onto her lap that she was indeed Kris Kringle.

These stories were sly spoofs on the stunt-girl reporting Nellie Bly had pioneered in the 1880s—back when the stunts were well and truly spectacular. Nellie Bly did things such as feign mental illness in order to infiltrate and expose the inhumane conditions at the Women's Lunatic Asylum on New York City's Blackwell's Island, or circumnavigate the globe via steamship and railroad in a record-breaking seventy-two days.

In Nellie Bly's day, the fact that a woman was reporting the story was itself an integral part of the article. The very thought of a lady undertaking such dangerous tasks mesmerized readers. They didn't just want to know what Nellie Bly uncovered, they wanted to know what happened *to* Nellie Bly as she uncovered it. The risks to her perceived femininity and innocence were an essential part of the formula, injecting near-lethal doses of suspense into her every undertaking. And so in her stories, Nellie Bly was not so much a reporter witnessing the news as she was the main character of a drama in which she *experienced* the news.

Hick took hold of the trope and turned it on its head, mocking the fact that women were still too often deemed lesser reporters worthy only of lesser assignments. Everyone in town knew she was no simpering airhead, and yet Hick wrote her Girl Cub Reporter stories as though some of her brains had trickled out of her ear.

Mostly, she poked fun at the frivolous "news" that was so often relegated to women staffers. "It was one of those jobs they're always handing out to a girl reporter," she opened in a feature that required her to see if a woman could get away with smoking in the restaurants and cabarets of Minneapolis, as rumor had it they now could in New York and Chicago. When the Girl Reporter (Hick) protested, "I'll get thrown out—maybe arrested," The Boss (Dillon) retorted, "Great guns! Of course you won't get by with it! Minneapolis won't stand for it. But that's your story, girl—swell funny yarn! Let 'em throw you out—make 'em do it!"

Dutifully she trekked about town, trying to cause a scene with the smoke emanating from her purple ivory cigarette holder, but no waiters or managers would oblige. Half a dozen restaurants later, the Girl Reporter lamented to her friends, "Gimmie a cigar—oh gimmie something quick! Be tough! I've got to get in trouble somewhere! Tell the manager to throw us out!" No one did, but that didn't stop her from turning the whole escapade into just the kind of "swell funny yarn" Dillon had ordered.

Other assignments included uncovering the secrets of making fashionable hats out of paper, discerning whether women or men were ruder in elevators, and investigating whether you could get a piece of pie in

Minneapolis for only five cents. When she covered traditionally masculine endeavors like ice fishing or golf, she feigned a staggering ignorance that highlighted the absurdities of the sport.

Hick's Girl Cub Reporter features weren't news—they were comedy, and Minneapolis gobbled them up. When a Girl Cub Reporter story was in the paper, the *Tribune* put a notice on the front page to make sure readers wouldn't miss it. The *Tribune* even commissioned illustrations for several of them, enhancing their humor with drawings of Hick that mimicked the comic strips.

By the early 1920s, folks in Minneapolis were becoming accustomed to opening up the *Tribune* and looking for stories by Lorena A. Hickok.

And her audience was about to widen.

CHAPTER 20

istic recognition outside Minnesota. It started with an article headlined "Mrs. Peter Olesen May Have to Discard Husband's Name on Ballot, Ruling Indicates." In formal, objective language, the six paragraphs that followed alerted readers that married women running for office were encountering difficulties in putting their names on the ballot. Minnesota's Democratic candidate for the United States Senate had built her reputation as a nationally known suffragist under the name Mrs. Peter Olesen. But the state attorney general ruled that she must use her own full name—Anna Dickie Olesen—on the ballot instead. The problem, the article concluded, was that "none of her close friends in the capitol knew her by any other name except 'Mrs. Peter Olesen.'"

The story struck a nerve. A mere two years had passed since women had earned the right to vote and run for office, and already, brand-new bureaucratic hurdles were springing up in their way. Women in Minnesota were angry—angry enough that other newspapers wanted in on the story.

Hick might not have written the original article; without a byline it's impossible to be sure. Nevertheless, Dillon had her rewrite and expand it to eleven paragraphs in the punchier, more conversational style she excelled at. Then he promptly leased the updated copy to the Consolidated Press wire syndicate. The next day the "special dispatch" appeared in the *New York Evening World*, the *Decatur Daily Review*, the Washington *Evening Star*, and the *St. Louis Post-Dispatch*.

"Minnesota women are boiling over today," Hick's lead announced, and went on to detail the handicap that the attorney general's ruling placed on Mrs. Olesen. "Nobody ever heard of Annie Dickie Olesen, and Mrs. Peter Olesen is a whole lot better known than Peter Olesen." Every single achievement of note in her political career had been won by Mrs. Peter Olesen, Hick explained, and the attorney general had just put a heap of work in front of her: "By next election day she must make Annie Dickie Olesen as well known in Minnesota as Mrs. Peter Olesen is now." Only one of the papers, the *Decatur Daily Review,* included Hick's byline.

But as the story spread, Hick's name appeared more reliably beneath the headline, including in Winnipeg, Canada. With that story, Hick earned the right to say that her work had appeared internationally.

～

Four months later, Hick hit another milestone with a two-page illustrated exposé of a North Dakota politician, Alexander McKenzie, who had a secret second family in Yonkers, New York. The profile included photographs of the wife and children McKenzie had kept hidden for thirty-two years and a detailed family history provided by one of his newly discovered daughters. How Hick managed to secure the woman's story from halfway across the nation can only be speculated on, but secure it she did. Not only that, she also interviewed one of McKenzie's daughters from his first marriage, creating a balanced and sympathetic portrait of the entire McKenzie clan. This story, too, spilled beyond the *Tribune,* so that once again, people outside Minneapolis took notice of Lorena Hickok's work.

～

Hick's years at the *Tribune* had molded her into "a general utility reporter capable of handling any kind of assignment with her own kind of individual distinction." Six days of every seven found her in the office, working "for the glory of it" from four in the afternoon until midnight.

As she worked, Minneapolis became a part of her, and she became part of the city. A lion cub at the zoo at Longfellow Gardens was named Miss Hick in her honor. Every summer she judged the Pushmobile Derby, a *Tribune*-sponsored go-cart race for youngsters, and every winter she covered its seasonal twin, the *Tribune*'s Dog Derby for junior sled mushers. Forever after, she would consider Minneapolis her hometown.

At long last Hick also acquired a cadre of friends, most of them from work, for with recognition had come camaraderie.

"I never heard her name spoken without respect, admiration, and affection," recalled one University of Minnesota student who encountered Hick at the business club dining room where she often ate. "I remember Hick as a friendly, casual, responsive woman, utterly unconscious of the fact that she was even then a personage."

For all that she enjoyed solitude—particularly when it involved "a well-padded sofa and *The Saturday Evening Post* and a bag of gumdrops"— Hick also liked to have fun. Fellow *Tribune* reporter Bradley Morison remembered clowning with her at picnics—balancing long sticks on their chins, or making slapstick attempts at tennis. "Hick always entered into this sort of nonsense with gusto," Morison recalled.

Other sorts of nonsense also appealed to her. She, Ellie Morse, Bradley Morison, and three others formed the Violent Study Club, a spoof on the name of a group she'd read about in the paper that called itself the Violet Study Club. While the lavender-hued organization pledged itself to "self-improvement morally, socially, intellectually and spiritually," the six members of Hick's gang were "frivolously devoted to get-togethers and good times."

Good times were plentiful around Hick. With her "habitually amused, reassuring, and sisterly" manner, she made folks feel at ease. In a crowd, her presence was unassuming. She tended to dress in "starched blouses and sensible skirts which did nothing to call attention to themselves," partly due to her work, where being inconspicuous often had its advantages. But when the occasion did call for it, she'd brighten her wardrobe with a colorful scarf, a dab of lipstick, or a pair of French heels. "Dressing the part," as she dubbed it.

꙳

The news that buzzed over the wires on August 2, 1923, shook the nation. President Harding had died in California in the middle of a transcontinental trip dubbed the Voyage of Understanding. Suddenly, the train that had carried him to Alaska and down the West Coast of North America became the funeral train that would bear his coffin back to Washington, DC.

Hick caught the scent of a human-interest story. From one end of the continent to the other, the train was trudging over tracks that were sometimes so closely crowded with mourners, the locomotive could hardly move forward. Hick wanted to report it. To get the angle she envisioned, she proposed to travel 360 miles south, where the Union Pacific Railroad met the Chicago & North Western line, and behold the spectacle on behalf of the *Minneapolis Tribune*. Dillon sent her.

Instead of targeting a metropolis like Omaha, Nebraska, Hick settled on Honey Creek, a village of about seventy-six residents perched on the very edge of western Iowa. The presidential train with its somber cargo was scheduled to pass the town at three o'clock in the morning, but alarm clocks were set for 1:45 a.m. The train would not stop on its way through, and no one wanted to risk missing it. Sleep was impossible in Honey Creek that night. Plenty of folks were up and ready to head for the station by 1:15.

For two and a half hours, Hick stood with the entire population of that small town as they waited and murmured by flashlight. She heard them talk of their crops and their children, watched them arrange stepladders and shinny up fences for the best view as the funeral train's headlamp finally came into view at 3:45 in the morning. In a matter of seconds, the great moment came and went.

Hick had gotten her story, but she had to travel another eighteen miles south to Omaha to type it up and file it. That turned out to be a task more trying than standing out in the dark all night. No sooner had she gotten her fingers poised over a keyboard in the office of the *Omaha Bee* than "some damn woman bookkeeper" from the newspaper elbowed in and insisted *she* had to use the typewriter. Hick's temper bubbled at a dangerous simmer as she stalked through town in search of someplace she could type the story that was fluttering desperately in the cage of her mind. "It was hotter than hell that day," she complained years afterward. Finally she abandoned the search altogether and went to a telegraph office. Instead of writing the story, she spoke it, composing it aloud to the operator as he transmitted it over the wires back to Minneapolis.

It was a story in which almost nothing happened. A train passed by a small town in the dead of night, just as dozens of trains did every night. And yet Hick conveyed the emotion of that earnest, patient crowd in a way that raised goose bumps. Reading that article, you felt as if you'd stood elbow to elbow with the women who had jangled their dinner bells to waken the neighborhood at 1:45 in the morning, the wide-eyed little boys in overalls, and the veterans holding their babies high as the funeral train shimmered by. "The long moaning whistle around the bend—the blinding shaft of light down the glittering rails—the roar and wind and trembling of the earth—the breathless wait for the rear car—the flashing vision of wreaths and flags and rigid figures in khaki—the red tail lights vanishing like pin points in the dark—yes, it was worth waiting for."

The story struck a powerful chord in the hearts of Americans—so powerful that it appeared the next year in a book entitled *The Best News Stories of 1923*.

CHAPTER 21

HICK HAD MORE THAN JUST SUCCESS NOW. SHE'D ALSO FOUND love. The object of her affection was none other than Ellie Morse, the *Tribune* society reporter who'd accompanied her to New York and back.

Beauty was not among Miss Morse's many admirable qualities. Hick herself described Ellie as "short, dumpy, with wispy, hard-to-manage blonde hair and grey-blue eyes too small for her squarish, full face." That didn't matter a bit. Hick worshipped her.

Ellie loved Hick right back with unabashed, almost childlike affection. Decades later, she would still occasionally address her letters to "Hickey Doodles."

"On first meeting people were apt to describe her as colorless," Hick recalled, what with Ellie's drab looks and her soft-voiced timidity. To Hick, though, Ellie would ever remain "the most unforgettable character I've met."

Ellie Morse had a heart valve that leaked so severely, the sound of it through a stethoscope made doctors jerk their heads back in surprise. And yet that heart was the seat of what Hick called "a very great genius in the art of friendship." Ellie was a kind of Cinderella—her mother had died giving birth to her, and Ellie had been brought up in the shadow of a pampered stepsister, never getting the affection she craved. Though Ellie had every material comfort, the emotional landscape of her childhood bore striking similarities to Hick's. They fit together like two pieces of a puzzle.

The pair set up housekeeping in a corner apartment suite at the Leamington Hotel, a "swanky place" funded by Ellie's father, and surrounded themselves with good books, good food, and good friends. Ellie was a fine cook and a fine reader, and Hick was "quite a gourmet." Together they hosted annual birthday parties in honor of Ellie's most beloved author, Charles Dickens. Even their cat, François Villon, was named after a poet.

For Hick, life with Ellie was a time of utmost happiness and security. Her career and her salary were on a steady upward climb. She had a fashionable address and no financial worries, thanks to Ellie's generosity. Together they amassed a library of novels, poetry, and plays worth almost $4,500. Their outings to the theater, where Ellie bought box seats, gave Hick immense delight. (These extravagances were also likely funded by Ellie's father, who'd "looked askance" when his daughter moved out to live with Hick, but paid the bills nonetheless.) Above all, there was Ellie's love—a gift that exceeded every tangible luxury.

Everyone knew that Hick lived with Ellie—she even referred to her "roommate" in her Girl Cub Reporter stories on occasion. How many people knew Hick and Ellie were a couple is a much thornier question. In the *Tribune* itself, queer people or relationships were simply erased from reality. "We did not even concede the existence of homosexuals," a *Tribune* city editor remembered of the paper's style code in Tom Dillon's days.

In the late 1970s, several of Hick's friends and coworkers denied having any inkling that Lorena Hickok was queer. So perhaps she and Ellie were firmly closeted. Then again, fifty years ago queer relationships were still taboo enough that Hick's friends might have felt compelled to withhold the truth to shield her reputation from anyone who might consider her sexuality shameful.

If Tom Dillon knew, he looked the other way. According to Minnesota law, homosexual acts were a crime. Though the laws were usually applied to men rather than women, the situation was still fraught with unpleasant possibilities. If word got out about Hick's relationship with Ellie, Dillon might have no choice but to fire her. The last thing the *Tribune* needed was for Hick to be persecuted, or even prosecuted. Hick was Dillon's star reporter now; anything that stood in the way of her success also hindered the paper's success.

~

Hick had not even reached her peak. With each assignment, the uncommon breadth of her abilities became clearer. Her articles could inform, entertain, or enrich—sometimes all at once.

She reported on a girls' track-and-field meet at the Minnesota State Academy for the Blind, detailing the accommodations that allowed the students to compete in sprints and jumping events. Athletics, Hick noted with admiration, had helped turn fearful girls who had once groped their way from place to place into young women with enough self-assurance to run races without using the ring-and-wire guide alongside the seventy-five-yard track.

When federal Prohibition agents seized four hundred cases of whiskey, draining forty-eight hundred quarts of liquor into the city's sewers, Hick wrote a piece of satire on the inebriated fish and rodents that resulted. "You can believe it or not, but 687 Mishishippi carp went home drunk Saturday night," the article began. All the sewer rats, she claimed, were so saturated with liquid courage that they'd climbed up through the grates to take revenge on the cats of Minneapolis.

Her sex rarely stood in her way now. Hick had a style all her own, a style the *Tribune*'s readers loved, and the only way to get a report in that style was to give Lorena Hickok the assignment.

For the sake of the news, she rode in speeding airplanes, motorboats, and race cars. Best of all was the night she donned cap and overalls and climbed aboard a steam locomotive known by her crew as Old Lady 501. The ninety-foot, 186,000-pound steel engine enchanted Hick. An engine, she informed her readers the next day, "is not a machine, but a living, breathing thing—a creature of intelligence and temperament, always referred to, not as 'it,' but 'she.'"

Hick's writing made that engine come alive, as if it were a benevolent beast that chuckled, sang, and breathed with every puff of steam and blast of its whistle. With Hick telling the story, steel and coal and fire and smoke felt like magic. To ride that engine alongside the engineer and the fireman, she wrote, was "a roaring, swaggering, joyous adventure."

CHAPTER 22

ONE ASSIGNMENT STOOD ABOVE ALL OTHERS, A BEAT HICK WOULD be proud of for the rest of her life: University of Minnesota football.

The idea of a woman covering sports, much less men's sports, defied comprehension in the 1920s. Other papers sent female journalists to boxing rings and racetracks "to deliver fawning 'feminine' perspectives" on what they saw there.

Tom Dillon already knew Hick could turn out that kind of fluff. She'd done Girl Cub Reporter features on golf, baseball, and football. "Football must be a mighty interesting show to watch—if you know what everything's all about," she wrote in the guise of her empty-headed alter ego in 1922. "Otherwise—you might just as well put in your time watching a lot of ants running in and out of their hole." The Girl Reporter didn't even know enough about the game to call what she'd observed a "practice" instead of a "rehearsal."

But Tom Dillon didn't want the so-called woman's angle. In a state that had no major-league teams to root for, college football was serious business. Fans of the gridiron depended on the Gophers to satisfy their football fix, so why wouldn't Dillon want his star reporter to cover the games?

Hick's first serious try at a football game came just three weeks after her satire about a football "rehearsal," when Dillon assigned her to watch the Gophers face off with the University of Michigan Wolverines. Her article landed in the sports section rather than with the features, a strong suggestion that Dillon was pleased with her efforts, for the sports page was no place for feminine frivolities. But if Hick covered any more football games over the next two years, the articles have yet to come to light. Perhaps she wrote without a byline while she honed her skills and knowledge of the game. Perhaps the men in the sports department raised a ruckus about sharing their turf with a woman.

Whatever the cause of her absence, November of 1924 found Hick back in the Gophers' grandstand. Not in the press box with the fellows from the sports department, though. Allowing a woman into that sacrosanct box, even a woman as capable and accustomed to working in an office full of men as Hick was, might have sent the male reporters into a tantrum of some sort. She had to content herself with a seat in the stands, right down among the fans. If the exclusion wounded her ego, it certainly didn't hurt her writing. Sitting in the thick of things put Hick that much closer to the heart of the game, which turned out to be the best place for a reporter of her particular strengths.

Hick left the play-by-play to the official sportswriters—the men. Her skill lay in re-creating the atmosphere of the stadium, the whole experience of attending a sporting event. And when Hick combined technical knowledge of the game with her superb eye for detail and mood, a new style of sports reporting emerged.

Hick's stories made the folks at home feel as though they were right there in the stands, shouting, cheering, or groaning as the events unspooled on the field in full color. She didn't just describe the plays and the stats—she expressed how it felt to experience them, so that the tension, the excitement, the thrills and disappointments leapt off the page and invaded readers' emotions.

Rather than relying on the familiar phrases and metaphors many sportswriters used to liven up their stories, Hick invented her own descriptions to convey the same happenings far more vividly. Instead of "the Minnesota line fighting like wildcats," for instance, Hick called the Gophers "a team with a fighting spirit that must have won a game against 11 gorillas."

Players didn't just run or dash in Hick's stories. She transformed the Gophers into forces of nature intimately familiar to the Minneapolis fans. "And then the Minnesota prairie fire was off," she wrote. "Right down the field they went, plowing, plunging, prancing through." Hick could even make something as intangible as a lucky break into something alive, something fans could cheer or boo. "And then—An old hussy named Lady Luck got into the game," she groused in the *Tribune* after a particularly crushing defeat.

For three seasons, Hick's football coverage regularly made the front page, sometimes with a full-page banner headline. Technically, it ought to have gone in the sports section. That placement might have been a testament to the quality and popularity of her work. Or the surging football craze might have demanded the topic's greater prominence. Or it might have been a clever way to avoid placing a woman's story on the sports page—a taboo almost as unthinkable as allowing a lady into the men's locker room. A bit of all three could have come into play.

Regardless, Gophers fans loved Hick's articles. As it had done with her Girl Cub Reporter stories, the *Tribune* proudly advertised her coverage of upcoming games on the front page. "To top the climax, Lorena Hickok will 'do' a feature on the Iowa-Minnesota game as only 'Hick' can do it," the *Tribune* bragged in the run-up to the 1925 Big Ten championship tournament. Whether the Gophers won or lost, fans counted on "Miss Hickok's rollicking sketch of the contest and crowds" as part of "The Supreme Thrill of the Football Season."

To the team, Hick became an unofficial mascot—their "Auntie Gopher." Hick reveled in the adulation, adopting the players as her "dear nephews" and christening herself "the Gophers' poet laureate." (The Wolverines coach, meanwhile, ribbed her good-naturedly with a nickname of his own: "Miss Goofer.") When the team played in Michigan, Wisconsin, or Iowa, Hick rode along on the Gophers' train and stayed in the same hotel. In an era when unattached women were expected to travel separately from men, that was a feat in itself.

After the Gophers lost the 1925 championship game to the University of Michigan Wolverines on the Ann Arbor field, she consoled fans back home with a report that exemplified sportsmanship. The Gophers had been woefully outmatched, plain and simple, and rather than complain, Hick made sure her admiration of both teams shone through her disappointment. "A lot of folks are probably going to feel just a wee bit sad about Minnesota's line," she wrote when Michigan's cheers had died down. "Well, don't." Sure, the superior muscle and brains of the Michigan team had demolished the Gophers. "But listen," Hick insisted with fierce pride. "There were a couple touchdowns Michigan never got because that Minnesota line held 'em. Twice the Wolverines had the ball almost on top of our goal posts, and the Gopher line held." Against a team as powerful as the Wolverines, she insisted, these small triumphs deserved as much praise as a win. Without ever saying so outright, she imparted a clear message: those boys—*her* boys—from Minnesota had played their hearts out in the face of certain defeat, and that alone was worth a heroes' welcome.

Perhaps that's why the fans loved Hick's coverage so much—she put her love of the game and the players on display, letting them live it through her. For her own part, Hick cherished her achievement in sports reporting as if it were a trophy. In the decades to come, she rarely failed to mention her football coverage both as an example of the breadth of her skill and as a symbol of how far she'd managed to advance in the traditionally masculine field of journalism.

If she hadn't known it before, she knew it now: there was nothing she couldn't cover.

CHAPTER 23

EVERYTHING CHANGED IN THE SUMMER OF 1925. ELLIE'S FAther died, bringing her a reported inheritance of three-quarters of a million dollars—the equivalent of $12.5 million today. With that kind of money, Ellie could do anything she wanted, and what she wanted was to pack up and move with Hick to the sun-kissed coastline of California. That was the same year Hick learned she had diabetes. A change of pace in a more forgiving climate was just the thing to revive her flagging health.

With Ellie taking care of the financial end of things, Hick could quit running all over the place after news stories, keep decent hours for once, take it easy, bask in the sun. Most tempting of all, she could try her hand at writing a novel, just as Edna Ferber had done.

The two set out together in late 1926 or early 1927, bound for the West Coast.

~

Hick had exactly two words to say about her time in California: "No go." Hidden behind that curt sentence was a world of heartbreak.

At first things went well. Hick and Ellie settled in an apartment on San Francisco's Russian Hill that boasted a picture window with marvelous views out across the bay. They soon made friends with another happily paired female couple—a librarian and a writer. Beyond that, there isn't much to tell until Ellie set off on what should have been an innocuous visit to her cousin Arthur in San Marino. When she returned, Ellie was married.

Hick never saw it coming. No one could have. The coincidence that triggered this abrupt turn of events had been impossibly slight. While touring Ellie around Pasadena, Cousin Arthur spotted a familiar face in a passing car. Ellie recognized him, too. She'd known Roy Dickinson back when she was a ten-year-old child living with Arthur's family. Roy was one of Arthur's schoolmates. Back then, Ellie'd had "quite a crush" on Roy.

The two cars pulled over, and just like that, Ellie and Roy rekindled their childhood friendship. Before anyone else knew what was happening, they eloped in Yuma, Arizona.

~≈~

Hick fled east—just about as far east as she could get. Her train steamed past Minneapolis, and all its memories of those eight wonderful years with Ellie, and deposited her in New York City.

There, Hick found a job with the *New York Daily Mirror,* a paper that "took the tabloid formula and put it on full blast." At its founding in 1924, publishing mogul William Randolph Hearst had promised the *Mirror*'s readers "90 percent entertainment, 10 percent information—and the information without boring you." Giant headlines and photographs crowded its front page, guaranteeing that no one could pass by a street-corner newsstand without at least noticing the *Mirror.* Excitement and sentiment dominated the *Mirror*'s focus, with aviators and babies frequently gracing the front page. If a murder, kidnapping, or high-profile divorce should happen to occur, all the better.

It wasn't quite the kind of journalism Hick was accustomed to. Only a few of the *Mirror*'s two dozen pages were devoted to actual news, and those articles tended to be quick and punchy summaries for people in a hurry. But it was a job, and Hick went at it with her usual aplomb. *Variety* magazine called her a "by-line sobbie," an indication that she was writing tearjerkers and gaining some notoriety at it. In reality, "Lorena A.

Hickok" bylines are almost nonexistent in the *Mirror,* and the two that have been unearthed are straight news stories. But even those scant bylines are notable, since the *Mirror* rarely credited any single reporter for a news item. Several times, Hick said, she joined the "wild, boisterous, unmannerly crew" of journalists that "would sweep down on some defenseless little town unfortunate enough to be the scene of a good murder, trial, [or] page-one divorce story," like the vanishing of college freshman Frances St. John Smith in Northampton, Massachusetts.

Hick was likely putting her abilities to use behind the scenes, contributing to uncredited news stories like the Smith disappearance, and perhaps ghostwriting "as told by" features, such as a series narrated by Josephine Brown, the mother of murderer Ruth Snyder, who was executed at Sing Sing Correctional Facility after strangling her husband with a picture wire. A trio of articles recounting the Christmastime plight of striking miners in Pittsburgh also seems to bear Hick's fingerprints, echoing her December 1922 coverage of Minneapolis's poor, from its striking ledes to the lingering emotion at its conclusion. Those are the only clues we have.

CHAPTER 24

IN AUGUST OF 1928, HICK MADE A LEAP FROM THE MOST TYPI-
cal of tabloids to a news agency that represented a pinnacle of respected
journalism—the Associated Press.

How on earth did she do it? Hick left no explanation behind. A chapter
of her life ends at the *Daily Mirror* and the next begins at the Associated
Press, with no bridge or transition between them. One of her *Minneapolis Tribune* colleagues suspected that their editor had recommended her
to the AP. It was just the sort of thing Tom Dillon would do, especially
given Dillon's respect for Hick's breadth of ability. That possibility repre-
sents only one fragment of the equation, though. More than anything, it
was sixteen years of solid performance and persistence that had brought
Hick to the doorstep of one of the world's preeminent news agencies.

⁂

"There are only two forces that can carry light to all corners of the globe,"
Mark Twain quipped in 1906, "only two—the sun in the heavens and the
Associated Press down here." The Associated Press was not a newspaper,
but a news service. The reports its staffers wrote were sent out by wire
to hundreds of newspaper offices all across the country. Compared to
the papers Hick had worked for before, the AP was a behemoth known
as a "great octopus" with tentacles extending into every continent. Its
unprecedented reach gave the AP a power tantamount to that of "an engine that causes 30,000,000 minds to have the same thought at the same
moment, and nothing on earth can equal the force thus generated."

The size of the AP's sixth-floor headquarters at 383 Madison Avenue mirrored the expanse of its influence. The office consumed half a block of floor space. Desks for the New York local staff; the financial, sports, and feature writers; and the foreign news reporters filled the center of the great open room. Some seventy-five clattering teletype and telegraph machines took up a horseshoe-shaped bank of desks where editors ceaselessly typed and tapped copy into wires that carried AP reports to metropolises and hamlets across the country. Around the edge of the room, reporters from England, France, Germany, and Canada worked in cubicles assigned to their various foreign agencies. "One noisy joint," as AP reporter Gardner Bridge recalled it.

Hick dove straight into the thick of things. Six days a week, she donned her tweeds, stuffed a sheaf of folded copy paper into her pocket (spiral-bound reporters' notebooks had yet to be invented), and prowled the city for news. That very first week Hick found herself assigned to the coveted arena of politics, a topic typically reserved for male reporters. And ironically, sexism got her the beat.

⁓

New York governor Al Smith, the Democratic Party's first Catholic nominee for president, was ramping up his campaign for the White House that summer. Although the AP's staffers were supposed to be objective and unbiased, the Southern Protestant reporters kept "infuriating" the Democratic leaders when their ingrained anti-Catholic sentiments leaked into their Smith stories.

"Why not send that girl over there?" the AP's general manager proposed one day, indicating Hick. They'd at least have to be polite to her, instead of "bounc[ing] her out of the twenty-third floor on her head" if another anti-Catholic reporter embarrassed the company. Hick wasn't about to refuse.

The look on the national chairman's face at the sight of a woman strolling into his press conference was "something to remember," Hick recalled. Even female Democrats were segregated to their own division, on a lower floor.

It turned out that aside from those press conferences, there really wasn't much news happening at Democratic headquarters. The real political reporting belonged to the more experienced AP men who traveled with Smith as he campaigned.

"Sometimes, on particularly dull days," Hick remembered, "I would wander down to the women's division looking for a feature story."

Instead of a story, she found Malvina Thompson, a secretary with "a rather forbidding New England exterior" and a walk that said "you'd better get out of my way." Friends called her Tommy, and soon Hick did, too. Once you got past that all-business front, Tommy was warm, funny, and touchingly devoted to the woman she called "my Boss"—Eleanor Roosevelt.

Hick couldn't help feeling curious about Tommy's boss, mostly because Mrs. Roosevelt's uncle was President Theodore Roosevelt. Despite the fact that he'd died nine years earlier, Teddy Roosevelt was still "THE president" in Hick's mind. Yet her first encounter with her hero's niece left Hick underwhelmed. Mrs. Roosevelt's teeth stuck out just like her famous uncle's, and though her clothes were stylish, they hadn't been properly tailored to suit her nearly six-foot height or her willowy frame. "I got the impression that she didn't care very much how she looked, so long as she was tidy," Hick recalled.

A few days later, Hick spotted Mrs. Roosevelt again. She was on her way to a luncheon where she would debate a prominent Republican society matron known for her keen wit and impeccable wardrobe. With a note of pity, Hick noticed the grayish tint Mrs. Roosevelt's green dress lent to her skin, and the hairnet gripping her light brown hair so tightly that its band left a visible crease across her forehead. Her hat, Hick thought, "looked like a black straw pancake." If all that wasn't enough, Mrs. Roosevelt had an erratic voice that launched itself into the higher registers without provocation, like an aria gone wrong. She also had a cringe-inducing habit of laughing inanely when she was nervous.

"You poor thing," Hick lamented to herself. "It will be murder for you at the luncheon."

Hick was wrong. The next day Tommy told Hick how the famously poised Republican lady had fumbled during her speech, somehow losing track of the statistics she'd meant to quote. Rather than let the speaker embarrass herself, Mrs. Roosevelt provided her opponent with the missing information. The diplomacy of that unselfish gesture made Hick think that perhaps Mrs. Roosevelt might be something more than just a president's niece.

New York State politics took a surprising turn on election night, and to Hick's everlasting satisfaction, she was there to watch it happen. The instant Al Smith conceded to his rival, Hick was on the phone to the AP to report that Republican Herbert Hoover would be the next president of the United States.

Smith had lost more than his bid for the White House. Confident he'd win the presidency, Smith had persuaded Eleanor Roosevelt's husband, Franklin, a state senator, to run for New York's governorship in his place, in hopes of keeping the state in Democratic hands. Roosevelt won, and Smith's strategy backfired in his face. Smith was out of a job, and Franklin Delano Roosevelt was bound for the executive mansion in Albany.

With her connection through the Women's Division of the New York State Democratic Committee, Hick was the natural choice to get the new first lady of New York's thoughts on FDR's win. "To my amazement, I was escorted up to the drawing room, where a handsome silver tea service was set out," Hick remembered. Never in her life had she been treated to tea—as if she were there by invitation—by a woman of Mrs. Roosevelt's standing.

The interview was not one of Hick's great successes. For all that her hostess divulged, Hick might have been chatting with any New York society matron over the election results. Oddly, Mrs. Roosevelt didn't appear particularly jubilant about her husband's victory. Al Smith's loss of the White House rankled her, though. In spite of how tactfully she expressed it, Hick could tell that Mrs. Roosevelt was "indignant" over the anti-Catholic sentiment that had contributed to Smith's defeat. That was about all Hick could pry out of her where politics were concerned. "I felt that she didn't trust me," Hick recalled.

Nevertheless, Hick found Mrs. Roosevelt's company unexpectedly pleasurable. Her hostess, who at first glance came across as awkward and ungainly, was so adept at serving tea that she could pour from two pots at once—one in each hand. The fluidity of this feat was simply mesmerizing. As the conversation turned away from politics, she chatted amiably with Hick about her five children, and especially about Meggie and Major, her Scottish terrier and German shepherd. Mrs. Roosevelt even looked different at home, in a lace-trimmed gown more becoming to her long, slender frame. Only another one of those dreadful hairnets distracted from her charm.

"I failed to get much news out of her," Hick recalled, yet Mrs. Roosevelt's personality had once again left Hick quietly astonished. Despite her obvious reluctance to be interviewed, the soon-to-be first lady of New York had treated Hick as a guest rather than a bothersome distraction to be shooed away as quickly as possible.

The article Hick turned in that day concluded with an unusual verbal flourish: "The new mistress of the Executive Mansion in Albany is a very great lady."

Hick's editor drew a decisive slash through that sentence without hesitation. "Too editorial," he declared.

He was right. It was an uncharacteristic slip for a reporter as good as Lorena Hickok. Something about Eleanor Roosevelt had ever so slightly loosened Hick's grip on her own objectivity.

CHAPTER 25

OUTSIDE OF DEMOCRATIC NATIONAL HEADQUARTERS, NEWS IN the late 1920s revolved around gangster shootings, speakeasy raids, and the corruption of New York City mayor Jimmy Walker. Ships arriving in New York Harbor also provided a rich source of potential information and interviews. Getting the story meant rising before the sun and taking a cutter to the waters off Staten Island, where incoming ships anchored for quarantine inspection prior to entering port. After scrambling across a ladder to the ship's hold, reporters like Hick were rewarded with a "sumptuous breakfast" and the opportunity to roam the decks in search of newsworthy passengers.

That was how Hick managed to nab an exclusive angle on the biggest story of November 1928. The morning after the steamship *Vestris* sank two hundred miles off the coast of Virginia, spilling 328 passengers and crew members into the Atlantic Ocean, Hick met the rescue liner *American Shipper* at the Battery docks and got an interview with Paul Dana, one of sixty passengers who survived the wreck. Dana had spent nearly twenty-four hours adrift, clinging to a disintegrating piece of wreckage alongside a woman named Clara Ball. Even before they arrived in New York Harbor, the pair had been dubbed by their rescuers the "two pluckiest people ever." Dana gave Hick the interview of a lifetime. The next day, Paul Dana's ordeal, as relayed by Hick, captivated the nation.

The story appeared on the front page of the *New York Times*. Its byline read "by Paul A. Dana, as told to Lorena A. Hickok, Associated Press Staff Reporter." That day, Hick became the first woman ever to see her byline on the *New York Times*'s front page.

⁂

Hick's article wasn't the first *Vestris* survivor's tale to hit the papers, but it was far and away the best. A passenger in another article recalled the instant before the ship sank with such formality that he sounded as though he'd been delivering a treatise on boat safety instead of preparing to plunge into the Atlantic: "Davies and myself walked along the railside of the *Vestris* right up to the last moment . . . commenting regarding the phlegmatic slowness as well as the inexperience shown in the life-saving manoeuvres aboard our ship."

Hick, on the other hand, used plain words and concise sentences that put her readers right into the water alongside Paul Dana as unsettling sensations swished past his dangling legs: "Toward sunset it began to cloud up, and then a thought flashed into my mind that made me feel a little sick all over—sharks."

To the casual reader, it might have looked as though Hick had done no more than type out every word Dana had said. But journalists knew better.

The *Raleigh News and Observer* immediately praised Hick's *Vestris* story as "A Masterpiece of Reporting." Paradoxically, her very invisibility in the article was exactly what proved her skill. Hick knew how to get everything out of the way of a good story, and she hadn't allowed one speck of clutter into the narrative. What Paul Dana told her didn't need any embellishing, any added drama. She relayed his experience so cleanly and directly that even a camera couldn't have captured the scene with more clarity. In words alone, the *News and Observer* said, "she painted a picture that will stand when the lurid writing of this calamity of the sea with all its picturesque detail and harrowing adjectives, is forgotten."

⁂

In a matter of just a few months at the Associated Press, Hick had proven that "she could tackle anything and she wrote with color, finish, a keen news sense, and good judgement."

The trouble was, despite her skill and experience, men were still ushered to the front of the line when hard news assignments were doled out. "The AP wouldn't let me handle a big story, not if there was a male cub, not yet dry behind the ears, within 50 miles of the place!" she griped in 1930. "Sometimes it hurts like hell. Sometimes I just get—savage."

Deprived of substantial news to sink her teeth into, Hick continued to make interviews her trademark. Here, too, sexism hindered her opportunities. Hick seethed every time a famous man arrived in New York and she was assigned to profile his wife or mother while a male reporter got dibs on the celebrity himself. Famous women were the only subjects Hick could reliably count on. Her array of interviewees included female aviators, athletes, politicians, police officers, champion bridge players, singers, and astronomers. At long last, she interviewed Geraldine Farrar, just as the diva was on the verge of retirement. None of it satisfied her. "If only they'd let me be a reporter, dammit, instead of sending me to do blah-blah features," she railed to a colleague.

⁘

In 1930, Hick once again found herself a guest at the Roosevelts' tea table for yet another feature on a famous man's wife. This time Hick was tasked with turning her attention to Mrs. Roosevelt's unusual range of nonpolitical activities. The first lady of New York, Hick learned, was not only the mother of five children, ranging from age fourteen to twenty-four, but also assistant principal of a private girls' school in New York City, where she taught classes in history and English literature three days a week. In addition to that, she was co-owner of a small factory in Hyde Park that specialized in reproductions of classic American furniture.

"The idea seems to be that when a woman reaches 45, and her

children are grown up and out of the way, she suddenly finds herself with nothing to do," Mrs. Roosevelt told Hick. "It's a wicked, wicked thing for a woman to concentrate all her interest in her children," she declared.

The more Hick saw of her, the more Mrs. Roosevelt intrigued her. This was a woman who wasn't afraid to fly in a single-engine plane or try out an Olympic bobsled run, a woman who kept coffee and sandwich makings in her kitchen so she could provide a bolstering meal at a moment's notice to the hungry job seekers she encountered on the street. She even edited a monthly magazine for the Women's Division of the New York State Democratic Committee, making her something of a fledgling journalist. While many women her age behaved as though life were winding down, Eleanor Roosevelt conveyed the attitude that she was just now getting to the juiciest, meatiest part of it. "I used to hope that we might at least get a little bit sociable," Hick confided. "But all I could ever get out of her was a very polite 'Good morning' or 'Isn't it a lovely day?'"

CHAPTER 26

SOMEHOW, HICK MANAGED TO KEEP HER DISAPPOINTMENTS AND setbacks from poisoning her attitude in the newsroom. "An excellent newsperson, a professional in every way," remembered Jane Eads, Hick's neighbor and the only other female reporter in the AP's New York office. "She worked 'like a man' and could handle the desk jobs and other regular wire service chores as well as any of the top male staffers—which in those days few women had a chance at, capable or not."

While some women journalists might have jealously defended their hard-earned turf, Hick welcomed new female colleagues aboard as if they were sisters, once telling a fresh recruit from Kansas City, "I'm going to teach you to play poker and swear—you might need it."

Another of her quirks occurred on her occasional Sunday shifts on the local desk, when Hick brought her German shepherd, Prinz, to the office in the freight elevator. He either napped by her side or sedately patrolled the office. Her affection for that dog was boundless, as Jane often observed when she and Hick returned from their shared grocery shopping trips. "She'd open the door and [Prinz] would be at her side instantly," Jane remembered. "She'd go absolutely ape over him—talking as a mother to a beloved, favorite child." While Hick put down her grocery bags, Prinz bounded up onto the table, ready to paint her face with kisses from his long wet tongue. The welcome-home ritual revolted Jane, but Hick gloried in it.

Hick was a good neighbor, too, the kind who not only lent pots and pans and shared her favorite recipes, but also helped her friends master them. Jane learned the knack of cooking "thick huge steaks in the oven with catsup and A1 sauce on top. (Sounds not so gourmet—but it was wonderful!)"

On off-duty Sundays, Hick hosted brunch for a half dozen of her pals, serving stinger cocktails out on her balcony at 10 Mitchell Place. Hick's place might have been small, but an apartment that size was easy to cram to bursting with friends.

✺

It took three or four years of tenacious persistence, but Hick eventually inched her way to the top of the ladder, becoming the first woman at the Associated Press whom editors "trusted with straight news leads on big stories." Her editor, Martin A. White, "never hesitated to give her the best story that came along."

When a twenty-five-year-old model named Starr Faithfull washed up dead on a Long Island beach in 1931, Hick got to report on the sordid twists and turns of the investigation and murder trial. Every time Governor Roosevelt came to New York City, Hick covered him, occasionally working as a correspondent on his trips around the state as well. (Her skill was also enough to shield her from the worst ravages of the Great Depression. The AP's 10 percent pay cut certainly pinched, but it was nothing compared to the financial ruin other folks were facing.) Hick even won a speaking role in NBC Radio's tour of the Associated Press office in March of 1931, describing her greatest thrill as a reporter—the moment during the 1928 presidential election when she called the AP with the news that "Al Smith had thrown up the sponge."

By 1932, Hick was recognized as one of "six perfect examples of the successful front-page girl." Hick knew it as well as anyone else, and wouldn't hesitate to call herself "just about the top gal reporter in the country."

The prestige didn't come without its frustrations, however, and that word "gal" headed the list. No matter how good she was, she'd come to realize she'd always be considered a woman first and a reporter second, as if male and female journalists were separate species. "The trouble is that, being a woman, I never should have gone into this business," Hick had griped in 1930. "My God, how tired I get of being a woman reporter!"

If that wasn't galling enough, the job was as punishing, both physically and emotionally, as it was rewarding. "Every time I go out on a story I'm scared stiff," Hick admitted. "I expect hell." Of course she could have taken less taxing assignments, assignments considered more suited to a woman's allegedly lesser energies, but where was the satisfaction in that? There wasn't any, as far as Hick was concerned. "The fascinating 'surprise' element," as she called it, was the very thing that kindled her interest and kept her coming back for more. "If you're built as I am mentally, temperamentally, nervously, or however you want to put it," she explained, "and you don't get any kick out of it except the thrill that comes out of working on news—real, honest-to-gawd stories—then it's just hell."

Hell or not, Hick kept at it. She'd built a life around newspaper reporting, and a darn successful one at that. There wasn't any other kind of work she'd rather do. And unbeknownst to Hick, the story of a lifetime was just around the corner.

CHAPTER 27

other jolted with the news on March 2, 1932:

"Lindbergh Baby Kidnapped from Home of Parents on Farm Near Princeton; Taken from His Crib; Wide Search On."

The twenty-month-old son of Charles Lindbergh, America's illustrious aviator, had been snatched from his upstairs nursery without arousing a hint of alarm from his parents or nursemaid. A note found beside the open window demanded $50,000 in ransom for Charles Jr.'s safe return.

"Lucky Lindy" was America's hero, the first pilot in history to fly solo across the Atlantic Ocean. At his son's birth, the whole country had adopted the curly-haired little "Eaglet" as if he were their own baby. And now they reacted as if the infant Jesus had been stolen from the manger.

The press went wild. Reporters swarmed to the scene of the crime. The *New York Times* alone carried over a dozen articles on the kidnapping that same day.

A day and a night passed before the Associated Press bothered to put Hick on the story—an eternity when every second toward apprehending the kidnapper counted. The delay incensed her. "Every reporter in the country was aching to get a crack at [it]," Hick remembered. But she was stuck with some political to-do at Al Smith's office in the Empire State Building that afternoon. Afterward, she stalked down Fifth Avenue, "cursing under my breath all the way and wondering if I would be justified in quitting the AP!"

Hick was beyond mad. She was downright furious. She sat before her typewriter like a steaming volcano, silently threatening to erupt if no one assigned her to that story. Jane Eads remembered sitting behind her, watching Hick grind her elbows into the surface of her desk as the back of her neck slowly turned red. Hick "expected and invariably got to work on all the top assignments," Jane recalled, which made the needless delay that much more antagonizing.

Thirty-six hours after the story broke, the AP finally gave Hick the go-ahead. Without stopping to pack a bag, she sped off to the secluded village on Sourland Mountain where the privacy-craving Lindberghs had built their home.

"Never in my life did I see anything like Hopewell, New Jersey, at the time of the Lindbergh kidnaping story," Hick recalled. Hopewell was hardly more than a speck on the map. A filling station, grocer, barbershop, and hotel made up the entire business district. Newspaper folks thronged the place so thickly, it looked to Hick like they outnumbered actual residents.

Within an hour of the first news bulletin, every room in the hotel had been booked, leaving three to four hundred reporters scrambling for a place to sleep. The AP managed to install its staffers in part of an apartment over the grocery store, rented from the local barber. The barber and his wife had one bedroom, while Hick shared another bedroom, the living room, and the dining room with five other reporters and photographers. A specially installed phone line connected them directly to New York. Hick and one of the men took charge of the story, working in twenty-four-hour shifts relieved by twelve hours of rest.

Frustration reigned supreme from the instant Hick set foot in Hopewell. Nobody knew a blasted thing. The Lindberghs were inaccessible, encamped in their hilltop estate behind a police barricade, and the officers weren't talking, either.

That first day, Hick and an AP photographer named Moe hired a car and tried to tail the police as officers combed a twenty-five-mile radius for any sign of Charles Jr. But their driver, whom they nicknamed Ambling Ashton, wouldn't push his ancient Dodge sedan above thirty miles per hour, no matter how urgently Hick and Moe prodded him. Discouragement and thirst alike eventually steered them into a rural speakeasy. Over their beers, they heard tell of an abandoned house on the Princeton highway and took a notion to investigate it themselves.

Ambling Ashton drove past twice before they spotted it through a screen of trees. The place looked like something out of a ghost story. Shattered glass, fallen plaster, shredded wallpaper, and broken bits of furniture littered what was left of the floorboards. Whole steps were missing from the staircase, and doors dangled from single hinges. The two newshounds found something almost right away.

Muddy footprints, so thick you could pick them up and turn them over, tracked through the house. One of them, Hick discovered, was still damp underneath. Nearby was another wet spot—a little puddle of spit. Someone had been there recently.

Armed with a broken hockey stick and a length of lead pipe, they scoured the house, peering under gunnysacks and piles of leaves, poking at the crumbling walls, and lifting up floorboards. Twilight was falling by the time they stepped outside again, but still they weren't satisfied. Together they dug into several loose mounds of dirt scattered around the yard.

"Them's just moles!" Ambling Ashton scoffed from inside his Dodge.

Law enforcement officials weren't any more impressed than Ashton when Hick and Moe reported what they'd found. "The police were not interested," Hick remembered. "They weren't even polite about it." Nor were her agitated editors back at the New York office, who bellowed every day for news.

Had the police heeded the tip, Hick might have scooped every reporter in the business. Hick didn't know it—no one would know it for another ten weeks—but she and Moe had been searching a mere two hundred yards from where Charles Lindbergh Jr. lay dead in the underbrush. Instead, the hunt and the Lindberghs' agony dragged on and on.

CHAPTER 28

"Everybody quit driving around the countryside searching abandoned houses," Hick recalled. "There were no more abandoned houses to search." But Hick kept cruising hopelessly along in Ambling Ashton's Dodge. What else was there to do? Good thing she did, for one day Ashton took it upon himself to pull over by a farm that backed up to the Lindbergh property. "There's a path up the mountain on this side," he announced. "Lindbergh, he uses it going in and out when he don't want nobody to see him. You go through this here barnyard—"

Hick didn't wait for him to finish. "I literally fell out of the car, rolled under a fence, raced across a barnyard, rolled under another fence and stared up the hill." There it was, just as Ambling Ashton had said. Hick didn't dare climb the path, though. "The cops had grown nervous, irritable, and, conceivably, trigger-happy," she reasoned. Anyone who showed up inside the barricade uninvited—especially someone creeping up the back of the property—might be greeted with bullets instead of questions. But if ever she needed to get around that barricade in a hurry, now Hick knew how to do it.

The odds of her making use of that path were slim. Already it had become clear to Hick that the Lindbergh story was "a grim and hopeless assignment." But it wasn't only the ghastliness of the crime itself.

Usually, New York reporters from rival papers had "an altogether gay and companionable time" on out-of-town stories. They "worked in a pack," sharing information during working hours and getting sloshed together on applejack liquor after chasing down the day's leads. The

Lindbergh story was different—"every man for himself," as Hick put it. "The story was too big, the leads too few." Drooping morale and fierce competition conspired to make a difficult assignment all the worse.

The editors back in their comfortable offices had no sympathy. "The New York office was constantly yipping at our heels, day and night," Hick recalled. "In all my twenty years in the business, I never knew city desks to get so hysterical over any other story." Every reporter in town seemed to have the same sentiment: "If you got beaten on the story, you might as well not go back to the office."

With nothing else to do, the dejected newspeople drank too much and ate too little. It wasn't only the lack of restaurants—there actually weren't enough provisions on hand in Hopewell to keep them all fed. The only thing less plentiful than food was sleep.

❦

Nearly a week passed. Monotony and frustration devolved into a hive of mistrust, anxiety, and paranoia. Every hour that trickled by increased the likelihood that whatever news did turn up would be as bad as it could get. Hick found herself waking in the night, "out of the sleep of exhaustion," to the imaginary cries of a baby.

"Day after day there would be nothing to write except what you could draw out of your imagination, and after three or four days imaginations began to wear pretty thin," she recalled. Her editors didn't care about that; she still had to turn out hundreds of words of copy daily. Hick took to humming Brahms's "Lullaby" as she typed, "to get myself worked up to the proper pitch."

Hick had never had a more difficult assignment. Nor would she ever cover a tougher one. "It was heartbreaking, unrewarding, fantastic."

Just about all she could report on were the rumors and theories swirling through the town. Phrases like "Still Missing" and "Still No Clue" dominated headlines. If the police so much as answered a question about the Lindberghs' Scottish terrier, Hick turned it into inches of newsprint. More than once she described the emotional weight of the atmosphere in Hopewell as deftly as she'd conveyed elated crowds of cheering Gophers fans. Even a Hopewell blizzard turned into front-page Lindbergh news.

And yet, with so little information to relay, Hick still managed to write at least eighteen articles during her nine days in Hopewell. All across the country, when readers opened their newspapers each morning in search of Lindbergh updates, Lorena A. Hickok's byline was there on the front page.

⌇

And then one howling and frigid midnight, the telephone rang in the barber's apartment. The AP's New York office had reports that Charles Jr. had been found and was right that minute safe in his parents' arms. Hick was dubious. How could such a heart-stopping scoop have slipped past the hundreds of reporters in Hopewell without setting off a feeding frenzy?

The man Hick sent out to the barricade at the foot of the Lindbergh driveway came back with nothing, just as she'd expected. The cops had nothing to say, and there wasn't a hint of excitement on the hilltop. That wasn't good enough for New York. Again and again the telephone rang, demanding that someone get the story. Hick and the city desk gave each other so much hell that the night executive editor finally got on the line. The man "sounded positively hysterical." Hick gave up the fight and promised to go after a story she had every reason to believe didn't exist.

The snow from the previous day's blizzard had begun to thaw, then froze again as the wind whipped back in that night. Hick armored herself against the cold with every garment she'd brought to Hopewell, along with anything anyone would lend. It was close to two in the morning when she and Eddie O'Haire, an AP cameraman who usually snapped pictures at the White House, piled into Ambling Ashton's sedan. If ever there was a moment to risk using that hidden path to the back of the Lindbergh property, this was it.

CHAPTER 29

EVERY PATCH OF SNOW THAT HAD BEGUN TO SOFTEN INTO A puddle that afternoon had turned into a black slick of ice. In her bulky layers and the giant overshoes she'd borrowed from Ambling Ashton, Hick wasn't exactly sure-footed. Nor could she detect the difference between the packed dirt and the frozen puddles until her feet flew out from under her. "I think I managed to fall down on every one of them," she remembered. Eddie couldn't help much when she hit the ground. He was a short, slight man with a heap of expensive equipment to wrangle—a camera and tripod and pockets weighted down with glass plates and flash powder.

Hick soon abandoned the path in favor of wrestling her way through the tangles of underbrush alongside it. Scratching her legs to bits was better than falling on her face or her backside every few steps. Up the hill they slipped and slid, practically crawling as the grade grew steadily steeper.

The trees thinned, and suddenly there it stood—the Lone Eagle's nest, as the press liked to call the Lindbergh home. Light from the windows fell on the snow in yellow rectangles, barely illuminating the building's spare outlines. For a moment, Hick and Eddie were stunned by the fact that it really was there, that the path had actually worked. They were standing in Charles Lindbergh's backyard. There wasn't a reporter within a hundred miles who wouldn't writhe with envy at the thought of being in that spot.

Eddie got to work without a sound. He set up his camera, took a six-minute exposure of the house, and then retreated to the cover of the tree line to wait. If Hick got caught, they'd agreed, he'd hightail it down the mountain with his photograph.

Hick's nerves screamed for a cigarette, but even the flare of a match might sabotage her mission. Hick looked, listened, and tried to gather her courage. No armed sentries patrolled the exterior as she'd half expected. The sole movement on the property came from an upstairs window— "the calm, unhurried motions of someone getting ready for bed." With one final gulp, she went down on her hands and knees and crawled over the snow until she reached the edges of the glowing outlines thrown by the windows.

Only the wind rippled the air. If it blew just right, she could catch a murmur of voices from the garage, where the police had their headquarters. The commotion that the editors in New York insisted she'd find was absent. As she crouched just outside the perimeters of light, the upstairs windows went dark.

There was no story.

Down the hill she and Eddie tumbled, losing the path and fumbling through the brush until they were thoroughly lost. Hick had no choice but to sit shivering with the camera equipment while Eddie tracked down the route and came back to get her.

When they finally returned to the barber's apartment, Kay Beebe, an AP recruit from the *Kansas City Star,* was in the kitchen with a pot of hot coffee, and eggs ready for scrambling. Hick called New York while Kay cooked a breakfast to heat them from the inside out. "The man on the city desk only grunted sourly when I told him where we had been," Hick wrote later. "I don't think he believed me. The only fact of which he was conscious was that I had no story."

~

Hick promptly got the flu, and didn't have an aspirin to her name. Kay Beebe wasn't surprised. It was just like Hick to think of nothing but the story and neglect to pack anything practical. So Kay went shopping and picked up some of the necessities Hick had overlooked.

The gesture touched Hick—so much so that she took it for a romantic overture. After all, back in New York she'd seen Kay openly carrying a copy of a controversial new novel about a lesbian love affair. Kay had even been surprised when Hick said she wouldn't want to be seen in public with that book in her hands. And now here was Kay, doing everything she could to make Hick more comfortable. Hick took a chance.

". . . she made for me," Kay revealed with great reluctance years later. Hick's unexpected advance rattled her. "I had never had *any* such experience," Kay recalled. But she gave herself a shake and asked herself, "What am I afraid of?"

Hick recognized her blunder and apologized immediately. "You were just so sweet to me that it undid me," she explained.

With her biggest secret suddenly out in the open, Hick began to confide in Kay. Her childhood miseries spilled free, including her father's rape and other abuse, as well as her abiding insecurities about her size and appearance. "She considered that she was a mess," as Kay put it. Hick also confessed to some of the romantic ventures she'd had since moving to New York. With men, she'd merely "experimented," but when it came to women, Hick "went off the deep end." Kay thought that Hick "didn't herself wish to surrender to these tendencies." But it was like trying to resist an ocean current. When her guard was down, as it had been with Kay, Hick was swept away.

To Kay's relief, the two remained friends, never speaking of the incident again.

CHAPTER 30

HICK STAYED SICK. FOR SIX WEEKS, SHE HAD NO VOICE. IF SHE'D been able to work up enough volume to do it, she would have quit. But the AP couldn't hear her, no matter how "furiously" she whispered. Instead, they relieved her of the dead-end Lindbergh assignment and shipped her back to New York. "A week later, still whispering, I was back covering politics."

Politics that year meant the presidential campaign. On the Democrats' side, Al Smith and Franklin Delano Roosevelt, now rivals, were both eyeing the nomination. Hick had covered Governor Roosevelt regularly since 1930, but now Louis Howe, the governor's closest advisor and a former newspaperman himself, arranged for her to profile FDR more closely.

~

Hick arrived at Springwood, the Hyde Park, New York, estate where FDR had been born, escorted by a state trooper. FDR and his wife awaited her in the library with the tea service Hick was growing accustomed to. "A good, substantial tea," Hick recalled with appreciation, "usually with chocolate cake."

Mrs. Roosevelt sat on a couch, knitting, as Hick interviewed the governor. FDR's wife had a way of being present yet somehow invisible, joining the conversation without ever contributing anything weighty enough to leave a firm impression. Yet Hick knew from everything she'd observed of Mrs. Roosevelt in the last two years that she had opinions, interests, and projects of her own—valuable and intriguing ones. Eleanor

Roosevelt knew politics as well. She *had* to. She was constantly working at Democratic headquarters, raising money for the women's division. Besides that, her uncle had been the president of the United States. Her husband had held office as a state senator and assistant secretary of the navy and run for vice president before becoming governor of New York. And yet there she sat, placidly clicking her knitting needles as if there were nothing more compelling in the world than teapots and yarn. It drove Hick just a little crazy.

After tea, a pair of state troopers carried Governor Roosevelt out to his car. It was a convertible, fitted up with hand controls for the accelerator and brakes. If Hick hadn't known the full extent of the governor's disability before she arrived at Hyde Park, she certainly did now.

It was common knowledge that in the summer of 1921, FDR had come down with a fever and paralysis that left him bedridden for months and absent from politics for nearly three years. Doctors diagnosed polio. In those days, a debilitating disease usually spelled a political death sentence. But FDR refused to surrender his career to the era's prejudices against physical disability.

The public believed that after years of therapy and strength-building exercises, he'd "beaten" polio and learned to walk again. That was a sham. FDR remained a paraplegic, paralyzed from the waist down, for the rest of his life. At home, he used a wheelchair. For public appearances, he strapped on a pair of steel-and-leather braces that weighed five pounds apiece and stretched from his hips to the soles of his feet. Hours of grueling, sweat-soaked practice with those braces had taught him how to create the illusion of walking.

It was an illusion fraught with risk. With his braces locked so that his knee joints could not buckle unexpectedly beneath him, the governor would shift his balance to one foot and use the muscles of his torso to swing the other leg forward as if it were a pendulum attached at his hip. For the critical next step, he had to have support on both sides of his body. Some combination of a cane (or two), a handrail, and the arm of one of his four tall and handsome sons usually did the trick. When his outthrust foot landed, FDR threw his balance onto that forward leg. This was the moment when everything could go wrong. It was as if his legs were stilts—stiff, heavy, spindly stilts that he could barely feel, much less control. A miscalculation could fling him into a bone-rattling heap. With every step he took, FDR gambled his own physical safety for the sake of concealing the true nature of his disability.

Yet this precarious illusion was necessary for a presidential candidate, for in the 1930s, a man with a physical disability would be universally thought unfit for office, as if the paralysis in his legs could somehow seep into his brain.

Remarkably, the press was in on the fraud. An unspoken gentleman's agreement dictated that no photographs would be taken of FDR using his wheelchair, or of him getting in and out of his car. And so Hick would not write a word that even hinted at the state troopers, the custom-made wheelchair, or the hand controls FDR manipulated as he toured her across his eleven-hundred-acre estate.

After a four-mile trip along the Hudson and through the wooded acres, the car rattled across a log bridge spanning a brook called the Val-Kill. "I built that for my Missis," FDR said, indicating a neat one-and-a-half-story stone cottage with a swimming pool. Mrs. Roosevelt shared the cozy hideaway with her friends, Nancy Cook and Marion Dickerman, who were co-owners of the furniture factory Hick had heard about. Miss Dickerman was also principal of the New York City girls' school where Mrs. Roosevelt taught.

Mrs. Roosevelt, Miss Cook, and Miss Dickerman were there to greet them when FDR's touring car pulled up.

It might have been a curious moment for Hick. Before her stood two women very much like herself; Nan and Marion had been romantic partners for over a decade, and would remain so for the rest of their lives.

As they traded pleasantries, did Hick intuit that Mrs. Roosevelt's business associates were also lovers? Did she spot the tea towels monogrammed with all three women's initials and wonder how Mrs. Roosevelt figured into their relationship? The potential impact on Hick of that meeting is mind-shaking. In a society that shunned and erased same-sex couples, Eleanor Roosevelt welcomed Nan and Marion into her professional and private lives alike. Other prominent women—women like FDR's mother, Sara Delano Roosevelt—would have shied away from associating so closely with Nan and Marion, turning up their noses at differences as superficial as the women's short haircuts and fondness for sweaters and knickers. (Eleanor, by contrast, ordered herself knickers to match theirs.) Perhaps for the first time, Hick had stumbled across a place where it might be safe to let her guard down, where she might be fully accepted for who she was.

If any of the women realized just then how much Hick and Nan and Marion had in common, no one ever remarked on it. Mrs. Roosevelt took Hick on a tour of the factory, which stood only a few hundred feet behind the cottage. Once again she was welcoming and polite in what Hick called "an impersonal way," centering their conversation firmly on furniture. On the surface, the visit was as mundane as could be. Its significance was anything but.

CHAPTER 31

orbit once again, when the Democratic Party's national convention met in Chicago to choose their candidate for president. Al Smith and Franklin Delano Roosevelt were the top contenders. Whatever happened in Chicago, the AP wanted to know what the Roosevelts had to say about it, and so they sent Hick to work the story with Elton Fay of the Albany bureau.

Everything the press needed was rigged up in the garage of the governor's mansion: a radio to listen to the conference as it happened, and telephones and telegraph machines complete with operators to relay the news as fast as Hick and her colleagues could translate it into lines of print.

Inside the mansion, FDR, Mrs. Roosevelt, two of their sons, and Franklin's mother were gathered around their own radio and telephone. Word was, Eleanor Roosevelt was knitting. Her hands, Hick had noticed, were never fully still.

The clock ticked, the reporters listened, and the Democrats in Chicago talked and talked and talked. For hours, nobody so much as reached for a ballot. Coffee and sandwiches arrived around midnight, courtesy of Mrs. Roosevelt.

Hick and Elton sat up all night, listening to the radio crackle out the sounds of yammering politicians and boos from the gallery of spectators. The delegates finally got around to voting well after sunrise. Three times they tried to reach a consensus, and every ballot came up deadlocked between Roosevelt and Smith.

At eight o'clock in the morning, Hick and Elton snapped off the radio. The garage was empty. Everyone else had abandoned the story. Nothing was going to happen until the convention reassembled that evening. Groggy and ravenous from the long night, Hick and Elton headed for their car.

Mrs. Roosevelt spotted the two exhausted reporters and beckoned them onto the porch to join her for breakfast. One good thing about working the Roosevelt beat, the hospitality never failed.

But Hick sensed something different in her hostess's manner that morning. In the spring, Mrs. Roosevelt had made herself effortlessly inconspicuous while Hick chatted with FDR. Now she seemed absent in a different way—"shut up inside herself," Hick thought.

"That woman is unhappy about something," Hick told Elton after they'd gotten in the car.

"She's probably afraid her husband won't get it," he said.

Hick wasn't buying that.

At FDR's press conference that afternoon, Hick's suspicions increased. The governor laughed and joked so heartily that Hick figured Roosevelt knew something they didn't. Probably some kind of deal was brewing in Chicago—a deal that he liked the sound of. Hick also took particular notice of Mrs. Roosevelt. She did not speak, and her face did not mirror her husband's convivial mood. She simply knitted.

Something was indeed brewing. John Nance Garner, Speaker of the House of Representatives, had swapped ninety of Texas's votes in exchange for nomination as the vice presidential candidate on the Roosevelt ticket. The trade put FDR within twelve votes of winning the nomination. That turned the tide, and the Democratic Party chose Franklin Delano Roosevelt as its candidate for the White House.

Friends, neighbors, reporters, and photographers alike promptly thronged the executive mansion as though it were a public park on the Fourth of July. FDR basked in the congratulations. Mrs. Roosevelt, however, seemed to have vanished. A knot of reporters—Hick among them—scoured the place in search of her, eager for her reaction to the triumphant news. The kitchen was perhaps the last place they expected to find her, but there she was, scrambling eggs for her husband's supper without spattering a drop on her gown of light green chiffon.

One young reporter burst out, "Mrs. Roosevelt, aren't you *thrilled* at the idea of living in the White House?" All the governor's wife did in reply was look at her. Mrs. Roosevelt was *not* thrilled, and her face plainly said so.

Eleanor Roosevelt, Hick began to suspect, was not a typical candidate's wife.

⁂

Hick was so intrigued that she talked the AP into assigning a reporter to Mrs. Roosevelt. It wasn't easy. Candidates' wives usually went to luncheons and teas, where their duty was to sit at the head table, look benevolent, and possibly murmur benign things. Little was more mind-numbing for a reporter than covering those functions. They were all the same: chicken salad, watercress sandwiches, and orchid corsages. Only the lady's dress might be different from one luncheon to the next.

But Hick insisted, and Kay Beebe got the job. Hick took her over to headquarters, introduced her to Mrs. Roosevelt, "and went happily on my way."

CHAPTER 32

THE DAY FDR'S CAMPAIGN TRAIN, THE ROOSEVELT SPECIAL, pulled out of the station in Albany for a twenty-one-day whistle-stop tour of the continental United States, Hick was aboard—one of three AP staffers, and the only woman in the press corps assigned to cover FDR's presidential campaign.

Hick "did not try to be 'one of the boys.'" She was simply herself. That approach had never failed her before, and it didn't fail this time. Her male colleagues admired her skill and appreciated her company. In theory, her assignment was to write features on the women of the Roosevelt family. But she was "too good as a reporter" to content herself with that, fellow AP writer W. B. Ragsdale noticed.

"Those were grueling 12- and 16-hour days," Ragsdale remembered, "and we enjoyed every minute of them." Each time the train stopped, Franklin Roosevelt could easily step onto the platform at the back of the caboose to give his speech. Gripping the handrail as a band blared the cheerful chorus of "Happy Days Are Here Again," he presented the illusion of an ambulatory, able-bodied man. His confidence and his concern for his fellow citizens' well-being were genuine, however, just like his pledge to give Americans a "New Deal"—a host of projects and programs to bring relief, recovery, and reform to both the public and the economy—if they put him in the White House. While Ragsdale covered FDR's speech, Hick circulated through the crowd. These great masses of people fascinated her. They listened so quietly, so intently, it was almost unnerving.

Hick had seen firsthand what the Depression was doing to people back in New York City. Along the East River where she walked Prinz, a settlement of shanties had popped up in 1930, cobbled together out of everything from scrap lumber to flattened tin cans. Other New Yorkers tended to ignore the men who lived there, dismissing them as lazy drunkards. But Hick took the time to talk to the men and learned that they were mostly out of work and so hard up for cash that they couldn't afford so much as a rented bed on skid row. If not for the slaughterhouse workers who smuggled them scraps of meat, they might have starved. President Hoover hadn't done a darn thing to help them, which prompted the homeless to dub their makeshift communities Hoovervilles.

Two years later, the folks along the campaign trail weren't much different. If they weren't already living in Hoovervilles, they feared the possibility. Hick sopped up their hopes and anxieties like a sponge. "Many times she came back aboard the campaign train in 1932 fuming and almost tearful over a hard-luck story she had picked up from someone in the crowd at a whistle-stop," Ragsdale remembered.

At a stop in Oregon, Hick got so thoroughly enmeshed in the crowd that she missed the train. The signal for the press to board came, and the mass of spectators shifted somehow, blocking Hick's path. Ragsdale saw her "yelling and trying to fight her way through." In the confusion, he couldn't tell if she'd made it aboard. He and the other reporters searched the cars and figured out quickly that she hadn't—they'd have heard the bellow of her voice grousing about her close scrape if she'd managed to catch hold of the moving Roosevelt Special and swing aboard.

At the next stop, FDR's press agent held the train. "Everyone knew her well enough by this time to be certain she would be along soon," Ragsdale recalled. They were right. Hick had hailed a cab and careened through the mountains to get there.

Ragsdale soon came to regard Lorena Hickok as "two distinct people." The "blasé and shock-proof" hard news reporter forever hurling invective around her Pall Malls in the club car was Hick. Within that reporter lived the woman Ragsdale thought of as Lorena: "tenderhearted and, even, sometimes shy."

In between observing speeches and writing articles, Hick struck up a friendship with Mrs. Roosevelt's secretary, Tommy. Both of them were at loose ends in the evenings. Everyone else from the national press associations had a drawing room or a private compartment. Hick had gotten stuck with the railway equivalent of a bunkhouse—a berth in a sleeper car with the regional reporters. If she wanted to do anything but sleep or look out the window, she had to do it in the club car or the dining car.

Tommy was alone, and not at all used to it. Mrs. Roosevelt was ahead of the train in Arizona and had lent Tommy to take dictation for the campaign advisors. Without the "Boss" and her endless correspondence to attend to, Tommy found herself with unaccustomed hours of leisure on her hands. "Tommy was so suspicious that people might try to use Mrs. Roosevelt," one Roosevelt insider recalled, "that she personally avoided making friends." Hick became a rare exception.

The two of them chatted over dinner in the dining car, often lingering long after their plates were empty. Tommy reminisced about her childhood in the Bronx, and how she'd taught herself to type and take shorthand. Hick, in turn, shared stories of her hardscrabble years in South Dakota. Just how far into her past she let Tommy is impossible to know. But more than once, it was well after midnight when Hick finally clambered into her berth and shut her curtains against the chorus of snores that rattled the sleeper car.

The Roosevelt Special lumbered through Cheyenne, Butte, San Francisco, Los Angeles, Salt Lake City, and Seattle before reaching Williams, Arizona. There, Eleanor Roosevelt joined the campaign train. Ragsdale hadn't known Hick for more than a week or two, but even he could tell that Mrs. Roosevelt's presence had an effect on Hick. He saw it the moment she returned from speaking with Mrs. Roosevelt, "as excited as I ever saw her." Right away he realized that something about that encounter had cut straight through Hick the lobster-shelled reporter to reach the alter ego known in his mind as Lorena. "From this time forward it became difficult for her to write with the usual AP restraint about Mrs. Roosevelt," he recalled. Ragsdale figured "the feeling must have been mutual for Mrs. Roosevelt saw, and understood, the solid gold beneath the tough exterior."

～～

The press learned they'd have a day off at last in Prescott, Arizona, so that FDR's family could attend a barbecue at a local cattle ranch owned by a longtime friend of Eleanor Roosevelt's. That was just fine with everybody, until someone got wind that one young reporter from the *Chicago Tribune* had been invited.

It made no sense. Nearly every journalist on the train had more professional clout, and the *Tribune* was just about as anti-Roosevelt as a paper could get. The unfairness rankled every one of the men—and the woman—left behind. (The secret truth was that FDR's married daughter, Anna, was having an affair with the *Tribune* reporter.)

Hick had a good mind to raise hell. She marched through the train until she found Mrs. Roosevelt and aired her complaints. FDR's wife listened keenly and decided that the best way to even the score was to invite Hick to come along as well.

Hick didn't witness much to report. It was just as they'd been told: barbecued beef, with some broncos and steer roping for entertainment. Mrs. Roosevelt did come and talk with her for a long time, but it was all about her friendship with their host, Isabella Greenway, who'd been a bridesmaid at the Roosevelts' wedding.

By the time Hick got back to the train, FDR's public relations man was every bit as mad as the broncos she'd watched that afternoon. What business did she have going to that barbecue when every reporter on the train had been told to stay behind? he demanded. The Washington correspondents were in a fury and holding him responsible. Hick lobbed right back that Mrs. Roosevelt was a Roosevelt, too, and if she wanted to bring someone along, she had as much right to do it as any other member of the family. The PR man backed down, and Hick cooled everyone else off by sharing what "precious little" news she'd picked up that day.

As the train swung back east through Nebraska and Iowa on its way toward Chicago, Hick turned out a few more stories about Mrs. Roosevelt. Her stamina alone could fill columns of newsprint. Anytime the terrain was too rough for FDR to risk touring—such as a Midwest farmer's fields—Mrs. Roosevelt stepped in to pinch-hit, as Hick called it. There wasn't anywhere she wouldn't go, and there didn't seem to be anything that could wear the woman out.

The way she strode through a cornfield left Hick in awe. She moved with incongruous elegance, as though she were strolling down a freshly paved New York City avenue. "Puffing, panting, and perspiring," Hick struggled along behind, watching in despair as Mrs. Roosevelt slipped through a barbed wire fence as gracefully as a sparrow riding a breeze. Hick followed—or tried to. She was not so lithe, or so nimble. Her stockings caught in the wires, tangling so badly she needed help to free herself.

Where in blue blazes was Kay Beebe? Hick wondered in the midst of it all. Shouldn't *she* be trotting along behind Mrs. Roosevelt on this trip, ripping up her silk stockings instead of Hick sacrificing hers?

It wasn't just that Eleanor Roosevelt was inexhaustible. She was also apparently unflappable, as Hick witnessed the evening the Roosevelt Special arrived in Chicago. Mayor Cermak, a fellow Democrat, had arranged for one of the most enthusiastic welcomes of the entire campaign tour.

Despite the late hour, an undulating wall of people crammed the streets of the Loop. Cheers, brass bands, and flares erupted as FDR's open car cruised toward his lakefront hotel. Copper urns filled with burning kerosene swung from poles, lighting the way down the avenue. Ticker tape and bits of paper sifted, snowlike, through the air. The crowd swelled, breaking through the police line and surging so close that the motorcade was forced to crawl.

Inevitably, one of the policemen's horses spooked. Up it reared, its forelegs hovering above the Roosevelts' car. In the instant before the mounted officer brought the horse back under control, it seemed that the creature's pawing hooves would land smack in Mr. and Mrs. Roosevelt's laps. To Hick's astonishment, Eleanor Roosevelt didn't flinch. Her spine stayed perfectly straight, her head pointed forward as the car rolled directly into the path of danger.

"Were you frightened when that horse reared over you last night?" Hick asked her the next day.

Mrs. Roosevelt looked as though the idea of being afraid had never occurred to her. There hadn't been time to get scared before it was all over, she said. "If I had been frightened, I'd have been frightened for Franklin," she added. "I can move quickly, but he can't."

CHAPTER 33

THE NEW YORK REPUBLICANS HELD THEIR STATE CONVENTION in Buffalo that year, and Hick disembarked from the Roosevelt Special to cover it. She was in the thick of political reporting now, and reveling in the accomplishment. Between the Roosevelt campaign and the Lindbergh kidnapping, 1932 had rewarded Hick with the most prominent stories a reporter of any sex could hope to land.

She returned to the New York City office to find everything in a scramble. The AP, figuring that Roosevelt was going to win the election, had imported several Washington, DC, staffers to jump-start its coverage of FDR, swamping him with reporters. Not only that, but Kay Beebe had resigned and hightailed it to San Francisco. That left the Eleanor Roosevelt assignment conspicuously empty. What happened next was maddeningly predictable.

"She's all yours now, Hickok," the city editor informed Hick. "Have fun!"

"Fun" was not the first word that came to Hick's mind. As interesting as Mrs. Roosevelt might be, covering a woman always felt like a step backward—just the kind of "women's page stuff" she'd shied away from for years. And this assignment meant she'd have to devote every hour to Eleanor Roosevelt for the better part of a month, giving her no chance to nab any of the more prestigious beats.

Trailing her constantly like that, Hick figured Mrs. Roosevelt would either regard her as a mortal enemy or succumb to friendship. Hick hoped for friendship, and not simply for the sake of making her waking hours more pleasant. "While I had no occasion to write stories about her, I wanted very much to know Mrs. Roosevelt," Hick admitted. "But she always held me at arm's length—and her arms were long."

Mrs. Roosevelt was just as dismayed when Hick explained her duties. The ever-gracious Mrs. Roosevelt conceded that Hick must be permitted to do her job. Anytime she had a public engagement, Hick could follow.

Coincidentally, Hick's first day on the Eleanor Roosevelt beat was Mrs. Roosevelt's forty-eighth birthday. "It's good to be middle-aged," she told Hick with a certain satisfaction. "Things don't matter so much. You don't take it so hard when things happen to you that you don't like." Hick felt her interest pique in spite of herself. Most women did not greet this phase of life so cordially. And the unspoken disappointments Mrs. Roosevelt alluded to practically begged for a follow-up question. Hick didn't ask. She knew by now that Mrs. Roosevelt wouldn't divulge anything more. There wasn't an article in it, especially without further details, but the remark burrowed itself into Hick's mind anyway.

There would be plenty of time to think about it in the days to come. Mrs. Roosevelt went about her business, and Hick followed.

Mostly, Hick sat. Outside Mrs. Roosevelt's office, with Tommy or Louis Howe for company. At the Todhunter School in New York City, where Mrs. Roosevelt taught her classes three days a week. In the audience during the unremarkable speeches she gave to women's groups—speeches in which she never mentioned her husband's presidential campaign. And hours upon hours on the train between New York City, Hyde Park, and Albany.

⁓

Just as she was reconciling herself to the Roosevelt assignment, a shadow came rearing up out of Hick's past. The body of a man thought to be around sixty-five years old was discovered behind a billboard just off Main Street in Aberdeen, South Dakota. He wore pin-striped trousers and a brown coat. A .32-caliber bullet was lodged in his brain; his right hand clutched a matching .32-caliber bulldog revolver. His watch bore the initials *A.J.H.*

It was none other than Hick's father, Addison J. Hickok.

His body was held at the local morgue, awaiting funeral instructions from family. Four days later, no word had come. The *Aberdeen Daily News* reported that upon being contacted in New York, two of Addison Hickok's daughters (presumably Hick and Ruby) had disavowed any connection to the body lying in the morgue. They had buried their father eight years ago, the women declared.

To friends, however, Hick was more forthcoming about the dead man's identity. One of Hick's Minneapolis neighbors recalled her terse response at the prospect of making funeral arrangements: "Send him to the glue factory."

∼

For three weeks Hick struggled to find something worth reporting about Eleanor Roosevelt. Every day that she returned to the office without a story, her embarrassment soaked in deeper. Hick figured the AP would pull the assignment out from under her at any moment. She had a hunch that Mrs. Roosevelt was working behind the scenes to smooth out a rocky relationship between two of FDR's top campaign officials, but hunches weren't news. The AP cared only about facts, and the facts so far were nothing short of bland.

Nevertheless, Hick would not admit defeat. There was something about this woman—the niece of one president and perhaps the nation's next first lady—who wore $10 dresses, drove her own car, and regularly ate at drugstore lunch counters. "THE DAME HAS ENORMOUS DIGNITY," Hick wired to the AP in lieu of news. "SHE'S A PERSON." Hick just couldn't prove it yet.

And then one late-October afternoon as Hick sat in the AP's Albany office trying to wring a full-length story out of her typewriter, the phone rang. Louis Howe's voice informed her that FDR's secretary, Marguerite LeHand, had just lost her mother. Mrs. Roosevelt was going to accompany Miss LeHand to the funeral in upstate New York, and Hick could go along if the AP deemed it necessary.

Hick trashed her flimsy story and phoned up the New York City office.

"Stay with it, kid," her editor there advised. Hick boarded the train almost as quickly as she'd caught the one to Hopewell, New Jersey, that spring.

Nothing much happened at first. A night and a day went by with Hick trailing along behind Mrs. Roosevelt and Miss LeHand. As usual, Mrs. Roosevelt was thoughtful and courteous, and perhaps something more. There seemed to be almost a whiff of friendliness in the air. After the funeral, Mrs. Roosevelt tracked Hick down in the restaurant where she'd stopped for lunch, wondering if Hick would like to go for a drive along the St. Lawrence River.

"I don't see many Democratic posters around," Mrs. Roosevelt said as they motored back into town. "Franklin is going to be dreadfully disappointed if he loses this election. For a while he won't know what to do with himself."

It was as if a tightly locked door had creaked open, just a sliver.

CHAPTER 34

ONLY A SINGLE DRAWING ROOM REMAINED ON THE TRAIN WHEN Hick and Mrs. Roosevelt boarded that evening. Every other berth and seat was taken. The two of them would have to share the compartment. To Hick's mortification, the first lady of New York insisted that Hick should take the bed. She herself would sleep on the skinny couch that stretched across the length of the opposite wall. "I'm longer than you," Mrs. Roosevelt pointed out. "And not quite so broad!" Hick could not argue with that logic, or with Mrs. Roosevelt's teasing smile.

The women put themselves to bed, only to realize that despite the lulling rhythm of the train, they were not going to fall asleep anytime soon. So they talked, a little self-consciously at first. Hick learned that her invitation on this trip was Tommy's doing. All those chats over supper on the Roosevelt Special had been more than just idle conversation to Tommy. "She's very fond of you," Mrs. Roosevelt said, "and Tommy is a good judge of people. So I decided you must be all right."

Her own reluctance to be interviewed wasn't personal, Mrs. Roosevelt explained for the first time. It had been bred into her by her grandmother, a woman with rigidly old-fashioned ideas about the impropriety of a lady's name appearing in the newspaper. "Franklin used to tease me about you," she confessed. "He'd say, 'You'd better watch out for that Hickok woman. She's smart.'"

As the dark seeped in around them, the words began to flow more freely from the other side of the compartment. Hick listened, and Eleanor Roosevelt, who had artfully sidestepped personal and political questions for four solid years, began to narrate the story of her childhood.

Her earliest memories were of feeling awkward and homely. Eleanor's mother, a socialite whose beauty was the toast of New York, had mocked Eleanor's plain looks and serious personality from the time she was a toddler. Eleanor could still remember, with a curdle of shame, her mother's voice calling her "Granny" as she stood shyly in the doorway with her finger in her mouth. "She is such a funny child, so old-fashioned, that we always call her 'Granny,'" Anna Roosevelt would explain to her visitors as Eleanor wished for the ability to "sink through the floor." Anna's shock and dismay at having produced such a thoroughly ordinary-looking child formed "a curious barrier" between Eleanor and her mother and her two younger brothers, just as Hick had felt a barrier between herself and her mother and siblings.

Like Hick's, Eleanor's childhood had been upended by her father's failings. The difference was, Eleanor worshipped Elliott Roosevelt. Elliott, in turn, had adored Eleanor—his Little Nell—as no one else in the world did. He also bullied her for her timidity, and once left her on the doorstep of the Knickerbocker Club for six hours while he drank himself into oblivion. But her father's boundless affection contrasted so sharply with her mother's disappointment that Eleanor was insensible to Elliott's faults, even when his drunkenness, infidelity, and increasingly erratic behavior broke the family in half. "Attention and admiration were the things through all my childhood which I wanted, because I was made to feel so conscious of the fact that nothing about me would attract attention or would bring me admiration," Eleanor later wrote.

While Elliott ricocheted from one sanitarium to another as his family tried to rid him of his addictions to alcohol, morphine, and laudanum, Eleanor awaited his occasional appearances at her grandmother's house in New York with eternal glee. "I slid down the banisters and usually catapulted into his arms before his hat was hung up," she recalled. No one told Eleanor why her father was so often away for months at a time. They only whispered, leaving her to wonder what was wrong with him, and perhaps with herself, that kept them apart. "If people only realized what a war goes on in a child's mind and heart in a situation of this kind,

I think they would try to explain more than they do to children; but no-body told me anything," she later mused.

Unable to bear Elliott's mysterious lingering absences, Eleanor created a fantasy world for herself, a world in which her father was the hero and she the heroine. When eight-year-old Eleanor's mother died of diphtheria, the immensity of the loss hardly registered. "Death meant nothing to me, and one fact wiped out everything else—my father was back, and I would see him very soon," she recalled. Elliott did come home to bury his wife, and he lavished Eleanor with promises of a day when they would have a life together, filled with travel and contentment. But Eleanor and her brothers remained in Grandmother Hall's care.

The next twenty-one months foisted one tragedy after another upon the shy and sensitive youngster. First, one of her little brothers died of scarlet fever. Just over a year later, Eleanor's world shattered entirely when Elliott succumbed to alcoholism. Eleanor "simply refused to believe it," and retreated further yet into her dream world.

Though Mary Hall had her orphaned grandchildren's best interests at heart, her own circumstances prevented her from giving Eleanor and her surviving brother the stability they so desperately needed. Mrs. Hall was a widow, already coping with financial woes and four unmarried adult children with difficulties of their own. The strain of it often sent her to her bed.

Uncle Eddie and Uncle Vallie were playboys, tennis champions with a fondness for liquor that nearly rivaled Elliott Roosevelt's. When drunk, Vallie sometimes amused himself by shooting buckshot out of his bedroom window at passersby. As Eleanor grew into her teen years, three stout locks were secured to her bedroom door. No member of the family ever revealed exactly what those locks protected her from, but their presence speaks volumes. Eleanor rarely invited any of her few friends to visit. "Every moment that they were there, however, I held my breath for fear that some unfortunate incident would occur."

The aunts were little help. One of them routinely wielded her emotions as weapons. At times she used kindness to bribe favors from Eleanor, but she could just as easily lash out with vindictiveness or disappear into fits of crying that lasted for days. This was the same aunt who informed Eleanor point-blank that she was "the ugly duckling" of the family. It wasn't news to Eleanor, but that didn't make it sting any less. "I knew I was the first girl in my mother's family who was not a belle, and though I never acknowledged it to them at that time, I was deeply ashamed."

No one bothered to praise Eleanor's most becoming features, like her luminous blue eyes or cascade of golden-brown hair. They only looked at her towering height, her protruding teeth, her small chin, the curving spine that had to be straightened with an expensive steel brace, and abandoned her appearance as hopeless. "Poor little soul, she is very plain," wrote one of her aunts. "Her mouth and teeth seem to have no future." At parties and dances, she felt like a child, with her too-short skirts and the old-fashioned flannel underthings her grandmother insisted she wear.

Only when she went abroad to a British boarding school at fifteen did Eleanor begin to find the confidence her childhood had deprived her of. Allenswood Academy and its charismatic, progressive headmistress, Mademoiselle Souvestre, gave Eleanor Roosevelt the space and encouragement to grow into herself, to recognize the power of her intellect and the value of her character. No one would give her a greater gift. "I think I was a curious mixture of extreme innocence and unworldliness with a great deal of knowledge of some of the less attractive and less agreeable sides of life," Eleanor concluded of her early years.

～

The circumstances of their lives were vastly different, but the emotions Eleanor had felt as a child were all but twins to Hick's. Here was a woman who understood how it felt to always be the wrong size, the wrong shape, a woman who knew that same bone-deep sense of rootlessness that came from craving a home of your own. She, too, had abandoned reality for a time to inhabit a gentler world of her own making.

Hick could not have known it in that moment, but Eleanor Roosevelt had just inducted Hick into her inner circle. Sharing the hurts of her childhood had become a ritual of friendship for Eleanor, a way of indicating the depth of her trust in another human being. Emotionally, it was akin to stripping herself naked before another's eyes.

Hick was almost afraid to ask, but she did. The reporter in her couldn't help it. "May I write some of that?"

Eleanor's voice was soft in the dark. "If you like," she said. "I trust you."

⁓

Something profound had happened on that train that would resonate through every moment of Hick's life. The conversation they'd shared forged the first unbreakable link in an ironclad bond between Lorena Hickok and Eleanor Roosevelt.

Hick had either fallen in love with Eleanor that night or was poised on the brink of it. Though she never said precisely when she lost her heart to Eleanor, Hick always considered that train trip the official beginning of a friendship that outshone all others.

The feeling would soon be mutual. Overnight, Eleanor elevated Hick from mere acquaintance to a position of intense trust—though when and how quickly her affinity for Hick turned to affection and then to love is impossible to pinpoint. What's certain is that within the space of a week, Hick had become Eleanor's closest confidante.

On the surface Hick and Eleanor seemed an unlikely pair. Yet their hearts' desires fit together like lock and key. Hick had an unrivaled ability to simply listen to people. Anyone who opened up to Lorena Hickok couldn't help but feel her opening up in return, as if her every pore expanded like a sympathetic sponge. And when Hick was touched by sorrow, she couldn't help but absorb some of it, experiencing others' pain as if it were her own.

For someone like Eleanor, who longed to be heard right down to her depths, Hick's empathy was a revelation. "I never talked to anyone," she would eventually marvel to Hick. "Perhaps that is why it all ate into my soul."

Eleanor, in turn, had a heart as vast as the horizon. Those who earned her devotion were rewarded with an all-encompassing love—just the kind of affection Hick had thirsted for her whole life long. The lonely, abandoned, and self-conscious teen who still lived at Hick's core had never known anything like the bewildering force of Eleanor's love. More bewildering yet, Hick found that she mattered to someone, more intensely than she had ever mattered to anyone before.

CHAPTER 35

LATE ON THE NIGHT BEFORE THE ELECTION, HICK WATCHED WITH admiration as FDR spoke at a rally in Poughkeepsie, a town just five miles down the Albany Post Road from his home. The kind of man who would not take for granted the support of his own neighbors seemed to Hick just the right kind of man to be president.

It was nearly midnight by the time FDR finished. Eleanor didn't waste a minute. She was ready to spring into her two-seat roadster and head to New York City. Election or no election, she had classes to teach at Todhunter the next morning.

Her husband protested. Eleanor liked to drive, and she liked to drive fast. FDR didn't relish the thought of her careening through the rain in the dead of night. He finally let up, on the condition that Eleanor take Hick with her to make sure she didn't nod off behind the wheel.

As they approached Eleanor's car, Hick noticed a reporter, a woman from one of the AP's rivals, waiting for them. The other press agencies had finally realized that Mrs. Franklin D. Roosevelt was worth covering in her own right. This woman was assigned to Eleanor, just as Hick was, and wanted to ride with them into the city.

Eleanor kindly refused. There simply wasn't room in the car for another person, she apologized. The reporter volunteered to ride in the rumble seat, and Eleanor put her foot down, more firmly this time. Hick ought to have squirmed. It looked an awful lot like the situation on the campaign train in Arizona, when one reporter out of the whole press corps had been invited to a barbecue for very personal reasons. A month ago, Hick had refused to stand for it. Now she was on the other side of the same predicament.

"You aren't going to be able to do that sort of thing after tomorrow," Hick warned as they drove off, leaving the woman dripping in the parking lot. "That girl is furious, and I can't say I blame her."

Eleanor dodged the rebuke—or tried to. Not a single vote had been cast yet. Nothing guaranteed that her husband would win the White House.

Hick had been from one end of the country to the other, mingling with the people as they listened to FDR's promise of a New Deal. Her every political instinct shouted to her that Franklin Delano Roosevelt stood on the verge of winning the presidency. "Want to bet?" she challenged.

Eleanor didn't. But there it was again, that discordant note of hope that slipped free anytime she mentioned the faint possibility that Franklin might lose. This time, Hick learned its source. Just as she had on the train the week before, Eleanor opened up. Once more the two of them sat side by side as the miles rolled by in the dark, and the soft tendrils of their conversation twined into the space between them.

Two of Eleanor's keenest worries bubbled up to the surface as she drove over the shining blacktop roads that night. Millions of hungry, jobless, frightened people were going to put their faith in FDR at the ballot box the next day. How could her husband possibly do enough to halt the downward spiral of the Great Depression if he won? People would starve and freeze during the coming winter if he couldn't organize help for them quickly enough. The magnitude of that responsibility daunted her.

And then there were her children. For a while they'd be the darlings of the media, and no doubt they'd lap up all the attention. They were accustomed to being spoiled—Franklin's mother doted on them so lavishly it drove Eleanor to distraction. But the same reporters and photographers who simpered over them now would turn into vultures the moment Anna, James, Elliott, Franklin Jr., or John made a mistake. "I know what they'll be up against," Eleanor said. "I've seen it happen."

Hick didn't have to ask. Eleanor's six cousins had grown up in the public eye during Theodore Roosevelt's eight years in the White House, delighting and scandalizing the country by turns with their antics. The eldest, Alice, was Eleanor's age and still hadn't tired of stirring up controversy—most recently by campaigning *against* FDR. "I can either run the country, or I can attend to Alice, but I cannot possibly do both," Theodore Roosevelt had famously declared of the ungovernable debutante.

Did the reporter in Hick still marvel at the change? Hardly more than a week ago, Eleanor had been as vague and guarded as she had been since 1928. Now she confided freely in Hick, trusting her implicitly not to quote anything too personal. Eleanor's faith was not misplaced. Already, the trust itself had become more precious to Hick than any newsworthy Roosevelt secrets she might learn.

⁓

Election night 1932 brought Hick to the Roosevelts' New York City town house on East Sixty-Fifth Street. The ever-hospitable Roosevelts had invited relatives and friends and even newspaper people for a buffet supper. In a few hours, FDR and his family would head to the Hotel Biltmore to watch the returns with the campaign staff. Hick would be there, too, as a representative of the Associated Press.

As she entered, Eleanor gave her a kiss, saying softly, "It's good to have you around tonight, Hick."

The sight of Eleanor Roosevelt in an evening gown was a revelation. How could this woman so indifferent to clothing be so transformed by it? Eleanor looked to Hick as if she could have been crowned and placed upon a throne right then and there.

⁓

Everything played out as Hick expected that night. In the ballroom of the Biltmore, the results for Roosevelt kept flashing up. Again and again, Roosevelt prevailed. The only moments of suspense came when Hoover captured most of New England. After that, a great tide of Roosevelt votes from every state west of Pennsylvania rolled across the continent. The congratulations and backslapping started before midnight. The American people had not so much elected as demanded a new president in FDR.

Now and then Hick managed a glance into the suite where FDR sat surrounded by his family and closest friends. Eleanor greeted each well-wisher with the same flawless graciousness Hick had experienced in her earliest encounters with the next first lady. Always a smile, always a kind word. But in the brief lulls when there was no one to speak to, the smile dissolved into a sober expression. Hick thought she detected a hint of sadness.

Hick also watched as Eleanor sat for her first press conference. Klieg lights glared down on her like magnifying glasses in the sun as reporters, photographers, and newsreel cameramen clamored about. Eleanor sat up straight, her head high, as if she could somehow hold herself away from it all. Hick had already learned what that rigid posture meant. When she looked serene and still as an ancient Greek statue, Eleanor Roosevelt was unhappy.

The reporters shouted a barrage of questions. Again, Hick watched Eleanor's gracious smile appear. Hick could not see the strain, but she knew it was there. For a brief instant their eyes met. Eleanor gave the slightest shake of her head. "I was reminded of a fox, surrounded by a pack of baying hounds—of which, of course, I was one," Hick remembered.

PART THREE
HICK & ELEANOR

CHAPTER 36

watched Eleanor leave the Roosevelt town house, just as she did every Wednesday morning. Her current events class at Todhunter began promptly at nine. As usual, Hick did her best to keep up with Eleanor's long, swinging stride. Eleanor's five-year-old granddaughter, Sisty, trotted along in her brand-new green raincoat, carrying her matching lunch box.

Eleanor proceeded into the school as though nothing the least bit extraordinary had happened the night before. But at chapel, Eleanor's friend and the principal of Todhunter, Marion Dickerman, made an announcement: "I know that some of you were heart and soul yesterday with the man who was defeated. But I think that we are all glad that a friend whom we have grown to love in the year that she has been with us is going to Washington as the first lady of the land." The room filled with applause, and one of the students presented Eleanor with a corsage and a small white box. Nestled inside lay a brooch shaped like an Egyptian scarab.

"This means good luck," Eleanor said, and promptly affixed it to her blouse.

Hick followed Eleanor to her classroom, where things went on largely as usual. After a lively discussion, one of the girls ventured to say, "We think it's grand to have the wife of the President for our teacher."

"But I'm not the wife of the President yet," Eleanor replied. "That doesn't happen until next March, and anyway, I don't want you to think of me that way." Thirty years later, Hick would also write that she'd heard Eleanor say with a hint of sadness, "But I haven't changed inside. I'm just the same as I was yesterday."

⁂

The very next day, Lorena Hickok introduced the American people to their new first lady. The Associated Press had tasked her with writing a series of three articles on Eleanor Roosevelt that ran in newspapers across the nation.

Hick had scored an enormous coup. First ladies did not grant interviews. It simply wasn't done. Bess Furman, an AP reporter from the Washington bureau who'd covered President Hoover during the election, couldn't get a thing out of Mrs. Hoover. Even when the Hoover campaign train pulled into Mrs. Hoover's parents' hometown, all she would divulge was a few facts about the place itself. Sharing even that small dribble of information felt taboo to Lou Hoover. "I was not to quote her directly," Furman remembered, "I was just to set [the facts] down as though I'd read them at a library." Hick's articles, by contrast, were crammed with direct quotes from Eleanor herself.

The American people had no idea that they were seeing Eleanor Roosevelt through the eyes of someone who had feelings for her. Hick and Eleanor's friendship, and their growing affection for each other, guaranteed that Eleanor would be presented to the reading public in a way that she *wanted* to be seen. Not only could Eleanor count on Hick to quote her words accurately, but perhaps more crucially, she could trust Hick to portray her emotions.

Hick did just that. For the first time, Hick described what Eleanor was thinking and feeling, rather than restricting herself to what Eleanor was doing. Hick put the reluctance she had sensed in Eleanor for weeks at center stage. Her first article in the series opened with a breathtaking statement from Eleanor: "If I wanted to be selfish, I could wish that he had not been elected." Of course she was married to the man who had just won the presidency, "but there isn't going to be any 'first lady of the land,'" Eleanor insisted. "There is just going to be plain, ordinary Mrs. Roosevelt. And that's all."

It could have been offensive. To some Americans, it would be. A staggering majority of the country was celebrating Franklin D. Roosevelt's election to the nation's highest office, and here was his wife, practically mourning it. But in Hick's hands, Eleanor Roosevelt's denunciation struck gently. Hick carefully guided her readers to picture the smile on Eleanor's face, the conviction in her eyes, and the softness of her voice as she declared, "I never wanted to be a president's wife, and I don't want it now."

She was glad the election had turned out the way it had, Eleanor hastened to explain, and not only for her husband's sake. As a Democrat herself, she believed in the promises FDR had made to change the country for the better. She wanted a Democrat in office for the good of the American people. "And now—I shall have to work out my own salvation. I am afraid it may be a little difficult. I know what Washington is like. I've lived there. I shall very likely be criticized. But I can't help it."

As most of the country saw it, the role of first lady was purely social: a hostess presiding over luncheons and teas and dinners. Eleanor couldn't bear the thought of restricting herself to such a limited sphere. Work sustained her. And when she could use her vast reserves of energy for the betterment of others, as she had with the Red Cross and Navy Relief Society during the Great War, she gloried in it. "I loved it," she said of her war work. "I simply ate it up."

Eleanor Roosevelt was not about to stop working. She wanted to keep making money of her own, so she could keep giving it away. "I have a lot of fun doing things with money," she said. Whether it was a $5 bill handed to a hungry man on the street or hundreds of dollars to a worthy organization didn't seem to matter. Eleanor positively delighted in using her earnings to help people.

Giving up her job at Todhunter pained her more than anything. "I hate to do it. I wonder if you have any idea how I hate to do it. I've liked it more than anything else I've ever done. But it's got to go." The demands of her position in Washington wouldn't allow her to continue commuting to New York City three days a week.

〜〜

The next installment read very much like Hick's recounting of the *Vestris* shipwreck. Eleanor told her own story without interruption, glossing over the emotional hardships of her childhood in favor of the bare facts: orphaned at eight, raised by her grandmother, sent to school in England at fifteen. She'd married, borne six children and buried one in ten years, and carried out the duties of a politician's wife during her husband's terms as state senator, assistant secretary of the navy, and governor of New York.

〜〜

The final article in the trio centered on what would soon become Eleanor's trademark characteristic: her energy. "She is, to use the expression of one of her friends, 'a whirlwind,'" Hick wrote. "She gets along perfectly on five or six hours' sleep, and apparently doesn't know the meaning of the word 'fatigue.'" The number of engagements she could cram into a single day boggled the mind. Hick also highlighted Eleanor's spartan practicality. The last thing Mrs. Roosevelt wanted was any sort of fuss or extravagance. If she could do something for herself instead of troubling someone else to do it, she would, whether that meant hailing a cab or shooing away police escorts. What mattered to her above all was people, and what she could do for *them*.

CHAPTER 37

HICK'S PORTRAIT OF ELEANOR WAS OF A WOMAN EXTRAORDI-
nary in her ordinariness—unconventional in the most matter-of-fact ways.
But because she'd soon be mistress of the White House, all the humdrum
things Eleanor did drew more attention instead of less. If she walked
down the street rather than taking a cab, or sat among the public on the
train instead of reserving a private compartment, some reporter wanted
to make a story of it.

The constant scrutiny drove Eleanor to a rare show of irritation when
a young reporter trailed her all the way from Albany to New York City
and accosted her in Grand Central Terminal, demanding to know where
she was headed. As it happened, Eleanor was on her way to Hick's apartment for dinner. She wasn't about to let that fact slip to one of Hick's
competitors. Eleanor stoutly refused to be followed, or to divulge the
name of her dinner companion.

The young woman wheedled. Couldn't she follow and wait outside
until the dinner was over? Didn't Mrs. Roosevelt understand she had a
job to do?

"If you insist," Eleanor threatened, "I shall spend the rest of the
evening right here in the station. But I am *not* going to be followed—by
you or by anybody else." She wasn't bluffing, either. Eleanor was perfectly capable of sitting down with her students' papers until the reporter slunk away. As kind as she was, when something really mattered
to her, Eleanor Roosevelt did not give a fraction of an inch. Sensing
she'd been beaten, the reporter retreated—for the moment, anyway.
The next morning she'd probably station herself right outside Eleanor's

office, waiting with all the other newspaper people for Mrs. Roosevelt to make a move.

Hick didn't have to bother with that sort of guesswork anymore. Eleanor told Hick where she'd be and when, and Hick met her there, ready and waiting to report it.

Sometimes all Hick could do was stand by and wince, for Eleanor hadn't yet learned how to handle questions from the press without making a mess of things. During an interview regarding her stance on Prohibition, she made an ironic quip about young ladies drinking gin, and the public took her literally. When she expressed her personal opinion that a lavish inaugural ball would be in poor taste with so many Americans suffering, reporters took it to mean there would be no ball at all. Major or minor uproars promptly followed, provoking yet more unwanted attention in the newspapers. A hefty chunk of the population soon began to wonder if this "plain, ordinary Mrs. Roosevelt" business was in fact a sly ploy to get her name in as many headlines as possible.

Even some of Eleanor's relatives fussed about seeing her name and face splashed all over the papers. Hick recalled one incident most vividly, at a lunch in the Roosevelt house.

Hick herself was in the enviable position of being paid to spend every minute of the day with the woman she was falling in love with. That position was not without its difficulties, however, especially with the line between professional and social occasions growing blurrier by the day. This particular afternoon, Hick was seated next to a Mrs. Collier, who happened to be Franklin's aunt Kassie. Mrs. Collier was "very much perturbed" by the attention Eleanor was getting in the press, and she did not hesitate to make her opinions on the matter known.

"And there I sat," Hick recalled, "chief perpetrator of the crime!"

Hick tried to ever so gently shift Aunt Kassie's perspective, suggesting that a woman about to occupy the White House could hardly avoid publicity.

"Nonsense!" Aunt Kassie protested with the vehemence of someone who does not know she is dead wrong. "I have never talked to a newspaper reporter in my life!"

If Hick could have drowned herself in her soup, she would have. That would have been preferable to sitting there, wondering if anyone at the table would accidentally blab the truth.

CHAPTER 38

HICK HAD MUCH MORE THAN HER OCCUPATION TO HIDE FROM people like Aunt Kassie. Behind the scenes, Hick and Eleanor's relationship was fast blossoming into a romance.

The exact trajectory of their emotions is impossible to trace, for virtually no tangible remnants of Hick and Eleanor's earliest months together have come to light. Just two letters from 1932 are known to exist, and they are almost strictly business. Only the signatures hint at more—Eleanor concluded her note with an abbreviated version of "affectionately," and Hick's is signed "Hicky."

But sometime between November of 1932 and March of 1933, the tone of their correspondence made a monumental shift.

Where their earliest surviving letters are addressed to "Mrs. Roosevelt" and "Miss Hickok," by the early spring of 1933 Eleanor opened hers with "Hick my dearest" and "Hick darling." (Hick's side of the correspondence is missing until November of 1933, and by then she'd taken to addressing Eleanor as "My Dear.")

Each time they parted, they punctuated their goodbye with their own tender "little saying" if no one else was in earshot. "Je t'aime et je t'adore," Eleanor told Hick—French for "I love you and I adore you." As a symbol of her commitment, Hick gave Eleanor a sapphire-and-diamond ring. Hick herself had received it from Ernestine Schumann-Heink, the great Bohemian contralto, whom she had befriended during her years in Milwaukee. That history made the ring all the more meaningful, especially to Eleanor, who only cared for jewelry if it carried sentimental significance. Eleanor wore Hick's ring on her smallest finger (a location many female couples of the time used as a secret code to conceal their equivalent of a wedding ring in plain sight) for the rest of her life.

~~~

From the outside, this bright proliferation of intimacies might seem as abrupt as a lightning bolt, especially on Eleanor's part. After all, Eleanor Roosevelt appeared to be a happily married mother and grandmother. She had nursed her husband day and night through his bout with polio, and supported FDR when he stubbornly pursued his political career in defiance of his mother's wishes that he retire to Hyde Park as an invalid. Eleanor and Franklin were about to celebrate their twenty-eighth wedding anniversary.

But Eleanor's private reality did not match the couple's public face. Few beyond the family circle knew that romance had permanently vanished from the Roosevelts' marriage well before polio had interfered with the trajectory of their lives. Just as crucially, Eleanor Roosevelt was not only familiar with, but also accepting of, romantic love and lifelong commitment between women.

Mademoiselle Souvestre, Eleanor's beloved and idolized teacher, had founded Allenswood Academy with her long-term partner, who doubled as the boarding school's Italian instructor. Eleanor also kept an apartment of her own in New York City's Greenwich Village, a progressive neighborhood known for a thriving queer community that included many members of Eleanor's circle of reformer friends. Eleanor's landlord, Esther Lape, whom she'd befriended in the 1920s through her work with the League of Women Voters, shared her brownstone and her life with suffragist Elizabeth Read. And of course, two of Eleanor's closest companions, Nancy Cook and Marion Dickerman, had been in a committed relationship for over a decade. Molly Dewson and Polly Porter, activists who lived just down the hall from Nan and Marion, were a couple as well.

Hick and Eleanor's romance resembled these couples' partnerships in all sorts of ways. Hick and Eleanor loved each other, and said so frequently. That love would evolve through the decades, enduring through death itself. Their letters state outright that they also shared kisses, caresses, and embraces. How else they might have expressed their affection in person, behind closed doors, is known only to them.

All that's certain is this: Hick and Eleanor not only loved each other, but were *in* love with each other. Intimacy of the heart and mind formed the abiding bedrock of their romance. Above all, they were friends—first, foremost, and forever.

Hick and Eleanor knew that the intensity of their affection and devotion would not be understood by outsiders. It had to be concealed from public view.

That was easy enough as long as Hick remained assigned to cover Eleanor's daily doings. As Hick rather mildly put it, "We continued to see a great deal of each other." When Eleanor chose the fabric for her inauguration gown and went to fittings, Hick was there. When she attended the theater, Hick sat beside her. No one batted an eye at a reporter's constant presence in Eleanor's home, office, school, train compartment, or car. The fact that they had also become what Eleanor publicly called "warm friends" made Hick's company all the more natural.

But Hick wasn't at Eleanor's side solely at the behest of the Associated Press anymore. By now, Eleanor was relying on Hick to help her find her way through the tangle of emotions that stood between her and the White House.

When she'd lived in Washington during Franklin's term as assistant secretary of the navy, the thought of calling the White House home had seemed almost like a fairy tale to Eleanor. "Now I was about to go there to live, and it felt anything but marvelous."

The nation's expectations of a president's wife ran contrary to the identity she'd built for herself over the last fourteen years. Americans were accustomed to seeing a grande dame as mistress of the White House, someone as luminous and refined as Eleanor's impossibly beautiful mother. The fact that Eleanor's uncle Ted had been president made matters even worse. Theodore Roosevelt's elegant wife had elevated the first lady's role to that of the nation's hostess—the absolute last thing Eleanor wanted to be. Comparisons to her aunt Edith were inevitable, and Eleanor shrank from the thought of what people would say when they saw all the ways in which she didn't measure up. The only thing she could half-heartedly look forward to was the possibility of catching up on her reading.

≈≈

The more Eleanor confided, the more Hick began to wonder if any of Eleanor's other friends knew of her qualms. So many of them had helped with Franklin's campaign and naturally were downright gleeful over his victory, Hick realized, that Eleanor could hardly expect them to listen to her misgivings the way Hick did. "I'll just have to go on being myself, as much as I can," Eleanor told Hick. "I'm just not the sort of person who would be any good at that job."

CHAPTER 39

ANTICIPATION CRACKLED THROUGH THE AIR THE MORNING Eleanor went down to Washington for the traditional meeting with the outgoing first lady. Hick felt it, too. Before Eleanor even set out for her appointment, a kerfuffle arose over transportation. Mrs. Hoover had offered to send a limousine, which Eleanor kindly declined. But State Department officials got wind of that and showed up at Eleanor's hotel to chauffeur her in one of their cars. Again Eleanor refused. She was going to walk, and that was all there was to it.

"You can't do that," the chief of protocol protested. "People will recognize you! You'll be mobbed!"

"Oh yes I can," Eleanor retorted. "Miss Hickok is walking over with me." Nobody'd told the State Department man that Hick was a reporter, but still she felt the chief radiating disapproval as he regarded her.

Transportation might have seemed a trifle to everyone else, but it was the principle that mattered to Eleanor. She wasn't first lady yet, and already everyone expected her to capitulate. Eleanor Roosevelt had no intention of surrendering before she even began. And as the chief of protocol learned that morning, when she put her foot down, not even an agency of the United States government could dissuade her.

～

Hick struggled more than usual to keep up as Eleanor's determination propelled her through the streets of Washington. Just as she'd predicted, Eleanor made it to the White House without incident. Hick watched Eleanor mount the steps with the magnificently perpendicular carriage that signaled her secret dread, then waited by the gate while Eleanor toured the private second-floor rooms that would be her home within a matter of weeks.

An hour later, photographers snapped a picture as she emerged. Eleanor hated being photographed, and Hick didn't blame her. The images the press captured maddened Hick. Camera lenses always drew attention to the least important facet of Eleanor—the Roosevelt mouth with its chin jutting inward and its teeth jutting outward. So much of what entranced Hick—Eleanor's generosity of spirit, her warmth, the grace of her movements—remained invisible in photographs.

Eleanor herself looked the truth straight in the eye. "My dear," she'd said when Hick complained, "if you haven't any chin and your front teeth stick out, it's going to show on a camera plate."

The photo captured on this day, however, would become Hick's all-time favorite image. Caught in a moment of relief and gratification—perhaps even the instant her eyes met Hick's—Eleanor beams out at the camera, looking very much as if she is on the verge of laughing. Her energy and movement are there, too, captured by the blur of her hands slipping into her gloves. Later, Eleanor would inscribe the photo for Hick: "We were only separated by a few yards dear Hick & I wonder which of us felt most oddly."

⁓

The story Hick filed with the AP that day downplayed the tussle between Eleanor and the State Department. It also revealed none of Eleanor's trepidations about moving into the White House. Hick's version painted a picture of an unfussy, self-assured woman breezing confidently toward her future. That was certainly the woman Eleanor wanted to be, and was striving to be. With practice, Eleanor would indeed become that woman in time. At that moment, however, Hick's portrait wasn't exactly accurate, much less objective.

If the Eleanor Roosevelt of Hick's articles seemed a little too good to be true, it's because she was. Hick was presenting Eleanor's ideal self to the world, rather than showing Eleanor for who she really was. Whether it was a deliberate sleight of hand is anyone's guess. Hick was in love with Eleanor, after all. Regardless of whether she realized it, her affection colored her perceptions. And thanks to Hick's prominence with the Associated Press, she was in a position to directly affect millions of Americans' view of their next first lady. More and more, the Eleanor that Hick adored and the Mrs. Roosevelt the American people read about in their morning papers were merging into a single personality.

The closer she and Eleanor grew, the murkier the ethics of Hick's job became. Hick had unprecedented access not only to Eleanor's day-to-day doings, but also to the Roosevelt family's private affairs, and Eleanor's own closely guarded thoughts and feelings. The Associated Press trusted Hick professionally, and Eleanor Roosevelt trusted her personally. How could Hick possibly write the unbiased truth *and* respect Eleanor's privacy? In short, she couldn't.

"Is Mrs. Roosevelt really the natural, unaffected person your stories make her out to be?" the chief of the AP's Washington bureau asked when Hick turned in another of her Eleanor Roosevelt stories.

"I think so," Hick said. "If I'm wrong, Bess Furman will find out."

❧

If Hick's conscience troubled her over any of these thorny questions, she must have figured that the assignment wasn't going to last long enough for it to matter. The moment Eleanor Roosevelt moved into 1600 Pennsylvania Avenue, Hick would land right back at Associated Press headquarters in New York City with a brand-new beat. Washington, DC, had its own AP bureau with its own staffers, and despite her feelings for Eleanor, Hick was not about to tread on their turf. After Inauguration Day, the Eleanor Roosevelt beat would belong to Bess Furman.

"Well, it won't be long before she'll be yours to worry about, not mine," Hick wrote to Bess early in 1933. "In some ways I envy you—I shall miss her terribly—but in other ways I don't envy you a bit." For all that she was smitten with Eleanor, newspaper work, the kind Hick called "real, honest-to-gawd stories," still tugged at her. Trotting along beside Eleanor lacked the thrill, the pulse, of rooting up leads and pouncing on breaking news. The reporter in her longed for the clatter and bustle of the newsroom again instead of being leashed to an assignment as tame as this one. When it came to the news, Hick was a lion, not a house cat. "Gosh, won't I love being back on a regular he-man assignment again!" she confided to Bess.

Hick made up her mind to turn Eleanor over to Bess with all the grace she could muster. Success for one woman journalist meant success for all of them, as far as she was concerned. Bess shared the sentiment. Although she and Hick had never met, every time Bess read an article of Hick's that she especially liked, she sent Hick a note to say so.

Hick's introduction, complete with a luncheon at the Roosevelts' Sixty-Fifth Street town house, made a lasting impression on Bess. "Here was an outstanding woman reporter, who had carried a sure-fire subject through years as a governor's wife and on through an historic political campaign," Bess wrote in her memoir. "She was handing the subject over with a gesture more than generous to another woman reporter who just happened to be 'geographically right.'"

Bess's gratitude didn't end there. At lunch that day, Mrs. Roosevelt asked Bess a question she'd never imagined hearing from a first lady's lips: "Would it be feasible . . . as wife of the President, to carry forward regular press conferences?"

It was as if Eleanor Roosevelt had just granted Bess Furman the keys to the White House. "Instantly I saw vast news possibilities opening before me—what you could do with a President's wife if she didn't have the Secret Service tagging along to fend you off—what you could do if you could ask questions and get answers." During the Hoover administration, the diminutive Bess had resorted to dressing up as a Girl Scout and infiltrating the troop's Christmas caroling event at the White House in order to get a glimpse of Mrs. Hoover in her home. Now here was Eleanor Roosevelt, offering to hold the door wide open for Bess and her colleagues once a week. More astonishing yet, Eleanor's plan was to admit only female reporters to her press conferences. "No newspaper woman could have asked for better luck," Bess marveled.

Luck had very little to do with it. It was Hick who'd conspired with Eleanor for the good of her sisters in journalism. Thanks to her, Eleanor had learned firsthand what women journalists were up against. Getting into the newspaper business was hard enough. Now, in the midst of the Great Depression, women in all kinds of professions were losing their jobs at terrifying rates. Men, so the logic of the 1930s went, had families to support; it wasn't seen as fair to fire a breadwinner, so working "girls" took the brunt of cutbacks. Never mind that women had bills to pay, too.

"Unless the women reporters could find something new to write about," Eleanor later explained, "the chances were that they would hold their jobs a very short time. Miss Hickok pointed out many of these things to me, because she felt a sense of responsibility for the other women writers." Hick had rigged up a scheme to ensure that any newspaper that wanted guaranteed access to the first lady *had* to have women reporters on staff, whether that meant keeping their existing female staffers or hiring new ones.

Together, Hick and Eleanor had scored their first victory, and an infinitely satisfying one at that. Hick had finagled job security for her colleagues; Eleanor got her first taste of how to lever her position as a force for positive change, and in exactly the direction she'd set her sights on.

"There are possibly a great many things which are not purely political in which I may be interested," Eleanor said two weeks before the inauguration. "I hope I shall be able to do a great deal for women." FDR hadn't even taken the oath of office yet, and already Eleanor was off to a running start.

CHAPTER 40

A FRENZY OF LAST-MINUTE PREPARATIONS FILLED THE FINAL TWO weeks before the inauguration. Eleanor also had her hands full behind the scenes, orchestrating the relocation of her entire household, from FDR's wheelchair to their horses and dogs, to Washington. Meanwhile, the economy was rapidly turning to quicksand. Banks in four states locked their vaults in a panic, then six. By the time FDR raised his right hand to take the oath of office on March 4, men and women in thirty-four states would be unable to access their bank accounts.

A snarl of warring feelings characterized those days for Hick. Half of her wanted to soak up every last second she could get with Eleanor. The other half salivated at the thought of returning to a newsroom. Covering a subject she had no emotional investment in would be one helluva relief.

The Associated Press had no idea it was engaged with Hick in a tug-of-war over Eleanor Roosevelt. To Hick's consternation, her editors expected her to keep them informed about every breath Eleanor took. Hick wanted to simply *be* with Eleanor, without the AP nipping at her heels for a story. To do that, she had to all but come right out and say it.

"No one except members of the family knows I am going with her," she wrote to the AP just before accompanying Eleanor on a weekend visit to her youngest sons' boarding school in Massachusetts. "I believe the understanding is that I don't have to put out anything unless a really good story breaks. About the only really good stories I can think of are: an automobile accident, attempted kidnaping of her, or something of that sort." In other words, Hick was telling her bosses, *Back off*. If there was news, real news, she'd get it.

Possibly Hick got the leeway she demanded because of the final Eleanor Roosevelt story she'd promised to deliver. Hick was going out of this assignment in a blaze of journalistic glory—an Inauguration Day interview with the first lady of the United States, *inside* the White House. Nothing like it had ever been done before.

Hick called it "the high spot of my newspaper career." This was bigger than the sinking of the *Vestris,* bigger than Geraldine Farrar, bigger than any of the meager scraps of news she'd managed to scratch out of the Lindbergh kidnapping.

Hick's scoop was big enough to incense the women of the Washington press corps. "Of all things, an exclusive to an outsider!" Hick's campaign train colleague, W. B. Ragsdale, remembered the local reporters lamenting. Something about it smelled ever so slightly off.

Years later, Hick would hotly denounce any insinuation that she'd gotten the interview through favoritism. "As though I was a nice, tame little gal who was somebody's pet," she fumed. She herself had requested and received FDR's personal approval for the interview, as she was quick to point out. "And I'd never have got it, had not he and Louis [Howe] and Mrs. R. all trusted me. I know that no other woman reporter could have got that story."

Hick was right . . . and wrong. Hick couldn't admit, even to herself, that her relationship with Eleanor had played any role whatsoever in securing the precedent-shattering interview. Of course she had established journalistic trust with FDR and his right-hand man. But because she had done it primarily through her stories about Eleanor, the tangled roots of that trust were bound up just as firmly in Eleanor's love as they were in FDR's genuine respect for her as a journalist.

The Washington press corps also didn't know that Hick had agreed to let Louis Howe okay her story before she turned it in to the Associated Press. An interview like that wouldn't exactly be objective. But even Hick hadn't realized yet that where Eleanor Roosevelt was concerned, her objectivity had already taken a precipitous tumble.

Eleanor spent what she called her "last night out of captivity" having dinner at Hick's New York City apartment. The following day she would board a train to Washington. The train had not been Eleanor's idea. She'd wanted to drive down herself, with Hick at her side, a plan that would squeeze every last second of privacy and freedom from the dwindling hours that remained theirs alone. FDR rarely complained about his wife's independence, but for once he did. The president-elect wanted his entire family to travel together for this momentous occasion. Eleanor gave in. But she also made sure there was a place for Hick on that train. Knowing how Hick felt about dogs, Eleanor asked her to look after Meggie, the Roosevelts' Scottish terrier, during the trip.

Hick did just as Eleanor asked, riding unobtrusively in another part of the train while FDR's family congregated in their private car. This was her first real taste of how it felt to be superseded by Eleanor's duty as first lady, to be reluctantly and lovingly set aside. For four more years, this was what she had to look forward to.

But that night, as Hick relinquished Meggie to her mistress, Eleanor asked Hick to meet her the next morning. Eleanor had barely more than twenty-four hours remaining before she entered the cage of the White House, and she wanted Hick to share one of those hours with her. Of course Hick agreed.

CHAPTER 41

HICK'S CAB PULLED UP AT THE SIDE ENTRANCE OF THE MAY-
flower Hotel promptly at eight o'clock on March 3, 1933. "There's something I'd like to show you," Eleanor had said the previous evening. "It's
something that used to mean a very great deal to me when we were in
Washington before."

The car had hardly come to a stop before Eleanor slid out between the
Secret Service men and into the backseat beside Hick, asking the driver
to take them to Rock Creek Cemetery. Silence enfolded the five-mile trip.
Hick sensed that Eleanor's mind was somewhere else—enveloped either
by her past or her future.

Once the cab passed under the black metal gates of the cemetery,
Eleanor guided the driver through the web of curving, intersecting path-
ways with practiced ease to a site partially concealed by evergreens.
Green-gold glints of metal peeked from the center.

Eleanor stepped past the greenery and settled onto one of a cluster
of benches arranged before a bronze statue. The deep folds of the seated
figure's robes left little more than the face visible. One hand rested at the
curve of the chin in a gesture suggesting contemplation or comfort. Its
hood shadowed a perfectly smooth face set in an expression of repose,
eyelids lowered. Known simply as the Adams Memorial, the sculpture
had been commissioned by a grieving husband after his wife had taken
her own life. The deliberately ambiguous design gave the androgynous
figure a chameleon-like ability to reflect a range of emotions, depending
on the observer's circumstances.

For a long time, Eleanor sat still and quiet. When she began to speak,

Hick understood from the hush in her voice that this was a sacred place to Eleanor.

Perhaps by now Hick already knew the story of Eleanor's most private wound. Or perhaps this was the moment when Eleanor revealed the secret of FDR's infidelity. Back in 1916, Franklin had carried on an affair with Eleanor's social secretary, Lucy Mercer. Eleanor's worst suspicions were finally confirmed in 1918, when she stumbled across a packet of love letters Miss Mercer had sent to Franklin. The breach of trust had shattered Eleanor's ideals so completely that she offered her husband a divorce.

Divorce in the 1910s had crushing consequences for a man with his eye on the highest office in the land. A scandal of that magnitude would have quashed FDR's chances for any sort of political career. Not only that, but if he sullied the family name by leaving Eleanor for Lucy, his mother promised she'd withhold every cent of his inheritance. Franklin surrendered to his wife and his mother, vowing never to see Lucy Mercer again—a pledge he ultimately would not keep.

Ever after, the Roosevelts' youngest son observed, Eleanor and Franklin's marriage resembled an "armed truce." An underlying affection— "an understanding, a closeness, a bond," one friend said—would always remain between them, but whatever passion or romance Eleanor felt toward her husband was forever snuffed out in 1918.

In the midst of her emotional crisis, Eleanor had found an ocean of solace in the statue she and Hick now regarded. When the tides of anger, betrayal, and brokenheartedness threatened to sweep her away, she confided to Hick, "I'd come out here, alone, and sit and look at that woman. And I'd always come away somehow feeling better. And stronger. I've been here many, many times." Anyone who had ever suffered could see their own pain mirrored in the figure's every contour. The simple act of looking at it conjured an unspoken empathy.

Hick felt it, too. "All the sorrow humanity had ever had to endure was expressed in that face," she wrote of her first encounter with the statue. "I could almost feel the hot, stinging unshed tears behind the lowered eyelids. Yet in that expression there was something almost triumphant. There was a woman who had experienced every kind of suffering known to mankind and come out of it serene—and compassionate."

Eleanor needed that serenity and strength. Franklin's affair had upended her carefully cultivated identity as a wife and mother, snatching the rug out from under her feet. It had taken Eleanor years to rebuild herself, to forge a new place for herself in the world.

Work had saved her. Work, and the friendships she found among the ranks of the Red Cross and Navy Relief Society volunteers during the war, and then the League of Women Voters, the Women's Trade Union League, and the Women's Division of the New York State Democratic Committee. Striving to contribute to the greater good gave Eleanor a new sense of self—a self whose worth was entirely independent of her husband or children.

Publicly, she would always credit the Great War as "my emancipation and my education." It was half true. She had indeed thrown herself into war work, but it was Franklin's betrayal that had prompted Eleanor to look for fulfillment outside her home and family.

This was the true reason Eleanor so dreaded becoming first lady. The prospect of relinquishing that hard-won identity to become a dutiful, unobtrusive wife and hostess all over again shook Eleanor Roosevelt to her core, and Lorena Hickok was quite possibly the only person on earth who knew it.

CHAPTER 42

THE TURMOIL OF ELEANOR'S EMOTIONS MATCHED THE TURMOIL in the public mind the night before the inauguration. In a matter of days the country had toppled into what Hick remembered as "the lowest ebb in the Great Depression." People were not shouting or marching through the streets of Washington, and yet Hick forever recalled that "the clamor of a desperate, frightened public rose louder and louder." Their very fear seemed to have a sound, even if their voices were not raised in protest.

All of that agitation swirled through Hick's mind as she sat in Eleanor's hotel room, listening to her read the words of the speech FDR intended to give the next day. The dangerous power of the people's anxiety, the president-elect's immeasurable responsibility, and the secret freight of Eleanor's emotions overwhelmed any possibility that she and Eleanor might enjoy these last precious moments together.

"Let me assert my firm belief that the only thing we have to fear is fear itself," Eleanor read aloud. They would become the most famous words FDR ever spoke, and Lorena Hickok, star reporter of the Associated Press, did not think for an instant of phoning her editors to report them.

~✺~

Hick's nerves thrummed as she approached the great columned portico of the mansion that Abraham Lincoln and Theodore Roosevelt had once called home. Eleanor had teased her about worrying, but Hick did not possess the power to keep herself calm. It wasn't just the thought of entering the White House for the first time. Hick couldn't suppress the feeling that the streets were filled with tinder, that the tiniest of sparks could set the people's fear ablaze. Eleanor and her husband were out in those streets, heading toward the Capitol in open touring cars.

Plain old White House jitters aside, it was hard not to feel uneasy, especially at such a distance from the historic proceedings. Hick's assignment that day was not to cover the ceremony, but to wait for Eleanor's return to her new home and capture her very first impressions of the inauguration experience.

The head usher, Ike Hoover, welcomed Hick and led her to the chamber Eleanor intended to turn into her sitting room. Both its hollowness and its temperature made Hick shiver. Hulking, mismatched pieces of temporary furniture lent the space an odd air of emptiness. Faded marks on the walls showed where the former president's picture frames had recently hung. Nothing else in the room so much as hinted that anyone had ever lived there. No books or magazines to leaf through, no pictures or knickknacks to admire. Not even a radio to tune in to the inauguration ceremony. The place felt as institutional and anonymous as a hospital waiting room.

Ike Hoover soon reappeared with a tall, frosty glass of orange juice on a silver tray. A cold drink was the last thing in the world Hick wanted just then, but she didn't have the heart to refuse his kindness. All Hick could do to stave off cold and boredom was pace while the radiators let out inhospitable thumps and hisses. A plate riveted to the fireplace informed Hick that the room had once been Abraham Lincoln's. Out the south-facing windows, the Washington Monument pointed into the damp and dreary skies.

One silent minute after another crawled past until cheers and the rumble of motorcycle engines heralded the new president's arrival. Hick peered out and saw a touring car containing Eleanor, FDR, and their eldest son, Jimmy, pull up to the South Portico. Relief rocketed through Hick as she saw the smiling trio, and a lump rose in her throat. Nothing had gone wrong.

By the time Eleanor reached the sitting room, her broad public smile had faded. The day she had recoiled from since November had caught up with her at last.

"It was very, very solemn," she told Hick as she peeled off her gloves, "and a little terrifying. The crowds were so tremendous, and you felt that they would do *anything*—if only someone would tell them *what* to do."

The interview itself was almost a formality. Hick already knew better than anyone how Eleanor felt about her new role. Watching her husband recite the oath of office had changed nothing.

❧

In her article, Hick tempered Eleanor's evident misery, presenting it as earnest responsibility instead. "No woman entering the White House, if she accepts the fact that it belongs to the people and therefore must be representative of whatever the conditions the people are facing, can light-heartedly take up her residence here," Hick quoted Eleanor. Hick could see from Eleanor's expression what she wanted to say next: "Least of all *this* woman." But that, of course, couldn't be printed.

Hick bestowed upon the public a first lady with every intention of holding herself to the same circumstances that confronted the rest of the country. If everyday Americans had to pinch their pennies, the president's household would tighten its belt, too—by 25 percent. Eleanor had also resolved to set a national example by following the dietary guidelines Cornell University was developing for people struggling to buy enough groceries with their diminishing incomes. "The important thing, it seems to me, is our attitude toward whatever may happen," Eleanor said. "It must be willingness to accept and share with others whatever may come and to meet the future courageously, with a cheerful spirit." That was Eleanor Roosevelt's core message to her fellow citizens, and Hick made sure it rang out loud and clear.

CHAPTER 43

HICK LINGERED IN WASHINGTON FOR ONE MORE DAY. THE NIGHT after the inauguration, Eleanor managed to whittle out a moment between her obligations for a private farewell. *Je t'aime et je t'adore,* they no doubt recited to each other, as they always had before. Whatever else Hick and Eleanor said or did to bolster themselves for the separation is known to them alone. The only surviving mention of it is contained in four words in Eleanor's engagement book: "Said good-bye to Hick."

The leather-bound engagement book itself was a gift from Hick. She had bought blank loose-leaf pages and painstakingly laid them out herself, hand-dating each one and marking off individual lines for the first lady's appointments at every half hour from eight o'clock in the morning until eight o'clock at night. Every day when Eleanor saw the handwriting across the top and down the side of the page, she'd think of Hick.

Hick had a calendar devoted to Eleanor, too. Just a small, cardboard-backed pocket calendar from the National Life Insurance Company of Montpelier, Vermont. Beginning in March, Hick marked each date with an X or an O. Every day spent with Eleanor earned a circle. Every day without her, Hick crossed out. Monday, March 6, began a whole row of cross-outs.

After weeks of spending nearly every waking hour together, Hick and Eleanor both hungered for daily connection. Long-distance telephone calls were too pricey to indulge in with any regularity, so they relied on pen and paper to bridge the physical distance between them.

Letters, Eleanor always believed, "keep up a kind of intimacy which wipes out time and space." It was an intimacy Eleanor clearly prized, for she sent Hick a deluge of letters beginning mere hours after Hick left the White House.

"Hick my dearest, I cannot go to bed to-night without a word to you," Eleanor wrote that evening. "I felt a little as though a part of me was leaving to-night. You have grown so much to be a part of my life that it is empty without you even though I'm busy every minute."

The sight of Eleanor's handwriting was a balm all its own. Handwritten letters from Eleanor were a special luxury, one she reserved for those she loved most. Her daily mail was so voluminous that the vast majority of her correspondence had to be dictated to and typed by Tommy, otherwise she couldn't possibly keep up. When Hick opened an envelope and saw Eleanor's distinctive scrawl beneath the gold White House emblem, she knew these were words no other ears had heard, no other eyes had read.

A curious mixture of intimacy and mundane details characterizes Eleanor's letters to Hick. After the first rush of passionate endearments, Eleanor usually proceeded to describe every minute of her day in an almost businesslike style. That was partly Hick's doing. Eleanor had agreed to write Hick a sort of diary of her daily engagements, a record Hick could use to re-create Eleanor's White House days if she ever tried her hand at writing Eleanor's biography. Mostly, though, writing "often & about little things" was essential to Eleanor, who believed that friends "must know what we are mutually feeling & thinking & going through or the ties between us will loosen." At the end of each letter came another burst of affection.

"Oh! darling, I hope on the whole you will be happier for my friendship," Eleanor concluded that first night without Hick. Their parting had not been an easy one. The pain it caused Hick stung Eleanor, too. "I felt I had brought you so much discomfort & hardship to-day & almost more heartache than you could bear & I don't want to make you unhappy."

She hoped to ease Hick's pain by sending her love over what she called "thought waves," starting that very night.

Hick's side of their 1933 correspondence is gone, possibly destroyed in the 1960s by Hick herself. Even with half of the conversation missing, their mutual affection is impossible to deny. "Hick darling, Oh! how good it was to hear your voice," Eleanor wrote after indulging in a telephone call the very next day. "Jimmy was near & I couldn't say 'je t'aime et je t'adore' as I longed to do but always remember I am saying it & that I go to sleep thinking of you & repeating our little saying."

⁓

Eleanor set to work that week, filling her sitting room walls with the dozens of photographs she cherished. Hick's face was now among them. "I can't kiss you so I kiss your picture good night & good morning!" Eleanor confessed. "Don't laugh!"

Hick wrote to Eleanor just before bed. If she had overnight guests, she waited until they'd gone to sleep. Hick hated to have her time with Eleanor interrupted, regardless of whether Eleanor was actually present. Even if they'd just spoken by phone, Hick would still sit down and write her a note as soon as they'd hung up. It didn't matter if there was nothing left to say. What mattered was making sure Eleanor always had a letter to open. All day long she had to be Mrs. Franklin Delano Roosevelt, first lady of the United States of America. When she read Hick's letters, she was simply Eleanor for a few moments.

⁓

Back in New York, Hick found herself adrift on a tumultuous sea of emotions. All her life, her feelings had come at her this way, in moods that threatened to drown her. Hick hated it. Whether the tides were made of anger, frustration, sorrow, or, in this case, loneliness, Hick loathed the way she gave in to her passions with tears and outbursts that left her exhausted and ashamed of herself.

"You have a stormier time than I do but I miss you as much, I think," Eleanor soothed after one of Hick's apparent flare-ups. "I couldn't bear to think of you crying yourself to sleep. Oh! how I wanted to put my arms around you in reality instead of in spirit." Instead, a tearful Eleanor settled for kissing Hick's photograph. "Please keep most of your heart in Washington as long as I'm here for most of mine is with you!"

It wasn't merely the physical separation. Jealousy plagued Hick from the beginning. She had to share Eleanor with Franklin, their children and grandchildren, and friends Eleanor had known for decades. Hick's reaction was all but inevitable. The seeds of her jealousy had been planted way back in her earliest years. The beaten and berated part of her simply refused to let Hick believe that she could possibly mean anything to someone as illustrious as Eleanor Roosevelt—someone who could now summon the company of any celebrity in the nation. Surely, that wounded part of Hick incessantly whispered, Eleanor had plenty of other, worthier people to love.

"Remember one thing always no one is just what you are to me," Eleanor reassured her during that first week apart. "I'd rather be writing you this minute than anyone else." Still, it was hard for Hick to fully believe.

Two days after she and Eleanor parted, Hick turned forty. "All day I've thought of you & another birthday I *will* be with you," Eleanor vowed. They'd talked on the phone yet again, but it felt faraway and formal. Eleanor, too, suffered through moments when she wondered if their love was too good to be true. "Your ring is a great comfort, I look at it & think she does love me, or I wouldn't be wearing it!"

~

Hick had to mark only eight Xs on her little calendar before she saw Eleanor again. On March 14, the first lady planned to return to New York City to attend the wedding of a former Todhunter pupil. "My dear if you meet me may I forget there are other reporters present or must I behave?" Eleanor wrote as her arrival neared. "I shall want to hug you to death."

Eleanor looked forward to more than smothering Hick in her arms. "The one thing which reconciles me to this job is the fact that I think I can give a great many people pleasure," she added, "& I begin to think there may be ways in which I can be useful. I am getting some ideas which I want to talk over with you." It had been little more than a week since her husband had taken office, and already her mind was stirring with thoughts that would reshape the role of America's first lady forever.

CHAPTER 44

THE WEEKEND AFTER ELEANOR'S VISIT TO NEW YORK, HICK returned to Washington for a dinner given by the Women's National Press Club. Although she was attending the event as Bess Furman's guest, Eleanor had insisted she spend the weekend at the White House instead of a hotel.

"I felt half choked," Hick recalled of her approach to the North Portico. "There was shyness in the sensation, and shamefaced elation. The tips of my fingers tingled."

Eleanor's visit to New York had almost been like old times. Hick had followed her about at the behest of the Associated Press, and turned in one last handful of Mrs. Roosevelt stories. This was something altogether different.

"It's just a house," she told herself. Hick could say that all she wanted; words did not chase away the immensity of the stillness, or the foundation-deep dignity that exuded through the corridors as an usher conducted her up to Eleanor's newly furnished sitting room. Every glimpse of the mansion's antique furniture, chandeliers, and paintings made her feel like "a crudely cut out comic paper doll pasted on a fine old tapestry."

The booming sound of her own name, announced as if she were a visiting dignitary, startled Hick as she stepped toward Eleanor's vast desk. Even the longed-for sight of Eleanor could not shoo away Hick's awe. Quite the contrary.

"What's the matter?" Eleanor asked. "Is there something queer about me?"

Hick couldn't answer. Here was her friend, her love. The very same Eleanor she adored stood before her. Hick knew that. And yet seeing her not only surrounded by the White House and all it symbolized, but suddenly *part* of it, Hick was overcome. Eleanor seemed somehow more than herself. Taller, statelier. Even her voice sounded far away. But Hick couldn't say so. She couldn't even fully form the thoughts just then. All she could do was shake her head.

Here she was, having exactly the kind of reaction Eleanor dreaded would overtake her friends. Hick, of all people, who knew Eleanor's fears about her new position better than anyone. Eleanor put a hand on Hick's shoulder. "Don't be that way," she said.

Hick tried. Talking on the sofa by the fireplace made things easier, until Eleanor insisted that Hick come say hello to Franklin.

Eleanor laughed at the look that came over Hick's face and offered a hand as if she were a child in need of coaxing. Hick could not feel the feet that carried her down the endless corridor to Franklin's study. Her eyes could not see the room she entered. The inside of her mind had become a screen, flashing with images of all the fleeting presidential encounters she'd had years before: Woodrow Wilson's arrival in Milwaukee. Calvin Coolidge's parade through Minneapolis. The funeral train of Warren G. Harding, barreling through the velvet Iowa night.

"Why, hello Hick!" a ringing voice interrupted. "Glad to see you!" Hick knew that voice. She'd heard the governor of New York speak hundreds, if not thousands, of times before and never once been intimidated. The trouble was, Franklin Delano Roosevelt was no longer governor of New York.

Hick felt her mouth move, but she could not hear her own thank-you. A chant boomed in her ears to the rhythm of her pulse, drowning out all other sounds and thoughts: "The President! The President! The-Pres-i-dent!"

After a mercifully quick exchange, Hick found herself back in Eleanor's study. They chatted a little more easily as Eleanor attended to a few more letters, then she and Hick rounded up the dogs for a walk.

❦

Meggie and Major dashed and scampered over the South Lawn while a misty rain enveloped Hick and Eleanor.

"You are very quiet," Eleanor said after a time.

History had overwhelmed Hick. Not only the history of the White House and all its occupants, but her own past and everything that had inexplicably led her to this place and the woman who stood beside her. "I wanted to tell her about a salmon colored schoolhouse set like a box in the center of a round, flat world," Hick later wrote, "of a green history book, of old men in blue marching along a blazing, dusty street on Memorial Day, of a child huddled close beside an old base burner coal stove on a bitter February night writing an essay for a school prize on the hundredth anniversary of the birth of Abraham Lincoln." Hick couldn't. It was all so big and yet so small, she could not put it into words.

❦

Not until breakfast the next morning did Hick truly begin to feel at ease. With little more than a few screens and some comfortable chairs, Eleanor had partitioned off a cozy sitting room at one end of the immense second-floor corridor. There, amid the rustling of newspapers and the smells of coffee and bacon, Hick gradually realized that her trepidations had fled without her feeling them go. The White House really was just a house sometimes, after all—a house whose occupants enjoyed picnics and scrambled-egg suppers just as they always had. Even though everything around them had changed, somehow the Roosevelts were still very much the Roosevelts.

CHAPTER 45

UPON HER RETURN TO ASSOCIATED PRESS HEADQUARTERS, Hick landed herself a crackerjack assignment covering the trial of Charles E. Mitchell in New York City. Mitchell, of National City Bank fame, had gotten himself into hot water over illegal stock transactions, speculation in National City Bank securities, and income tax evasion that had allegedly contributed to the stock market collapse of 1929. "He, more than any fifty men, is responsible for this stock crash," one Virginia senator had said barely two weeks after the market plummeted.

This was the kind of high-profile assignment a woman wouldn't have dared to dream of back when Hick first got into the newspaper business, full of financial complexities and dirty-money scandal. The unfolding drama of the Mitchell story spoon-fed her everything she'd missed about reporting while covering Eleanor Roosevelt.

Hick ought to have been reveling in her accomplishments. Instead, her conscience was roiling. The memory of the night before the inauguration, when she hadn't leaked even a sentence of the president's speech, would not leave her alone. In all her years in the press, she'd never had a chance at a bigger scoop, and she'd let it pass by without a thought. Guilt plagued her.

She couldn't talk to her own bosses about the front-page story that had slipped through her fingers, so Hick decided to ask Louis Howe how to handle her conflict of interest. Howe knew two subjects at least as well as Hick did: the Roosevelts and the newspaper business. Before masterminding FDR's pursuit of the presidency and subsequently taking on the role now known as White House chief of staff, he'd spent a decade as a reporter.

A frail, disheveled man, Howe had a face so shriveled and craggy that Hick had likened him to a gnome in her campaign trail articles. Cigarette ashes constantly speckled his shirtfronts in defiance of the chronic asthma that was killing him inch by inch.

Howe's terse advice offered Hick no solace. "A reporter should never get too close to the news source," he told her.

Hick couldn't fool herself any longer. The line between reporter and source had officially vanished. The AP already suspected something was amiss. Weeks earlier, Eleanor's on-air comments about young people's drinking habits had caused a backlash after a radio interview. At Eleanor's request, Hick hadn't written a story about it. The less said about the whole mess, the better, Eleanor reasoned. Hick had bluffed, telling her supervisors that she'd do her best to get the story, knowing all the while that Eleanor wasn't going to so much as whisper about it. Then Eleanor fumbled again. Thinking she was off the record, she spoke about the controversy to a *New York Post* reporter. The *Post* printed the story. "I was given Hell and my salary was cut as a disciplinary measure," Hick remembered ruefully.

Then and there, Hick's real troubles at the Associated Press had begun. It didn't seem too worrisome at first, though that salary cut had pinched. She'd banked on the belief that all her Roosevelt complications would evaporate when she returned to New York. As long as she steered clear of Washington, Hick had figured, everything would be fine. But she was dead wrong.

The Associated Press knew full well that Hick was closer to Eleanor Roosevelt than any other reporter on earth, and they expected her to *do* something with that connection. There in the newsroom sat a woman who knew exactly what the Roosevelt family was up to on any given day of the week. In fact, Hick knew a great deal more about the president's family than the AP ever suspected. Eleanor was watching two of her children's marriages fail, and filled her letters to Hick with her woes over the situation.

Hick's editors and fellow reporters wanted tips. "Inside dope," reporters called it. But Hick wasn't about to set the press loose on Eleanor's heels. "Trouble with this outfit is that they're spoiled," Hick had written to Bess Furman back when she was still on the Mrs. Roosevelt assignment. "Think they have to have a beat on every story."

More and more, it looked like Hick would have to choose: either the AP or Eleanor.

Eleanor sympathized. "I do understand your joy and pride in your job, and I have a deep respect for it," she wrote in April. But she, too, could feel how Hick's loyalty to the Associated Press intruded on their relationship. "When you haven't the feeling of responsibility to the AP I know you have a happier time with me."

But if she quit, then what? Hick wasn't at all sure that the newspaper-specific skills she'd honed over the last two decades could get her a job anywhere else. "I hate to hear you say 'I'm only a reporter,'" Eleanor gently scolded. "You are a very good one." With Eleanor's encouragement, Hick toyed with the idea of writing for a magazine like *McCall's*—maybe a story on Ike Hoover, the White House usher who had served under six presidents. "I hope that, whatever your decision, it may be the right one for you," Eleanor wrote. "I want you to be happy in your work."

While Hick wrestled with her professional dilemma, Eleanor feuded with her own emotions. Anna's and Elliott's impending divorces weighed heavily on her conscience all through April and May. Eleanor couldn't shake the conviction that those breakups were ultimately her responsibility. Their failure was her failure, and it left Eleanor feeling "disgusted with myself" and "soiled."

"My zest in life is rather gone for the time being," she wrote to Hick at the end of May. "If anyone looks at me I want to weep." She'd gotten mired in slumps like this before, but now her position made it impossible to retreat into the comfort of solitude the way she usually did. "It makes me feel like a squirrel in a cage. I want to run, and I can't, and I despise myself." Hick was the only solace she could cling to. "You are my rock," Eleanor wrote. "I need you very much as a refuge just now."

No matter what her editors wanted, Hick would not feed them the "dope" they craved about the Roosevelts—especially not now, when Eleanor was so very vulnerable. But the higher-ups at the office refused to let it drop. The AP's expectations nettled and gnawed at Hick until she couldn't stand it anymore. "I got sorer and sorer," she recalled with bitterness, "and finally quit."

Hick quit with a capital Q, abandoning not only the Associated Press, but the newspaper business as a whole. There wasn't a paper in the country that would hire her without expecting to benefit from her Roosevelt connections, and she knew it.

Quitting pained Hick like nothing else. She had built her entire life, her entire identity, around newspaper reporting. The first place Hick had ever felt at home was the newsroom; writing news stories had taken her from a self-conscious schoolgirl to a confident professional. On the surface it sounded noble and romantic—Eleanor's love and trust meant more to Hick than the occupation she'd devoted herself to for twenty years. The reality was bleaker. Lorena Hickok had just voluntarily joined the ranks of the unemployed during the worst year yet of the Great Depression.

CHAPTER 46

LUCK WAS ON HICK'S SIDE. THE VERY SAME CONNECTIONS that cost Hick her job at the Associated Press landed her another one with the federal government.

As part of FDR's plans to shore up the economy, his administration had created a slew of "alphabet soup" agencies, each geared toward mitigating a specific facet of the country's financial crisis. Over a dozen debuted in 1933, including the AAA (Agricultural Adjustment Administration), the CCC (Civilian Conservation Corps), the TVA (Tennessee Valley Authority), the PWA (Public Works Administration), and the FDIC (Federal Deposit Insurance Corporation). The New Deal concocted an agency to cope with everything from plummeting crop prices to the safety of bank deposits. One of them, the Federal Emergency Relief Administration (FERA), took on the task of providing what became known as work relief to legions of unemployed Americans.

Most folks who had lost their jobs didn't want a government handout. They wanted work. Taking money without earning it left them feeling worthless and ashamed, on top of the humiliation of being out of work in the first place. That was where FERA stepped in, creating jobs almost any able-bodied man could do with minimal training. FERA employees built roads, cleared land for parks, and dug ditches. If a fellow could swing a pickax or wield a shovel, FERA could put him to work. The paychecks boosted the men's morale, and the projects boosted their communities' infrastructure—a win for everyone involved. On paper, at least. The reality wasn't so clear. Critics grumbled that the whole thing was a money-draining sham, that the men on FERA projects were good-for-nothing shovel leaners who weren't doing a lick of actual work.

FERA's administrator, Harry Hopkins, needed someone to go out into cities, towns, and farmland across the nation and see firsthand how the work relief system was really functioning. He needed to know whether the millions of dollars he was allocating to state relief agencies for FERA-backed projects were indeed making a difference in the lives of everyday Americans. Eleanor suggested Hick for the job.

It was unlike anything Hick had done before, but she leapt at the chance. The position paid $5,000 a year plus travel expenses, and no one with half an ounce of sense would turn down an offer like that in the middle of 1933.

"What I want you to do is to go out around the country and look this thing over," Mr. Hopkins told Hick. "I don't want statistics from you. I don't want the social worker angle. I just want your own reaction, as an ordinary citizen." The more kinds of unemployed folks she talked to, the better, whether they'd started off rich or had struggled to make ends meet for generations. "Tell me what you see and hear," he instructed. "All of it. Don't ever pull your punches."

If there was one thing Hick knew how to do, it was how to talk to people and write down what they told her. She'd been interviewing everyone from princesses to paupers since she was twenty-two years old. But more importantly, Hick knew exactly how it felt to be broke, homeless, and out of work when it seemed like nobody in the world gave a damn about you. She'd learned that when she was fourteen and never forgotten it.

Still, walking away from a twenty-year career was no easy proposition. Hick was so high up in the ranks of Associated Press reporters, it was a little like jumping off the Empire State Building. Even a risk as carefully calculated as this one could go bad. "I'm looking forward to the new job," she wrote to Mr. Hopkins in early June. "As a matter of fact, it's the only thing that has come along since I began contemplating the possibility of getting out of the AP that has really interested me."

Loyal to the last, Hick tied up every loose end she could at the

Associated Press. The Mitchell trial hadn't ended, and Hick didn't want to walk out in the middle of it after working the story every day for nearly three weeks. "It's such a darn complicated affair, and I am the only one who is thoroughly familiar with it," she explained to Mr. Hopkins. "Since it is the last newspaper assignment I'll have for a time, I'd like to see it through and do as good a job on it as I can."

Mr. Hopkins agreed. She'd need a week's training, and then, come August, he'd send Hick out on her first assignment, to the coal country of Pennsylvania.

≈

Hick arrived in Washington, DC, the last week in June, ready to be "indoctrinated," as she put it, for her new job. Eleanor had once again invited Hick to stay at the White House rather than a hotel. Only this time, she and the president would be away. Hick would have the place to herself, with no formal dinners or conversations to sweat over.

Washington was a hot and swampy place in the summer, so Eleanor had left instructions for Hick to be put up in her own sitting room, which boasted a portable air conditioner. Hick had never seen one before. The rectangular steel contraption filled the whole fireplace. Water dripped into a pan underneath it, which a servant emptied just before Hick turned in for the night.

After he'd gone, Hick opened both windows. Leaving them shut in such oppressive heat made no sense at all to her. And then, with fresh air streaming in, she went to sleep.

When Hick woke the next morning, she found the room awash. Her bedroom slippers floated jauntily by on what looked to her like a good three inches of water.

It turned out that the machine was not actually an air conditioner at all, but a dehumidifier. While Hick slept with her windows wide open, it had valiantly tried to strip every drop of moisture from the entire city of

Washington, DC. And since Washington was framed on two sides by the Potomac and Anacostia Rivers, there was no shortage of moisture for it to contend with. The drip pan had overflowed hours before, submerging the woolen rug with runoff that streamed under the doors leading to the president's bedroom and the hallway.

Hick was mortified down to her toenails. Men came with mops—a whole crew of them—and hauled the sopping rug away. The thought that she'd possibly ruined Eleanor's lovely blue rug was bad enough. Worse, Eleanor's sitting room was situated directly over the State Dining Room. Hick was sure the water would seep through the floor and stain the ceiling beneath. She'd thank her lucky stars if the entire sitting room didn't come crashing down onto the massive dining table. One night at the White House and here she was, putting the whole place in peril.

Sheet after sheet of White House stationery went into the trash can as Hick struggled to find the best way to admit to Eleanor what she'd done. But Eleanor hardly minded. She found the incident more amusing than anything. The president, too, took particular delight in ribbing Hick about the whole soggy affair.

"I never knew anyone who had a more mischievous sense of humor than Franklin Roosevelt had," Hick recalled. "He was an unmerciful tease." The ceiling never did leak, and the rug dried out with only a single ripple. With no real harm done, FDR saw fit to make the most of Hick's embarrassment.

Ever after, the president referred to the dehumidifier as "Hick's rug-washing machine." That alone would have been enough to make Hick squirm. But FDR didn't stop there. For the next few days, he'd pause in the middle of a meal—usually with some dignitary or other present—to sniff thoughtfully at the air. "It seems to me that Washington is a little less humid than it was," he'd observe. "What do *you* think, Hick?"

CHAPTER 47

IN BETWEEN ONE PHASE OF HICK'S LIFE AND THE NEXT, SHE and Eleanor treated themselves to a vacation—a road trip through New England and southeast Quebec. If it worked out the way Eleanor hoped, this would be the first time the two of them enjoyed more than a few hours alone together.

Thanks to her boundless faith in humanity, Eleanor believed that the press and the public would allow her to travel unharried, like any other tourist. Hick had her doubts, which she kept to herself. The Secret Service put up enough of a fuss as it was. They'd be kidnapped, the security men insisted. Eleanor scoffed at the very idea. "Where would they hide us?" she wanted to know. Between her unusual height and Hick's substantial breadth, Eleanor considered it too absurd to even bother worrying about. Once again, Eleanor stood her ground until the men gave up. There would be no Secret Service escort—just Eleanor and Hick, for three glorious weeks.

The two set off toward the Adirondacks in Eleanor's blue convertible roadster on July 6. To Hick's surprise, the days unfolded precisely as Eleanor had hoped. No one took the slightest notice of them as they motored through upstate New York and into New England. Hick could only presume that no one recognized the first lady. Eleanor took a different view. "My dear, they're all Republicans up here," she quipped.

Moving about so freely was perfectly delicious. No Secret Service men scuttling about. No risk of Eleanor being called away. No downplaying their love to fit anyone else's expectations.

There was no schedule, either, no adherence to Eleanor's fat little engagement book, which was usually so crammed with appointments that she had to hold it shut with a rubber band. Their ultimate destination was the Gaspé Peninsula, a curved finger of Canada extending from the northernmost tip of Maine into the Gulf of St. Lawrence, and they could take all the time they pleased getting there.

On one of their first evenings, Eleanor spied a little house on the road to Lake Placid with a sign out front welcoming tourists for overnight stays. Eleanor, the child of upper-crust city dwellers, had always wanted to try a night in this kind of place. So they turned the car around and did just that. The Secret Service probably would have spontaneously combusted at the thought of Eleanor Roosevelt entering a random private home on the side of the road. That might well have been half the fun for Eleanor.

The young married couple who owned the place swallowed their shock at finding the president's wife on their doorstep and led Hick and Eleanor to a small but immaculate bedroom. There was only one problem, the woman apologized to her guests. The new hot-water system was only partially installed and could provide but a single warm bath.

"Well—you're the First Lady," Hick declared to Eleanor, "so you get the first bath."

Eleanor didn't want any special treatment—that was why she and Hick had fled the capital. Eleanor thrust her hands toward Hick in reply, fingers extended like a sorcerer casting an evil spell. In an instant, Hick was at Eleanor's mercy. "I was so ticklish that all she had to do to reduce me to a quivering mass of pulp was to point her fingers at me." After she'd tormented Hick sufficiently, Eleanor acquiesced and bathed first. But when Hick took her turn, she found plenty of hot water left. Eleanor had taken cold baths since childhood; forgoing warm water was no great sacrifice to her.

That night Eleanor read aloud to Hick from one of Eleanor's favorite poems, a book-length epic called *John Brown's Body,* and the next day they visited the infamous abolitionist's grave near Lake Placid. Then on to Lake Champlain and Mount Mansfield. Eleanor also took Hick to see some of the famous sights of the Northeast that Hick had read about as a child—the Great Stone Face on the side of one of New Hampshire's White Mountains, and the Plains of Abraham battlefield in Quebec.

In Quebec City, they made one compromise and attended an official luncheon hosted by the lieutenant governor. When the meal and the obligatory chat with the press were over, the French Canadians left them alone. Not one reporter even attempted to follow them. The courtesy of the Canadians left Hick thunderstruck. All around the Gaspé Peninsula Hick and Eleanor meandered, and only twice did anyone let on to the fact that they'd recognized Mrs. Franklin D. Roosevelt.

It happened first at a Sunday Mass they'd decided to attend. Hick noticed Eleanor's cheeks suddenly flushing red during a prayer. Hick sat puzzled, unable to decipher enough French to guess what could have embarrassed her. The priest had prayed for them by name, Eleanor explained after the service. But outside the church, Eleanor's car stole the show. Convertibles were a rare sight in that corner of the province—rarer even than presidents' wives, judging by the crowd that gathered to admire every inch of it.

Days would pass before anyone drew attention to them again, days on which Hick and Eleanor hopscotched from one village to another, reveling in their anonymity. Each little town was as beguiling as the last. The sound of French and the smell of bread baking in stone ovens filled the air in every one of them. Hick felt as if she'd been transported to Europe.

But the greatest luxury by far was Eleanor's uninterrupted company. Every day she and Eleanor ate together, watched sunrises and sunsets together, read aloud together. They slept in every kind of lodging from a log tourist cabin to a posh hotel suite. One night they had an entire inn to themselves, thanks to a thoughtful proprietor who deliberately turned away other tourists to give the first lady complete privacy. They motored up mountains, through forests, and along the shores of the Gulf of St. Lawrence with the top down until they were gritty with dust and nearly intoxicated with wind and sunshine. And they laughed to-gether, once dissolving into tears of hilarity when Eleanor fashioned a makeshift head covering for Hick out of a knotted handkerchief so that she could enter the Basilica of Sainte-Anne-de-Beaupré. It was a kind of heaven.

CHAPTER 48

HICK AND ELEANOR RELUCTANTLY CROSSED BACK INTO THE
United States a few days later at the town of Presque Isle, Maine. As Eleanor swung the roadster onto the main drag, a cavalcade of vehicles suddenly fell into line behind her. Flags gripped in children's hands fluttered
from the curbs. It was a parade, of all things, lined up and just waiting
for their arrival.

Hick and Eleanor were horrified. After their long drive down through
New Brunswick, neither of them was in any condition to greet the public. Hick was nearly blistered with sunburn and had slathered her face in
white lotion in hopes of soothing it. Eleanor usually tanned rather than
burned, but for some reason her lower lip had taken exception to this
rule and puffed up to twice its size.

Eleanor couldn't back up, and she couldn't turn the car around. The
only way out of Presque Isle was through it. Flustering Eleanor Roosevelt was no small feat, but the citizens of Presque Isle managed it that
day. She tried her best to drive with one hand and wave with the other,
but the unwanted, unexpected attention distracted her from the road as
she rolled toward a temporary traffic signal standing in the dead center
of the street.

"Damn!" Eleanor said as the car bumped into the signal. The word
might have dropped from the sky like a thunderbolt. Eleanor Roosevelt
did not, as she so delicately put it, use "unbecoming language." Before
that moment, the closest Hick had ever heard her come to swearing was
"Oh spinach!"

The collision did nothing to dampen the town's enthusiasm. Hick and Eleanor could not escape Presque Isle until the mayor had given a speech and presented Eleanor with an armload of flowers.

As Hick and Eleanor finally pulled out of town, a dozen vehicles tagged along behind. "We've got to get out of this some way," Eleanor said. The string of cars followed them all the way to Houlton, forty miles south. In desperation, they abandoned their plans to stay at the hotel there, opting to take their chances farther on. Eleanor zigzagged around corners until she shook the other drivers loose from their tail.

Soon Eleanor's blue roadster was cruising between the potato fields of Aroostook County without another soul in sight. Instead of a hotel, Hick and Eleanor ended up on a potato farm for the night—a neat white farmhouse with a sign advertising rooms for tourists.

The farmwife displayed no hint of recognition as she showed Hick and Eleanor to their rooms. Staunch Republicans, Eleanor figured. A relaxing evening of anonymity would be just the thing to unwind from the afternoon's hubbub.

The registration book ruined everything. Hick tried like the dickens to wiggle out of signing her name and Eleanor's to that book, offering to register in the morning instead. But the woman insisted. "Don't you know who the lady is?" Hick finally asked.

Hick thought the farmwife would keel over where she stood when she heard Eleanor's name. The power of speech appeared to have deserted her. Hick ducked out onto the porch without another word to let their hostess collect herself.

Hick and Eleanor took a stroll down the road, idly wondering if they'd be thrown out. FDR's agricultural policies were winning him no friends among the apple and potato farmers of Maine, after all.

But when they returned, no ruckus awaited. They risked taking a seat on the porch swing, still unsure of their welcome. In a little while, the farmer joined them, wary yet curious, Hick noticed from the cautious way he took a seat on the porch steps.

None of the scenarios Hick had imagined matched what happened next. Before Hick's eyes, Eleanor began discussing the potato crop and its prices with an ease and confidence that left Hick baffled. Hick knew darn well that every bit of Eleanor's knowledge on the topic had come from the newspaper they'd bought in New Brunswick only that morning. Yet here she was, conversing with a potato farmer as confidently as if she were married to his next-door neighbor rather than to the president of the United States.

Hick listened all the more closely and realized Eleanor was performing a remarkable sleight of hand. The way Eleanor crafted her questions allowed her to extract all kinds of facts and statistics, which she reworked in such a way that the farmer did not recognize them as his own when she wove them back into their chat moments later. Everything he said gave Eleanor a crumb of information she could use to her advantage. Awe filled Hick from top to bottom.

The ploy could have been a cheap trick in anyone else's hands. But though Eleanor's knowledge was purloined, her interest was absolutely genuine. Eleanor's goal wasn't to fool the man—it was to get to know him and his circumstances. The real magic was that it worked both ways. As Eleanor talked, Hick could see the farmer's opinion of Mrs. Franklin D. Roosevelt altering before her eyes. Where there had been only wariness before, "respect and admiration" were now taking root. The talk eventually drew the farmer's wife outside, and the next thing Hick knew, the lady of the house was chatting amiably with the president's wife, too.

By eleven o'clock that night, the foursome were sitting around the kitchen table like old friends, with a bedtime snack of doughnuts and milk.

∼≫

Hick and Eleanor capped their vacation with a stopover at the Roosevelts' cottage on Campobello, an island in the Bay of Fundy. As if in welcome, the island's perpetual fog lifted that week, revealing a place of "unearthly beauty." Here, on an island accessible only by boat, where the Roosevelts had long been regarded by the locals as ordinary neighbors, she and Eleanor again enjoyed pristine solitude.

Both of them hated to leave, but the long-standing obligations cramming Eleanor's engagement book demanded it. The holiday had been everything Eleanor had hoped, everything Hick could have asked for. The memory of that perfect trip would glow, warm and golden, in Hick's mind for the rest of her days.

CHAPTER 49

HICK SET OUT FOR PENNSYLVANIA ON BEHALF OF FERA ON August 1 to see what she could learn about "the relief show," as she'd soon come to christen the government's efforts for the unemployed.

Hick didn't quite know what she was in for. Later, she'd call it "a three-year Odyssey through every man's land—and no man's land."

Chief in her mind were Mr. Hopkins's instructions regarding the people she was about to encounter. "Harry Hopkins had one remarkable quality," Hick recalled in later years, "and that was his ability to put himself in the place of the person on relief." He was adamant in his empathy toward America's millions of jobless citizens and demanded the same from Hick. The discussion they'd had about it would ring in her ears for decades. "When you're talking to somebody on relief," he'd told her, "you just say to yourself, *But for the grace of God, I'd be sitting on the other side of that table.*"

Hick's week began in the office of the State Emergency Relief Board in Harrisburg. As she mapped out her travels for the next five days, she overheard the folks who came in with complaints. "Kickers," she called them.

The loudest and most common complaints had to do with the grocery orders many relief agencies handed out to FERA workers in lieu of payments. Nobody had a single good word to say about those orders. Walking into a grocery store and handing over a food order instead of dollars and cents told the whole world you were on relief, and most people would rather listen to their stomachs howl than announce to their neighbors that they had no money for food. More galling yet was the fact that the orders spelled out exactly what goods the bearer was entitled to, as if they were children who couldn't be trusted to spend responsibly, not adults who'd been capably managing their households until the Great Depression yanked the rug out from under them.

The whole food order system admonished and humiliated folks who'd found themselves unemployed through no fault of their own. In its rush to avert an epidemic of hunger, the government hadn't taken people's morale into account, and the consequences had turned dire in a hurry.

"If they're not in a fighting mood, they're getting hopeless," a Republican county chairman told Hick. "If I were broke and starving, I don't believe there's a case worker in the country who could make me accept one of those damned food orders." Handing out paychecks instead would improve morale and eliminate reams of red tape. "We'd all be better off and feel more like human beings," the chairman told her. He knew fellows who refused to do "made work" for grocery orders but would be perfectly willing to do anything from planting trees to fixing up buildings if they were paid cash instead.

There was also the business of employers holding back pay for debts. It happened mostly in mining towns, Hick learned, where the company owned the houses its employees lived in and ran the stores where they shopped. Miners had no choice but to run up tabs for food and rent while the mines were closed. When they did get back to work, the company skimmed the debts right off the top with no regard for how much remained for a family to survive on until the next payday. "I actually saw yesterday one pay check for 8 cents," an appalled Hick recounted.

A paycheck like that was a sucker punch to a man who'd managed to get off relief and back on the job. "What's the use of going back to work if you're worse off than you were before," the chairman asked Hick. She had no answer.

Thanks to the food orders and the ludicrous paychecks, she learned, you could practically watch the self-respect drain away from unemployed men like water down a bath drain. "They'll never be any good any more, many of them," the chairman lamented.

～

For five days, Hick traveled through eastern Pennsylvania, interviewing everyone from her taxi driver to the governor himself in cities as large as Philadelphia and as small as Milford. She spoke with two dozen families on relief, often right in their homes. With her own eyes Hick saw the empty shelves in their pantries and the ragged overalls that hung from the shoulders of their hungry, barefoot children.

When she'd started, Hick later admitted, "they were not really people at all. They had no faces. They were just 'the unemployed.'" Not anymore. "One by one, sometimes bold, sometimes hesitant, sometimes demanding, sometimes faltering, they emerged—individuals," Hick wrote. "People with voices, faces, eyes. People with hope. People without hope. People still fighting. People with all the courage squeezed out of them. People with stories."

Hick looked, and she listened. She listened long and hard. People opened up to her, told her things they wouldn't say to a social worker. "Suppose you were my wife," one of the men Hick talked to during her FERA travels explained, "and I'll bet you're thanking your lucky stars you're not—run down, without any decent clothes, looking ten years older than you ought to look. How would you like it if some smooth-faced—not a wrinkle anywhere—young girl, nicely dressed, all made up, came into your house, sat down on the edge of a chair and began to ask you a lot of personal questions. You'd want to throw something at her, wouldn't you? The contrast is just too painful, that's all."

Once again, Hick's appearance worked in her favor. She was better dressed than most of the people she'd been sent to speak with, but she didn't have the kind of looks that made other women feel self-conscious. Her I've-seen-it-all manner encouraged the men to be forthright with her, too. People trusted her with their troubles and also with their shame.

Those stories stayed with her. "Tonight I feel like a great big sponge all filled with water," Hick wrote to Eleanor from Philadelphia. "I seem to have lost all my individuality and (To use another figure of speech!) become a sort of wax record for the recording of other people's ideas and complaints and hopes." A single conversation, like the one she had with Philadelphia's relief administrator that day, provided masses of information worthy of Mr. Hopkins's attention. "I could write a book on the stuff she told me, and the thought of how I am ever going to get it down on paper fills me with despair."

CHAPTER 50

HICK HAD TO FIGURE OUT HOW TO CONVEY WHAT SHE'D LEARNED to Mr. Hopkins. Her training hadn't covered how to go about it. There were no forms, no guidelines. So she decided to try writing out her impressions as a letter.

Hick sat down and started typing. Page by page, she told Mr. Hopkins what she'd seen, laying it out as if he were sitting across her dining room table, listening. Hick didn't bother with formality or try to make herself sound like some sort of expert. She reported, in plain, strong words, just as she'd done during her twenty years in the newspaper business.

Boiling down a week's worth of investigation to its essence was a monumental task, but Hick did it. She gave Hopkins a broad overview of the thorniest issues plaguing the relief situation, illustrating them with the most stirring examples she'd gotten straight from the people FERA's policies affected. She told Hopkins what she thought about the people she'd encountered—whether the complaints sounded legitimate, whether the relief administrators struck her as honest, and whether the folks labeled as agitators and radicals seemed likely to cause any real trouble.

"I doubt if you'll ever find time to read all this," she wrote as she finally wound down seven pages later. "Perhaps it isn't what you want at all." Hick thought she'd probably delved far too deeply into the details, but she couldn't bring herself to trim any of those stories out. "It's all new to me and therefore, to me, terribly important and extremely interesting. When I get back to Washington, perhaps we can talk it over," she suggested, "and you can tell me what I should have left out. Only don't tell me to leave it *all* out, please, because I like this job."

Although her report exuded professional confidence, Hick was about as nervous as a schoolgirl handing in a term paper. "I feel faint whenever I try to imagine the expression on Mr. Hopkins's face when he gets this report," she admitted to his secretary. "Of course it's too long, much, much too long for a man as busy as he is to read. Maybe he'll never read it, and perhaps that would be just as well. But I had to get some of it off my chest," she apologized. "Will you please pass it on to him if you think he can stand the shock?"

Hick sent a copy to Eleanor, too. All along, Hick had been writing to her. Everything she hadn't been able to cram into her official report, Hick put into Eleanor's letters. Those stories and details captivated both Eleanor and the president. "I read parts of your letter to Franklin," she told Hick, "and he read the report and was much interested." She marveled at how much insight Hick was gaining. "You must be simply worn out, putting so much into every day."

It *was* wearing, but Hick had learned fast that she couldn't let it show. Once, after an hour's discussion with a committee of unemployed men, she let slip that she was tired. An out-of-work miner shot back, "We're tired, too, lady—and we're living on 90 cents a week." Hick shut up and kept right on listening.

The more Hick worked, the more she got to know the folks who relied on FERA, and the more she allowed her own emotions to creep into her official reports. Anger, indignation, frustration, sorrow. Consequently, her reports didn't simply inform. "What a power you have to feel and to describe," Eleanor wrote her in late August. "I can see what you have seen and feel as you felt, just reading your letters."

Before the month was out, that power spurred Eleanor to personally inspect the most down-and-out community Hick had encountered.

CHAPTER 51

"IF YOU WANT TO SEE JUST HOW BAD THINGS ARE," THE EX-ecutive director of the American Friends Service Committee, a Quaker charity in Pennsylvania, had told Hick, "go down to the southwest part of the state and into West Virginia."

So Hick did. On her next trip, she visited Scotts Run, West Virginia, a mining town on its last legs. What she saw there left her slack-jawed.

"The Great Depression had never really hit me personally at all," Hick admitted later. Even her salary cuts at the AP "hadn't really hurt." With a few weeks of FERA investigations under her belt, she thought she'd gained a much clearer understanding of what the Depression really meant to millions of Americans. She'd seen stores with no goods on the shelves, and nobody in town with a nickel to buy anything anyway. She'd talked with homeless miners who'd fashioned themselves a camp out of abandoned coke ovens—"obsolete" men, living in obsolete coal-processing equipment that looked like "brick beehives falling into ruin." One Catholic priest's eyes still haunted her, a man who'd begged for the most basic of medical supplies for his parishioners—aspirin.

Even after all that, Scotts Run knocked Hick flat.

A coat of black coal dust stained all the houses, though the mines were barely operating a day or two a week. Inside those homes, rats and insects ran rampant. Many of the children had no beds, just rags piled up over the same floor where the vermin skittered and scampered. Sanitation was nonexistent. Water for drinking, cooking, or washing all came out of the gutter that ran along the main thoroughfare.

Hunger in Scotts Run had become as common and as vicious as the rats. The mountainsides were so steep, Hick couldn't see how folks got the seeds into the ground at all, unless they were shot from a gun like bullets. And then, after the unfathomable effort of planting, the people's ache for food was so keen, they could not wait for the vegetables to ripen. They pried minuscule potatoes out of the ground and devoured the tomatoes while they were still green.

The people were too hollowed out and listless to muster up the energy to hope anymore. Their despair and emotional torpor saturated Hick until she could think of little else. "The hills are still beautiful," she wrote of the rolling green landscape, "but I'm beginning to hate them for all the misery that the stuff inside of them makes for people." In her daily letters to Eleanor, she had hardly anything to say about herself. "Again tonight I have that sense of having lost my individuality," Hick explained. "What happens to us as individuals, what we think or desire or hope to do seems so trifling in the face of what I'm seeing these days!"

Hick could not force her mind to comprehend the reality of a country like the United States allowing entire communities to fall so far. How could there exist, in a nation as recently prosperous as America, a whole colony of people living in tents so tattered, the fabric wasn't fit for underwear?

Eleanor had been aware of the dire conditions, but after a week of reading Hick's descriptions of the region, she got in her car and drove to West Virginia. Hick met her at Morgantown with Clarence Pickett, the man who'd directed Hick to investigate the area.

The miners' wives, Hick recalled, "instinctively liked and trusted the tall, slender lady with the warming smile and soft, lovely voice," but none of them recognized Eleanor as the president's wife. These were people who didn't have enough spare change for the newspapers that carried her photograph.

One encounter, with a miner and his wife and six children, stuck with Eleanor for the rest of her days. She saw the man's pay stub, with its deductions for rent, his debt at the company store, and even the oil he used in his mine lamp to light the dark coal shafts as he worked. Less than a dollar remained to feed and clothe eight people.

The children, skittish and wary of the visitors, snatched handfuls of scraps—"the kind you or I might give to a dog," Eleanor observed—out of a bowl on the table as the adults talked. Those meager fragments were their lunch.

But the image that forever encapsulated the miners' plight in Eleanor's memory was the little boy who lingered in the doorway, holding a white rabbit. Eleanor could see by the way he cradled the creature that it was a beloved pet. His sister stood by, her rangy frame carved down by her unsatisfied appetite.

"He thinks we are not going to eat it," the little girl told Eleanor, her hungry eyes gleaming, "but we are."

❧

The misery in Scotts Run made a two-fisted impression on Eleanor. The miners needed help both for their own sake and for the well-being of the nation as a whole. If something wasn't done for people like this, she thought, the United States might well have a revolution on its hands.

And so, at Eleanor's urging, the government launched an experimental program based on a concept that had long interested FDR: subsistence farming. The idea was to take workers out of overcrowded industrial areas and move them to their own small farms, where they could grow enough food to support their families. Even if the Depression magically ended in a matter of days, workers of all kinds were still going to be faced with layoffs and decreased hours due to the rapid increase in mechanization. One machine—a bulldozer or an electric drill, for instance— could put a dozen men out of work. Hick was seeing these very effects in her travels already, and as the president knew from her reports, the consequences of mechanization troubled her mightily.

Subsistence farming looked like a promising solution. A man who owned a five-acre plot of land could work part-time in industry and spend the rest of his working hours raising animals and vegetables to eliminate his grocery and butcher bills. The unemployed miners of Scotts Run were a ready-made test case.

That autumn, the federal government purchased a twelve-hundred-acre farm to divvy up into individual homesteads and began accepting applications from Morgantown-area miners who wanted the chance to become residents of a subsistence community called Arthurdale.

Plans for Arthurdale included its own school, library, and church, with a community center, post office, barbershop, inn, and general store to follow. The houses boasted conveniences almost unheard of in coal camps—electricity, indoor plumbing, steam heat, and modern kitchen appliances. Furniture even came with the first fifty houses. Each homestead included a two-to-five-acre plot of land to accommodate gardens and livestock. Over the next four years, hundreds of local men got jobs building 165 houses. Future residents could count on work weaving rugs, building furniture, or metalsmithing in Arthurdale's cooperative businesses.

For the families who moved into Arthurdale, the change felt like something beyond reality. "We woke up one morning in hell, and went to bed the next night in heaven," one of them said.

It wasn't free. They had to pay rent on their few acres of heaven and work to help the co-op turn a profit, and eventually they'd be expected to buy their houses from the government. But that was a squarer deal than any they'd gotten working in the mines.

The project did have its faults. The $2,000-per-house budget ballooned to over $8,000, thanks to Eleanor's insistence on what some critics saw as outrageous luxuries like refrigerators and flush toilets. And to Eleanor's eternal dismay, Black people were not considered eligible for residency; Arthurdale would be a segregated community.

Eleanor took a deep and abiding interest not just in the fate of the experimental community, but also in its individual residents. She became a regular visitor, honored guest, and friend who danced at Arthurdale square dances, sent gifts to each family at Christmas, and presented diplomas to Arthurdale's high school graduates.

In the eyes of the government and taxpayers, Arthurdale would ultimately represent an abject failure. The government never did recoup its investment. Every one of the cooperative businesses lost money, and the community did not fulfill its aspiration of self-sufficiency.

Eleanor disagreed with that sort of thinking. "Only a few of the resettlement projects had any success," she conceded years afterward, "nevertheless, I have always felt that the good they did was incalculable." To Eleanor, Arthurdale was an experiment in *human,* not economic, development.

The residents of Arthurdale sided firmly with Eleanor. The difference the community made in the lives of the people who lived there was indeed impossible to measure by any tangible methods. Whole families were lifted from the filth, starvation, and despair of the coal camps and ensconced in spick-and-span little houses virtually overnight. Arthurdale restored their hope and their dignity and gave their children an opportunity to thrive.

Ever after, Arthurdale's residents and their descendants would see Eleanor Roosevelt as a kind of guardian angel, and rightly so. But it was that visit to Morgantown, prompted by Hick's distress calls, that had brought their guardian angel to their doorsteps and awakened her to their need.

Just one photo of the Hickok family is known to exist. Lorena sits at the far left, with her mother, sister Myrtle, father, and sister Ruby.

Courtesy of the Franklin D. Roosevelt Presidential Library and Museum, Hyde Park, New York

Senior high school portrait, 1912.

Courtesy of the author

LAWREAN

	Fell		*Harris*			*Cochrane*		
Mielke	*Richardson*	*Bussard*	*Frankel*	*Boardwin*	*Beach*	*Mielke*		*Cheney*
Faville	*Cade*	*Ketchpaw*	*Castle*		*Germond*	*Goodrich*		
Stevenson	*Wray*	*B. Ross*	*McNaughton*	*Semester*	*Lund*	*Hickock*		

Lawrence University's Lawrean Literary Society in 1914. Lorena is at the bottom right.

Courtesy of the author

"The Girl Reporter" grins as she meets an elephant named Alfred, rides a horse in the parade, and models Barnum & Bailey Circus costumes for *Minneapolis Tribune* readers in 1917.

Courtesy of the author

The public face of the Roosevelt family in 1919. Though all appears serene, Eleanor was secretly wrestling with the knowledge of her husband's infidelity.

Courtesy of the Franklin D. Roosevelt Presidential Library and Museum, Hyde Park, New York

Lorena and her roommate, Ellie Morse, rush to catch the elevator in this 1920 illustration from one of Lorena's Girl Reporter features.

Courtesy of the author

Eleanor Roosevelt shared close personal, business, and political ties with queer women long before meeting Hick. Here she holds hands with Marion Dickerman in 1926, while Marion's life partner, Nancy Cook, poses on the right.

Courtesy of the Franklin D. Roosevelt Presidential Library and Museum, Hyde Park, New York

"Lorena" no more—Hick during her star reporter days at the *Minneapolis Tribune*.

Hennepin County Library Special Collection

Hick on her thirty-third birthday, about to climb aboard Old Lady 501 for "a roaring, swaggering, joyous adventure" in the steam locomotive.

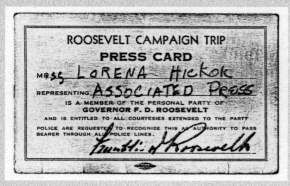

Hick's press pass from the 1932 Roosevelt presidential campaign. "Miss" is handwritten over the preprinted "Mr."

Courtesy of the Franklin D. Roosevelt Presidential Library and Museum, Hyde Park, New York

Eleanor Roosevelt, hairnet and all, looking much as she did when Hick first met her.

Eleanor Roosevelt leaving the White House in January 1933. She inscribed Hick's copy of the photo: "We were only separated by a few yards dear Hick & I wonder which of us felt most oddly!"

Courtesy of the Franklin D. Roosevelt Presidential Library and Museum, Hyde Park, New York

The Adams Memorial, where Hick and Eleanor sat in quiet contemplation before FDR's 1933 inauguration.

Stillman Rogers

THE WHITE HOUSE
WASHINGTON

Sunday night
March 5th
[1933]

Hick my dearest — I cannot go to
bed to-night without a word to
you. I felt a little as though a
part of me was leaving to-night.
You have grown so much to be a
part of my life that it is empty
without you even though I'm busy
every minute.

These are strange days & very
odd to me but I'll remember
the boys & try to plan pleasant
things & count the days between
our times together!

Eleanor to Hick, March 5, 1933: "Hick my dearest, I cannot go to bed to-night without a word to you. I felt a little as though a part of me was leaving to-night. You have grown so much to be a part of my life that it is empty without you even though I'm busy every minute."

Courtesy of the Franklin D. Roosevelt Presidential Library and Museum, Hyde Park, New York

Bx 1

Lycan Hotels

THE HOTEL CROOKSTON
CROOKSTON, MINN.

NEW HOTEL MARKHAM
AND ANNEX
BEMIDJI, MINN.

[LH to ER]
Wednesday night
December 5th [1933]

Dear:

Tonight its Bemidji, away
up in the timber country, not
a bad hotel, and one day
nearer you. Only eight more days.
Twenty-four hours from now
it will be only seven more —
just a week! I've been trying
today to bring back your face —
to remember just _how_ you look.
Funny how even the dearest
face will fade away in time.
Most clearly I remember your
eyes, with a kind of teasing smile

Hick to Eleanor, December 5, 1933: "I've been trying today to bring back your face—to remember just _how_ you look. Funny how even the dearest face will fade away in time. Most clearly I remember your eyes, with a kind of teasing smile in them, and the feeling of that soft spot just northeast of the corner of your mouth against my lips."

Courtesy of the Franklin D. Roosevelt Presidential Library and Museum, Hyde Park, New York

The pocket calendar Hick used to record her days with and without Eleanor, beginning in March 1933. She kept similar calendars in 1934 and 1935.

Courtesy of the author

Photos of Eleanor and Hick together are few and far between. Here Hick (right) and Eleanor (second from left) pose with two unidentified women in the 1930s.

Courtesy of the Franklin D. Roosevelt Presidential Library and Museum, Hyde Park, New York

Eleanor and Hick pause alongside Eleanor's roadster in Massachusetts during their July 1933 vacation to New England and the Gaspé Peninsula.

Courtesy of the Franklin D. Roosevelt Presidential Library and Museum, Hyde Park, New York

Hick and Earl Miller (Eleanor's friend and bodyguard from her days as first lady of New York) in 1933. Hick's uncharacteristic ease before the camera—in a bathing suit, no less—suggests that Eleanor may have been the photographer.

Courtesy of the Franklin D. Roosevelt Presidential Library and Museum, Hyde Park, New York

Hick and Eleanor's arrival in Puerto Rico on Hick's forty-first birthday.
Courtesy of the Franklin D. Roosevelt Presidential Library and Museum, Hyde Park, New York

Eleanor and Hick (wearing a long dark scarf) inspecting a neighborhood in Puerto Rico on behalf of FERA.

Courtesy of the Franklin D. Roosevelt Presidential Library and Museum, Hyde Park, New York

Hick trying to shrink from the camera as photographers intrude on her breakfast with Eleanor in Sacramento in July 1934. Tourists and reporters alike hounded them relentlessly in California.

Bettman

Hick's dread of photographers shines through in this image from the Pan American Day concert she attended with Eleanor in 1935.

Bettman

Sketch for a custom-made Christmas card featuring Hick's steadfast German shepherd, Prinz.
Courtesy of the author

A newly discovered photo of Hick with Eleanor at a Black choral concert in April 1935.
Afro Newspaper/Gado

A beaming Hick in 1936 with the Plymouth convertible she named Stepchild.
Courtesy of the Franklin D. Roosevelt Presidential Library and Museum, Hyde Park, New York

Hick and Eleanor on one of their increasingly rare outings together, this one in the Great Smoky Mountains in the spring of 1937.

Bettman

Hick gives the camera a dubious look from the sunporch at her Long Island cottage.

Courtesy of the Franklin D. Roosevelt Presidential Library and Museum, Hyde Park, New York

Hick showing off Prinz's good manners.

Courtesy of the Franklin D. Roosevelt Presidential Library and Museum, Hyde Park, New York

Marion Harron, whose love brightened Hick's life in the 1940s, at the Little House.

Courtesy of the Franklin D. Roosevelt Presidential Library and Museum, Hyde Park, New York

Hick playing with Mr. Choate, the English setter Eleanor gave her after Prinz's death.

Courtesy of the Franklin D. Roosevelt Presidential Library and Museum, Hyde Park, New York

Eleanor Roosevelt's favorite portrait of Hick.

Courtesy of the Franklin D. Roosevelt Presidential Library and Museum, Hyde Park, New York

Hick with her beloved Aunt Ella in 1947.

Courtesy of the Franklin D. Roosevelt Presidential Library and Museum, Hyde Park, New York

The ocean of mourners and floral tributes at Eleanor Roosevelt's funeral, November 10, 1962.

Courtesy of the Franklin D. Roosevelt Presidential Library and Museum, Hyde Park, New York

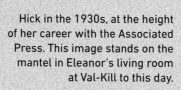

Hick's memorial plaque beneath a dogwood tree in Rhinebeck Cemetery.

Courtesy of the author

Hick in the 1930s, at the height of her career with the Associated Press. This image stands on the mantel in Eleanor's living room at Val-Kill to this day.

National Park Service

CHAPTER 52

AFTER SCOTTS RUN, HICK WENT ON TO KENTUCKY, UPSTATE New York, Maine, and New York City. Compared to what she'd seen in West Virginia, the folks in the Northeast had it made. Thousands of people were struggling, but the relief show out there was running like a steam locomotive at full throttle.

Conditions in eastern Kentucky bore a disheartening resemblance to Morgantown's coal camps. Eleanor had feared that a revolution might spring out of the destitute West Virginians, but there was nothing to fear from the folks in Kentucky. They were so near the edge of starvation, they didn't have the energy to riot. Their patience and decency despite limping along for three weeks without grocery orders nearly did Hick in.

"Don't forget me, honey! Don't forget me!" one malnourished and sickly old woman called Aunt Cora whispered to Hick with a hand on her arm as they parted. Aunt Cora's feet were bare, and she carried a paper bag containing a scant handful of string beans.

Hick didn't forget her. Not ever.

Between FERA excursions, Hick often bunked at the White House for a week or more at a time. During FDR's tenure, the private quarters of the executive mansion functioned like something between a hotel and a dormitory, hosting a regular cavalcade of staff, close friends, and relations. Some stayed a night or two; others remained for years.

Hick slept on the daybed in Eleanor's big sitting room on the second floor. It was part of Eleanor's three-room suite in the southwest corner, adjoining Eleanor's much smaller bedroom and bath. Customarily, the largest chamber in the suite served as the bedroom with the smaller as a dressing room, but Eleanor had flip-flopped their purposes. That left Hick sandwiched between the president's and first lady's bedrooms.

Hick settled right in. Mornings, she joined Eleanor in the cozy upstairs sitting area, sipping her café au lait out of an enormous blue-and-white willowware mug. On any given day, she might accompany the president and first lady to a formal White House dinner, a family scrambled-egg supper, or a cruise down the Chesapeake Bay on the USS *Sequoia*. Now and then Hick and Eleanor even managed to steal away to New York City for a weekend to take in a concert or play.

⁕

The Roosevelts were most gracious hosts, pleased to extend invitations to friends and relatives of their guests, so that they, too, might experience the thrill of a meal or a night in the White House. Hick's beloved Aunt Ella, by then in her seventies, was among them on at least one occasion.

"Now, Franklin, you behave yourself tonight," Eleanor told her husband before they took the elevator down to dinner one evening. "Hick's Republican relatives are here from Illinois. Don't you say anything to shock them."

Hick was more concerned about her aunt than anything FDR might do. Ella Ellis was almost scared stiff at the prospect of being seated beside the president of the United States. But to Hick's stupefaction, Aunt Ella and FDR laughed and chatted their way through dinner. Her shy and soft-spoken little aunt did not show a glimmer of unease. And FDR loved every second of it. Usually his female dinner guests were so tongue-tied he couldn't get a thing out of them except "Yes, Mr. President" and "No, Mr. President." Faced with such mind-numbing conversation, he'd often keep score of the yeses and nos just to give his brain something to do. Aunt Ella proved herself a vastly superior conversationalist. Charm positively radiated from the president as he and Ella talked—really talked.

Ella Ellis kept right on voting Republican, but never again would she tolerate an unkind word against FDR in her presence.

CHAPTER 53

MID-OCTOBER OF 1933 SAW HICK HEADING OFF TO THE MID-west for a two-month investigation of Minnesota, North Dakota, South Dakota, Iowa, and Nebraska. Morale among farmers out there was so shaky, Mr. Hopkins wanted Hick to wire her reports. Threats of strikes, agitation, and violence were gathering like smoke over the region. A situation that volatile couldn't afford to wait for the mail.

Hick drove a smart blue Chevrolet convertible Eleanor had procured for her secondhand. She christened the car Bluette, after one of her favorite White House maids, Bluette Pannell.

Minnesota had its potential bright spots. Back in what she considered her home state, there were scores of old friends to reconnect with during her off hours. She stayed at the Leamington Hotel, where she'd lived with Ellie Morse years ago, and visited with "Old Man" Tom Dillon's family, spending Thanksgiving in Minneapolis.

The Dakotas hit Hick hard. Desperation there rivaled what she'd seen in West Virginia, but there was likely more to it than that. Though she never seems to have said so outright, Mr. Hopkins's mantra, *But for the grace of God, I'd be sitting on the other side of that table*, must have echoed especially loudly in Hick's mind as she surveyed the hail-damaged, drought-stricken, and grasshopper-ridden farmland where she'd spent the bleakest years of her childhood. If not for the winding string of circumstances that had led her to Washington, DC, Hick herself would indeed have been among the weary, vacant-eyed people who now confronted her.

The people of Bottineau, North Dakota, she told Eleanor, were "in a daze. A sort of nameless dread hangs over the place." For two years in a row, grasshoppers had ravaged the crops. They'd even devoured the laundry off the clotheslines. Worse, the insects had left their eggs behind, guaranteeing another failure in the year to come.

Winter was months off and already children were purple-footed with cold. One house Hick visited was no more weatherproof than a colander. License plates and tin can lids patched holes in the floor. Wadded-up newspapers feebly blocked drafts from the windows, while two little barefooted boys ran about in nothing but threadbare overalls. "Their mother—bare-legged, too, although she had some ragged sneakers on her feet—is going to have another baby in January," a horrified Hick reported. "And in that house!" The whole family slept in a single bed, under two dirty flannel blankets, relying mostly on body heat to keep them warm. The rest of the linen had given out two years ago, the pregnant woman told her.

When she learned that the Red Cross had an untapped supply of blankets and clothing stocked away for emergencies, Hick turned livid. "Good God," she wrote to Eleanor, "I wonder what constitutes an emergency in the eyes of the old ladies who run the Red Cross!"

Hick sopped up the local mood as she always did. And the mood on these vast stretches of prairie as winter loomed nearer was universally desolate. "These plains are beautiful," she conceded to Eleanor. "But, oh, the terrible, crushing drabness of life here."

Eleanor's correspondence became Hick's lifeline. "Oh, my dear, I *do* get so hungry for letters!" she wrote. They had never been apart this long.

"Poor dear, what sad things you are living through!" Eleanor consoled. "But you will be able to help, things will be done, and it will be because you have the power to see and feel and write."

And write she did. Hick wrote to Mr. Hopkins at a furious pace, pounding home the urgency of "the desperate need for things to keep people warm up here in this ghastly climate." Where before she'd sent a report every week or two, now sometimes less than twenty-four hours separated them. "Dammit, I don't WANT to write to you again tonight," she typed from Winner, South Dakota. "It's been a long day, and I'm tired." But Hick couldn't sleep without telling Mr. Hopkins what she'd seen, and what people needed.

Even when Hick permitted herself time to sleep, she didn't get much rest. The hotels out there were horrors. Drab, worn-out little places sometimes infested with fleas or bedbugs. "There isn't—there can't be— any reason for a hotel to be so hopelessly uninviting as this one is," she wrote from Bottineau.

Only a handful of Hick's letters to Eleanor survive from this period, but it's clear from Eleanor's end of the conversation that the misery Hick witnessed each day was fraying her emotions to their limits. "I am prouder, dear, to know you than I can ever tell you," Eleanor soothed, "and you ought not only to be proud of yourself, but to have all the self-confidence in the world, because anyone who is 'you' after all you've been through need never be afraid of anything or anyone."

Even the weather conspired to darken Hick's state of mind. "I thought I'd already seen about everything in the way of desolation, discomfort, and misery that could exist, right here in South Dakota," Hick wrote to Eleanor in mid-November. "Well, it seems that I hadn't. Today's little treat was a dust storm. And I mean dust storm!"

When Hick woke after a night of ceaseless wind that "howled and screamed and sobbed around the windows," the sky was muddied with dust. A "queer brown haze" was building itself up from the ground, like a brick wall forming layer by layer. Only when she looked straight up could Hick see clear sky above her head. It took until nine o'clock before a lighter circle appeared in the haze, marking the place where the sun tried feebly to penetrate the grit.

Hick and the county relief director piled into the car to make the rounds they'd planned, only to turn back within a few miles as the storm shifted into high gear. "Terrifying" was the only word for it, Hick told Eleanor. As the thickening dust swallowed up the road and even the light itself, the wind shoved them along like a great ghostly hand; if they did not engage the emergency brake, the car moved forward on its own. "It was as though we had left the earth," Hick wrote. "We were being whirled off into space in a vast, impenetrable cloud of brown dust."

The streetlights were on by the time they crept back into town, hardly able to see a foot beyond the front fender. Noon that day looked more like a kind of supernatural nightfall. The buildings across the street had vanished into the gloom. Even the dim disk of the sun had disappeared. Later, as she lay reading in her hotel room, Hick looked up from her newspaper. The sky was midnight black. For an instant, fear zinged through her all over again. "It seemed like the end of the world," she said.

~

"What a picture you can paint!" Eleanor wrote back a few days later. "I nearly wept. If ever under any circumstances you give up writing, I'll flay you," she threatened, "whether I'm here in the flesh or flaying you from some other world!"

Eleanor worried, too. She fretted over Hick's mood, her lack of rest, and whether the restaurants served the right kind of food to manage her diabetes. But the only thing she could minister to from afar was Hick's spirits, and so she garnished each letter with generous helpings of comfort and affection. "You feel too much to live constantly in the midst of misery," she sympathized.

Eleanor was pining just as much as Hick. On Thanksgiving, she admitted, she'd "had a little longing (secretly) that FDR might think I'd like you to be here & insist on you coming to report to him! You know how one dreams? I knew it wouldn't be true but it was nice to think about!"

Hick soldiered on for two more weeks. Separated by thousands of miles, she and Eleanor counted down the days as their letters crisscrossed the nation. "I've been trying today to bring back your face—to remember just *how* you look," Hick wrote the first week in December.

"Funny how even the dearest face will fade away in time. Most clearly I remember your eyes, with a kind of teasing smile in them, and the feeling of that soft spot just northeast of the corner of your mouth against my lips."

"Funny everything I do my thoughts fly to you," Eleanor replied. A concert, a drive, or a sunset all stirred memories shared with Hick.

"We'll have tea in my room as soon as you get here Friday & then we'll decide about Sat. & Sunday," Eleanor promised. She also invited Hick to spend the night of December 21 at her apartment in New York City. "I'd like to have you here that night & celebrate a little X-mas of our own!"

Hick could hardly wait.

CHAPTER 54

HICK'S RETURN TO THE WHITE HOUSE HARDLY RESEMBLED THE daydreams that had kept her spirits afloat in the Dakotas.

Probably they had their joyful reunion over the Friday tea that Eleanor had proposed. (No letters from mid-December 1933 exist, making the details impossible to pinpoint.) But soon afterward, Hick got slapped with the realization that her time with Eleanor was going to be far less plentiful than she'd anticipated. The first lady's schedule was as chock-full of obligations as ever.

Through all the wretched hotels, barren fields, starving livestock, shivering children, and woebegone farmers, the thought of returning to Eleanor's waiting arms had sustained her. Now that refuge seemed to be available by appointment only. The promise of a special Christmas celebration alone with Eleanor on December 21 might have been the only thing keeping Hick from blowing her top.

And then it happened. Some crisis with Anna and her failing marriage intervened at the last minute, calling Eleanor away and thwarting their treasured plans.

Worse, Eleanor might not have shown a speck of dismay. Her grandmother had told her no so often in her childhood that she'd learned to protect herself by pretending not to want things. It was easier than having her fragile hopes dashed. Eleanor never fully grew out of the habit. She'd even said as much to Hick two weeks earlier: "Dear one it's getting nearer & nearer & I am half afraid to be too happy. It's the way I felt as a child when I dreaded disappointment!"

Judging by Hick's reaction, none of that went through her mind. She snatched up her suitcase and left. In a temper or in tears is anyone's guess. Perhaps she managed to hustle herself out of the White House before the grenade of her wounded feelings detonated. All the way back to New York City she fled, determined to spend the holiday with people who would appreciate her presence.

Eleanor found herself with a mountain of apologizing to do. "Hick dearest," she wrote two nights before Christmas, "I went to sleep saying a little prayer, 'God give me depth enough not to hurt Hick again.'"

Committing such a slight weighed heavily on Eleanor. "The greatest responsibility anyone can have is that of making someone else suffer," she'd written Hick back in April. And now she'd done exactly what she most dreaded to the person she most cherished.

On Christmas Day, Eleanor wrote again. By then they'd had at least one phone call and patched things up enough that Hick had agreed to return to the White House for the rest of her holiday. "You shall dine in bed & sleep all you want if you'll just stay here & be happy," Eleanor vowed.

⁕

Months later, Eleanor dug deep enough within herself to uncover the root of her mistake. "I think my real trouble is not that I don't care enough," she mused, "but that for so many years I've let my work engulf me so as to have no time to think & now when I should know how to shake it, it has become my master!"

Eleanor learned her lesson well. Never again would she take Hick's time, or her patience, for granted.

CHAPTER 55

of 1933 had. During the winter months, Hick made FERA trips into the balmy states of Georgia, Florida, South Carolina, and North Carolina.

A quiet January weekend with Eleanor in Warm Springs, Georgia— a town renowned for its mineral baths that FDR had converted into a rehabilitation center for polio patients—helped further heal the hurt of Christmas.

"Dearest, it was a lovely weekend," Hick wrote afterward. "I shall have it to think about for a long, long time. Each time we have together that way—brings us closer, doesn't it? And I believe those days and long pleasant hours together each time make it perhaps a little less possible for us to hurt each other."

"I loved every minute," Eleanor agreed, "& I am going to live on it during the next few weeks."

Parting so quickly yet again wrenched them both, leaving Eleanor with "a lost feeling." There was one benefit to being history's busiest first lady, though. She could always count on "the infinite succession of things" to take hold and numb the ache Hick left behind.

Hick's work kept her mind busy, too. "This *is* a fascinating job of mine!" she wrote in January. She toured the citrus groves of Orlando; assessed Miami's tourist industry; visited Georgia's turpentine belt and South Carolina's cotton mills, cigar manufacturers, and truck farms; and scrutinized the situation of domestic workers in North Carolina.

The South was showing her racial inequities as she'd never seen them before. In Savannah, she learned of the Black workers who preferred government relief over regular work. Most taxpayers believed that was just proof of how lazy Black people were. The truth, Hick discovered, was a different story. Relief payments added up to more money each week than white employers had been paying Black people *before* the Depression. Why work for $8 a week when the government allotted $12?

"Half-starved Whites and Blacks struggle in competition for less to eat than my dog gets at home, for the privilege of living in huts that are infinitely less comfortable than his kennel," Hick reported from Georgia. Jealousy and rivalries over basic necessities were so fierce that they sometimes ended with lynchings. "I just can't describe to you some of the things I've seen and heard down here these last few days," she told Mr. Hopkins. "I shall never forget them—never as long as I live."

Thankfully for Hick's state of mind, Eleanor's almost daily letters reached like an embrace across the Southeast as she traveled. Letters awaited her at hotel after hotel. "Oh, dear one, it is all the little things, tones in your voice, the feel of your hair, gestures, these are the things I think about & long for," Eleanor wrote. She also praised Hick's reports and sprinkled her letters with the tender endearments that helped keep her dear one's spirits from sinking. "Strong relationships have to grow deep roots," Eleanor counseled, "we're growing them now, partly because we are separated, the foliage & the flowers will come, somehow I'm sure of it."

~

The rest Hick needed to keep her on an even keel remained elusive. In South Carolina word got out that she was some kind of an investigator from Washington, and a flood of people came to talk to her—three reporters, a lawyer working on behalf of veterans, and a congressman's campaign manager. Her phone rang incessantly, until she told the hotel operator not to put any more calls through. "Believe me, the next state administrator who lets out any publicity on me is going to get his head cracked!" she railed to Mr. Hopkins.

But Hick couldn't crack the next head that set her off just eleven days later in North Carolina. She was not in a stellar mood that evening to begin with. She'd already bumped, scraped, and dented Bluette all in a single week, and entered her Charlotte hotel "half dead from fatigue and worry about the car."

A knot of people awaited her in the lobby. An unemployed delegation from the little Blue Ridge town of Old Fort had come down to meet her, hoping she'd carry word of their troubles straight to Mr. Hopkins. Tired as she was, Hick couldn't bring herself to beg off. They'd already been waiting for two hours.

"As I came in, they handed me, with beaming smiles, a copy of *Time*," she recounted for Hopkins's secretary. No doubt they thought she'd be thrilled to see her name and photograph in a national newsmagazine, unaware that Hick cringed at cameras and had been getting her name into print since 1915. "I read the thing and wanted to curse until the air was blue."

The two-and-a-half-page cover feature on Harry Hopkins and his relief efforts had devoted exactly six sentences to Hick. The second one incensed her on the spot. "She is a rotund lady with a husky voice, a peremptory manner, baggy clothes," *Time* wrote, as if any of that had the slightest bearing on how she did her job.

"I'm so fed up with publicity I want to kick every reporter I see," she fumed. "Which is a bad state for me to get into, since I'll probably be back in the business myself after I get through with this."

Hick's upcoming FERA trip to Puerto Rico got a mention, too. Eleanor was booked on that trip as well, and of course *Time* noted that "Miss Hickok would also go along," making it sound as if Hick were just trotting along behind Eleanor like some kind of afterthought, when the reverse was closer to the truth. And like a final slap, the paragraph contained an implication that Hick had gotten her job with FERA solely on the basis of her friendship with Eleanor. Hick sparked with fury at that most of all.

"I don't suppose I ought to kick," she groused to the secretary. "It's friendly and fair, on the whole, to the Boss and administration. Only— why the Hell CAN'T they leave me alone?"

CHAPTER 56

"I BELIEVE IT GETS HARDER TO LET YOU GO EACH TIME," ELEA-
nor wrote Hick after their return from the Caribbean. "It seems as
though you belonged near me," she went on, mourning the necessity
of their separations. "Just now what you do is of such value to the country that we ought not to complain, only that doesn't make me miss you
less or feel less lonely!"

Hick spent the next several weeks making her way across Alabama,
Louisiana, Texas, and New Mexico. Then she'd take the first half of the
summer to trek through Ohio, Michigan, Tennessee, and Colorado before finally landing in California in July.

Now and then Hick eked out a few moments of pleasure solely for
herself. "What a town for a glutton!" she crowed after a sumptuous meal
in New Orleans. "Two gin fizzes, some sort of a marvelous shrimp con-
coction known as shrimps Arnaud, pompano baked in a paper bag, potatoes soufflé, a pint of sauterne, crepes Suzette, and black coffee."

But just stepping into the waiting rooms at the relief office could
obliterate all the good an evening of culinary delights had done for her.
"Mr. Hopkins, did you ever spend a couple of hours sitting around an
intake?" Hick asked. "An intake is about the nearest thing to Hell that I
know anything about. The smell alone—I'd recognize it anywhere. And
take that on top of the psychological effect of having to be there at all.
God!" she fumed. "If I were applying for relief, one look at the average
intake room would send me to the river."

Hick conveyed the feel of the place in a fistful of words that hit like
a punch. And the honesty and forcefulness of her reports only increased
as she traveled across the Southwest. Once again drenched in people's

hardships, she relayed them back to Washington as perhaps nobody else could have done.

"I'll give you more on New Orleans tomorrow night," she promised her boss from Houston. "I'm too tired and too gloomy to do any more tonight. Perhaps I shouldn't have written at all when I felt this way. But, dammit, you want the state of mind of the nation—and I'm giving it to you."

"Oh, my dear, love me a lot! I need it!" Hick begged Eleanor that same night. Her spirits had taken another dive after learning the sordid details of how single women traded sex for money—sometimes as little as a dime.

Eleanor eagerly obliged. Back in Washington, she sent letters every day, always with a bit of sweetness at the beginning and the end. "Dearest, I miss you & wish you were here I want to put my arms around you & feel yours around me. More love than I can express in a letter is flying on waves of thought to you."

Rarely did a moment pass for Eleanor without thoughts of her Dear One. "I wonder if always I'm not going to feel that a day is incomplete which we don't start & end to-gether?" she wrote. "I miss you very much & I love you very much, more & more deeply as the weeks roll on."

On those days when everything in sight looked bleak and empty, Hick could at least count on a bright spot when she checked the mail at her hotel. "You give me so much more happiness than you realize dear," Eleanor assured her. "And I love to feel you love me just as you do & I do love you."

Hick lapped up every drop of affection, but words on paper could only go so far. Unlike Eleanor, she had no friends or family to help patch the hole her darling's absence left behind. Even Hick's beloved German shepherd was out of her reach. "I've been thinking a lot tonight about Prinz and wondering if he misses me as much as I miss him, the dear pup," she wrote from Fort Worth. "And now I'm going to bed—to try to dream about you. I never do, but I always have hopes."

CHAPTER 57

"OH! LORD, I'M GETTING TO FEEL MORE LIKE A GOLDFISH EVERY day!" Eleanor complained.

Although she was expanding the role of first lady faster than some Americans could comprehend it, Eleanor still chafed at the boundaries her position imposed upon her. In her mind, she inhabited two identities: the president's wife, whom she called *Mrs. R.,* and her true self, known as *E.R.*

"I've been very much 'Mrs. R.' all day!" she bemoaned to Hick in April of 1934. It was an act she hadn't yet learned to keep up at all costs. That day, during an inopportune moment, "E.R. who suddenly felt like herself & not like the first lady said several things the first lady shouldn't have said."

Hick understood completely. She was very much in love with E.R., and occasionally very much inconvenienced by Mrs. R. In a fit of frustration over the *Time* magazine article that had so rankled her, Hick had exclaimed, "I love Mrs. Roosevelt dearly—she is the best friend I have in the world—but sometimes I do wish, for my own sake, that she were Mrs. Joe Doaks of Olewein, Iowa!" Between the two of them, Mrs. Doaks, a Midwestern nobody, became a sort of inside joke—code for the underlying Eleanor who was no different from any other woman in the world who "would like a little privacy now & then!"

"I'm glad you don't mind being Mrs. Doaks' friend anyway but she must remain obscure!" Eleanor wrote after someone blew Hick's FERA cover by mentioning her friendship with the first lady.

Though Hick never blamed Eleanor herself for the publicity she attracted, that same notoriety often turned into headaches for Hick. "Poor dear, I am so sorry I pursue you so unpleasantly all over the country,"

Eleanor apologized when another newspaper had irritated Hick yet again with its Eleanor Roosevelt coverage, which always seemed to emphasize some inane thing instead of issues that really mattered. "Ever so much love & think of me only as Mrs. Doaks!"

⁓

On a stretch of road between Lordsburg, New Mexico, and Tucson, Arizona, Bluette's tires hit a patch of loose gravel. Hick lost control. The tires spun, and Bluette rolled over into the ditch.

Over the years, Hick would return to that moment more than once, recalling it as a perfect moment to bid the world goodbye. "I'd have died happy, as happy as I've ever been in my life, and it would have all been over. I'd never even have known that I was dying."

But fate wasn't particularly interested in Hick's idea of perfection. She escaped the wreck largely unscathed, spending a single day in bed as a precaution. According to the doctor, there had been an instant as the car flipped when Bluette's entire weight had rested on Hick's neck. "Incidentally, sir," she wrote to Mr. Hopkins, "you have to have a darned good neck to get away with anything like that. I think mine had no doubt got toughened up these last five or six weeks from carrying the weight of the world on it."

Eleanor didn't take the news half so well. Hick's near miss launched the first lady into the kind of state she herself called a "tizzy-whiz." As soon as she heard the news of the accident, Eleanor promptly wired, called, and wrote, hardly able to satisfy herself that Hick was truly all right.

"Hick darling, I've just talked to you & hearing your voice has saved me," she wrote. "The 'what might have happened aspect' I can't face even now."

Eleanor promised to help Hick replace Bluette, and even entertained a momentary fantasy of chauffeuring Hick herself. "Oh! dear one I love you & long to be with you when things go wrong," she lamented.

⁂

Whether she knew it or not, Hick was rattled. Nearly a year of observing economic devastation and its human toll had chipped steadily away at her emotional defenses. She simply couldn't rest while others suffered.

"Damn it, it's the same old story here, wherever I go," she reported to Mr. Hopkins from Arizona. Relief dragged white people down and lifted Mexican, Indigenous, and Black people up. Just as in the Southeast, wages for people of color were abysmally low—lower than relief payments. The lopsided economics increased tension between the races and muddied up the whole attitude toward government assistance.

Worries over workers her own age dogged her endlessly. Hick could just see how it would play out for people weathering the Depression in their forties. By the time the economy got back on its feet, younger men would get first crack at the jobs, leaving the older fellows with half-grown families to support. "A stranded generation," Hick called them.

"Pardon me for getting personal," she wrote to her boss, "but I believe you are a little past 40 yourself. Suppose at 45 you lost your job and couldn't get another one—probably never." Hick harbored the same uneasiness when she considered her own future. "I'm over 40 myself. Suppose after this job is finished I couldn't ever get another. How would I like spending the rest of my life on relief—provided, as a single person, I could get relief? I'd be damned rebellious, I tell you."

The more she witnessed the same problems in different places, the more the futility of the Great Depression dragged Hick down. Even when she marveled over a successful community project, she couldn't escape the invisible undertow pulling at her. "Always in the background, though, is this dreadful relief business—dull, hopeless, deadening. God— when are we going to get out of it?" she asked Eleanor.

Her confidence dipped right along with her mood. "With the possible exception of the one on Puerto Rico, this is probably the poorest report I've ever written," Hick moaned to Eleanor in June. "I must pull myself up. But *how*? I *am* so tired."

Individual tragedies hit her as hard as the big-picture problems, if not harder. The children weeding the beet fields of Colorado laid Hick especially low. She'd had a hard enough time earning a living for herself as a teenager. Here were eight-, ten-, and twelve-year-olds shuffling on their knees to keep their backs from getting too sore. Some of them started working twelve-hour days as young as six. The things she saw in those fields made Hick grind her teeth until her mouth was raw.

"You, Washington, the apartment in New York, Prinz—they all seem very far away this morning," she wrote in July. "I wonder if it will be like this when I die—a feeling of remoteness from everything. Oh, my dear, I'm so sick of the whole miserable business!"

Hick desperately needed a break. "You cannot get so tired," Eleanor scolded, "it always results in mental & emotional depression & that feeling of 'utter futility' of all things is a result of weariness." Fortunately, Hick and Eleanor had arranged to rendezvous in Sacramento for a three-week vacation in July. "One thing I'm sure about," Eleanor wrote Hick as the trip neared, "our holiday should be very calm & must be in one place as long as possible & not hurry."

Eleanor was as overdue for privacy and relaxation as Hick. Her schedule had already become famously relentless. For instance, the single nineteen-hour, two-hundred-mile day during which Eleanor gave a dozen speeches, toured two farm-factory communities, met two babies named Eleanor, and paid a visit to a Civil War battle site.

From the outside, Eleanor looked indefatigable as ever. Inside, she'd had about all the attention and publicity she could stand. Her patience had been thinning for months. "I'd like to put my arms around you and shut out the world," she'd written back in April. "We must be careful this summer to keep it out of the papers when we are off together."

Hick couldn't have agreed more.

CHAPTER 58

started.

By the time Hick reached her hotel in Sacramento, word of the first lady's impending arrival had already leaked. Reporters and photographers congregated in the lobby, waiting for their chance to nab an Eleanor Roosevelt scoop. "I then proceeded to do the silliest thing I ever did in my life," Hick admitted. As if she'd somehow forgotten her own newspaper days, Hick took it into her head that she could outmaneuver the press.

The next day unfolded like the plot of a Hollywood caper, with the hotel staff, the state police, and the Secret Service all in cahoots. Hick took a cab to the airport to meet Eleanor's 6:45 a.m. flight, leaving the keys to her car—a brand-new gray Plymouth convertible she'd dubbed Stepchild—at the front desk on the sly.

Naturally, the press followed, trying to elbow their way to the first lady. Hick entreated the reporters to give Mrs. Roosevelt a break. Wouldn't they just allow her time enough to get a cup of coffee and freshen up a little before pressing her for an interview? Hick asked. They could trust her, she implied ever so innocently, because "I used to be a newspaperman myself." They took the bait, and settled down to wait in the hotel lobby.

Hick had lied, of course. She and Eleanor skedaddled out the rear of the hotel, where Stepchild awaited with a state trooper in the driver's seat. Her DC plates had been switched for California ones. Hick and Eleanor wedged themselves into the passenger side and Stepchild sped off.

Before they had time to congratulate themselves, a car crammed with reporters and photographers appeared in the rearview mirror.

Hick cursed her own stupidity. Her clumsy attempt at outwitting the press had only ratcheted the stakes up higher.

Once they'd broken free of the city limits, the trooper behind the wheel leaned on Hick's accelerator. She watched with mounting trepidation as the speedometer climbed to fifty miles per hour and kept right on going. A police car pulled in front of them, its lights flashing to clear the way. The thought of what was happening inside Stepchild's motor as the chain of vehicles barreled northeast gave Hick fits. The lightweight convertible wasn't built for such speeds. Surely a policeman of all people would know that. Still he accelerated, past sixty-five and then seventy.

The irony of it had to have smacked Hick square in the face. A year or so ago, she might have been among the reporters speeding toward the Sierra Nevada in hot pursuit of a story. Now here she was, trying to outrun them.

At seventy-seven miles per hour, Eleanor called off the chase.

The little convoy eased over onto a shady section of the road. Eleanor thanked the troopers for their daredevil efforts and sent them on their way. Camera shutters snapped as the reporters demanded to know where Mrs. Roosevelt was headed. The press had every reason to believe the first lady was en route to Reno, where her daughter had temporarily relocated to obtain a divorce.

Eleanor refused, as kindly and firmly as no one but Eleanor Roosevelt could refuse. "This is my vacation and I expect to be treated as any other tourist would be treated," she told them. "I'll answer any other questions you want to ask, if I can. But not that one."

Anyone else might have given in to their temper under such incessant prodding. Eleanor did precisely the opposite. She fished her knitting bag from the jumble of luggage and settled herself comfortably in the shade. As her needles clicked and flashed, she informed the reporters that she'd be perfectly happy to spend the whole day knitting by the roadside. They could insist all they wanted—she was not going to budge from that spot until they gave up the chase. Just like that, she'd bamboozled them in the politest manner possible. In fact, they all ended up having breakfast together at a nearby restaurant ("with Hick scowling," Eleanor recalled) before the reporters dutifully motored off.

She and Eleanor proceeded to Ellie Morse Dickinson's home in Colfax without further interruption.

⁓

From the outside, their visit with the Dickinsons had all the appearances of a ticking time bomb. Here was Hick, presenting the woman she was in love with to the woman who had jilted her for a man—a good-for-nothing man, as far as Hick was concerned. Add in the intimidating fact that Hick's new love was the first lady of the United States, and some kind of disaster seemed inevitable. Even Eleanor couldn't help dreading just a little the prospect of coming face to face with Ellie. Nevertheless, Eleanor was determined. "I know I've got to fit in gradually to your past, meet your friends & like them so there won't be closed doors between us later on," she told Hick.

One surprising fact averted disaster: Hick and Ellie still loved each other. The nature of their love had changed, but their friendship had not abated. That enduring affection made it possible for the unlikely foursome to enjoy mountainside picnics, followed by peaceful evenings of Eleanor reading poems aloud from Ellie's copy of *The Oxford Book of English Verse*. Hick and Ellie had never encountered anyone who could bring poetry to life like Eleanor.

Hick did have one bad moment, though it had nothing to do with Ellie and her husband, Roy. When Eleanor handed her the itinerary for their upcoming camping excursion in Yosemite, Hick's horrified gaze fell upon the sentence: "Miss Hickok will require a quiet, gentle horse, since she has not ridden for some time." That was a colossal understatement.

Eleanor expected her to ride the trails at the national park, when Hick hadn't sat in a saddle since she'd reluctantly clambered aboard a circus horse named Norman back in her Girl Cub Reporter days. "How could you do this to me?" Hick asked, her voice prickly with reproach.

Eleanor waved off Hick's concerns. All Hick needed, she said, was a pair of trousers and a shirt. As if a pair of blue jeans would magically transform her into an expert trail rider. Hick was dubious, but she bought the Levi's and the shirt.

⁘

The next leg of the trip brought them to Pyramid Lake, Nevada, and the ranch of Bill and Ella Dana. These friends of Anna Roosevelt welcomed Hick and Eleanor into their private oasis like family. The house and lake were at their disposal, as well as any horse in the barn, including Ella's special pet, a palomino whose coat looked like it'd been spun from gold threads.

The Danas were so generous and genial, it was impossible not to like them. Everyone shared the housework so that they'd all have more time for leisure. Eleanor washed the dishes (poorly, Hick noticed), and Hick dried them.

Hick tried like the dickens to shy away from the horseback riding, but Eleanor insisted—Hick *had* to practice. Otherwise she'd be as sorry as she was sore when they hit the trails at Yosemite. Hick acquiesced.

Out of the pasture came a big gray horse named Old Blue. Nobody rode him much anymore; he'd done his work and earned the right to graze and stand drowsing in the sunshine for the rest of his days.

With help from a ranch hand and a box to stand on, Hick got herself positioned upon the towering old creature and took the reins. She listened politely as Bill Dana instructed her how to kick the horse to keep him going, then let Bill and Eleanor ride ahead. Speed was the last thing Hick wanted from Old Blue. If he preferred to amble while the others trotted and cantered, that'd be fine and dandy. However, Hick also didn't want to go tumbling off, as she had back in Dakota when she'd commanded a contrary mare to "whoa!" So when Old Blue started stumbling, Hick hollered up to Bill and Eleanor that something was wrong with her horse.

Bill circled back to see what was the matter. One look at Old Blue, and Bill's laugher echoed through the hills. "Hick, your damned horse is asleep!" he guffawed, struggling for enough breath to speak. "Kick him! Kick him hard! You have to, to keep him awake!"

Old Blue had not prepared her one bit for Yosemite.

CHAPTER 59

A WHITE-KNUCKLE DRIVE THROUGH THE SIERRA NEVADA KICKED off Hick and Eleanor's Yosemite excursion. At times the car motored along above the clouds, weaving between the sort of escarpments that gave the Saturday-matinee cliff-hangers their names.

Five rangers, seven horses, and five pack animals greeted them upon their arrival at the national park. The heap of gear and guides and animals looked to Hick like it'd be enough to sustain Teddy Roosevelt's famous yearlong African safari. Only then did Hick learn that their destination was higher yet up the mountains, accessible solely on horseback.

The path didn't just meander side to side, but up and down as well. Going up wasn't so bad. Coming down was something else altogether. Some of the grades were so steep that Hick couldn't see the next step—from her perch in the saddle it looked as though her horse had no choice but to plummet into thin air. Up ahead, Eleanor and two of the rangers rode blithely forward, actually enjoying themselves.

The thought that the national park rangers would not knowingly put the president's wife in danger placated Hick a little. With that in mind, Hick soon became so engrossed by the intelligence of her horse that her fears faded from her consciousness. The small brown mare seemed to think as a human would, surveying the trail and carefully considering her strategy before she tackled a sharp downhill slope. Anytime the trail gave her enough space to do it, the horse eased the ceaseless pull of gravity by zigzagging from one side of the path to the other. If the trail was too narrow for that, she paused to carefully paw the dust from the rocks, making sure that her footing was solid before chancing a step.

Two and a half hours later, Hick and Eleanor emerged from the trees. The shore of Lower Young Lake spread out before them, with a snow-drifted white granite mountainside as a backdrop. The vista was so pristine, so vividly colored and artistically composed, they might have been stepping into a painting instead of a living landscape. There wasn't another soul within miles. This—all of it—was their campsite.

The rangers pitched a tent for them, but after the first night Hick and Eleanor only used it to change in and out of their pajamas. They spread their sleeping bags along the shore and fell asleep beneath a sky so saturated with stars that the silver light seemed to rain down on them.

Each morning Eleanor plunged into the icy lake for a swim. Hick tried it once, and only once. The frigid water stole the breath from her lungs even after she'd shivered her way back to shore. In fact, Hick "more or less panted" the whole time, Eleanor noticed. All her years of smoking made the simple task of breathing at an altitude of nearly ten thousand feet into a workout for Hick. So while Eleanor hiked, striding across the mountaintops until even the chief ranger was purple-faced with exertion, Hick followed on her thoughtful little brown mare.

The activities weren't exactly to Hick's taste, but the time with Eleanor in a wide-open space miles and miles from the demands of the first lady's family, her work, and the public more than made up for that.

When the time came to reluctantly fold up the tents and break camp, the only way out was the same way they'd come in: on horseback. The route into the Yosemite Valley included fording a small river. A sandbar ran through it, and the horses knew how to steer their way through the water without sinking into the drop-offs. All the riders had to do was lean back and hand over the task of navigation to their mounts.

Hick did as she was told, loosing the reins to let her mare find her own way. Eleanor and the rangers had made it across when, without warning, Hick's horse lunged to the left and rolled gleefully into the deeper water. No one had remembered to warn Hick that her faithful mare rarely passed up a chance to plunge into cool water for a swim.

Hick never did know how she did it, but somehow she detached herself from the saddle and plopped seat-first onto the sandbar, dousing herself to the chin in the process. Hick's embarrassment could have made the river boil. There she was again—"Fatty," the girl from South Dakota who couldn't do anything in the saddle but make a fool of herself. But Hick didn't raise a fuss. She let the apologetic rangers hoist her out of the water and back into the saddle and finished the ride, sopping wet. Private embarrassment, she could handle with good grace. The intrusions that came butting in when they visited the public areas of the park turned out to be another matter.

～

Once she and Eleanor descended into less secluded territory, their Yosemite idyll began to sour. No reporters hounded them within the park's gates, but the tourists drove Hick crazier than the mosquitoes. "We were never alone at all—they just followed us everywhere," she groused.

There wasn't a thing they could do without being followed, watched, and photographed. On a path to the Lower Yosemite Falls, Hick happened across the tamest chipmunks she'd ever seen. She crouched down and offered a handful of breadcrumbs. One of them hopped up onto her wrist and proceeded to pick out the best-looking morsels. Hick was entranced. All her life the company of animals had offered her a level of companionship and trust that most of human society withheld. Watching a chipmunk eat from her palm with the pert dignity of a diplomat at a White House dinner had Hick awash in pure delight.

Until she heard the cameras clicking, that is. She turned to find tourists snapping photos as though her backside were some kind of natural wonder. Hick made a scene. Knowing Hick, she probably blistered the air with some of her favorite expletives. Eleanor, who rarely let profanity cross her lips, got stuck tugging a spluttering Hick away.

Things didn't go much better during their visit to the Mariposa Grove. The majesty of those giant sequoias awed Hick. Never in her life had she been in the presence of anything so ancient and sublime. "I felt almost prayerful," she remembered, "and above all, I wanted to be quiet." But the tourists' guides yammered out a constant stream of statistics—how tall, how thick, how old. Hick didn't care about any of that. Statistics couldn't tell you how it felt to stand there, dwarfed by living things that had quite possibly existed in the days when Cleopatra, Julius Caesar, and Jesus of Nazareth walked the earth.

And then a guide made the mistake of informing the group that the largest of the giant sequoias towering over them had been named after General William Tecumseh Sherman of the Civil War. Hick's barely contained irritation blew. To name such a venerable and enduring living thing after something so insignificant as a person stuck Hick as not only "positively sacrilegious," but the height of indignity. "And I said so, right out loud." Once again, an embarrassed Eleanor had to deal with the fallout.

Interference stalked them at dinner at the grand Ahwahnee Hotel, too. The very first night, as Hick and Eleanor settled in at their table overlooking the Sierra Nevada, in walked Secretary of the Interior Harold Ickes.

Hick's blood just about halted in her veins at the sight of him. This was worse luck than a whole flock of tourists and their cameras. Secretary Ickes had a reputation as a "blunt and peppery" man, and Hick had harangued him freely in her FERA reports for using big industry and heavy machinery to get critical infrastructure projects done fast. The idea of deliberately employing only a handful of people to operate bulldozers when the dignity of hundreds of unemployed men could be salvaged by hiring them to wield shovels and picks had galled Hick at every turn. "It took [FERA] longer to build a road," she conceded, "but, so far as I could see, it was just as good a road as Mr. Ickes' road."

To Hick's horror, Ickes joined them for dinner. Hick half expected the secretary to wag his finger in her face. Anytime the conversation drifted perilously close to the touchy topic of unemployment, she girded herself for the moment when his agreeable front would drop. It never did. They ate their dinner, then went out to the terrace to continue chatting.

Hick was almost willing to breathe a sigh of relief by then—until Eleanor was called away. Hick's guard shot right back up. Without Eleanor as a buffer, the secretary had the perfect chance to berate Hick up one side and down the other. A long and terrible moment passed. The secretary puffed at his cigar as Hick tried not to die of anticipation.

"I've been reading your reports," Secretary Ickes announced without preamble. Hick steeled herself for an onslaught. "Interestin'," he added. And that was that. Not another word passed between them on the subject.

CHAPTER 60

HICK HAD HIGH HOPES FOR THEIR NEXT STOP. SHE ADORED San Francisco. Here was her chance to take on the role of tour guide and introduce Eleanor to everything she loved about the city.

Their arrival at the small and inconspicuous hotel she'd chosen flustered the management at first (Hick hadn't told them who would be accompanying her), but no one made a commotion. The staff of the Worth Hotel discreetly parked Hick's car in a garage, and sent flowers to their room in silent acknowledgment of the first lady's presence.

That night she and Eleanor dined in a little French café Hick had loved for years. Nothing fancy on the inside, except for the best French food Hick had found in the United States. No one batted an eye or fawned over them during the entire meal. As they walked to the cable car, Hick noticed a few people looking at Eleanor with "a puzzled expression," as if they'd seen that tall woman somewhere before but couldn't quite place her. Mostly, though, the bustling crowds were engrossed in their own Saturday-night excursions.

On Russian Hill, Hick pointed out the apartment she and Ellie had shared. She couldn't show Eleanor what it was like to sit in the living room and gaze out at the bay through the picture window, so they went to a little park with a similar view instead. Across the water, the dark bulk of Alcatraz Island floated "like a big, lighted battleship." The two of them sat talking until eleven o'clock, when they caught the cable car back down the hill. Not far from the hotel, the lights of a drugstore beckoned, and Hick and Eleanor treated themselves to ice cream sodas at the counter. Both of them agreed it had been "a perfect evening."

Half a block from their hotel, the frenzied manager of the Worth intercepted them. Word of Mrs. Roosevelt's presence had leaked, he confessed. "I didn't tell anyone," Mr. Harter promised. "I didn't think you'd want to be bothered—if you had, you wouldn't have come to my hotel." Reporters were clogging his lobby even as they spoke. Hick immediately pinned her suspicions on the bellboy.

Eleanor shook her head as she and Hick made straight for the elevator. "No interviews," she said. "I'm still on my 'off the record' vacation."

A larger mob awaited them the next morning. "Really, I couldn't pose for any pictures," Eleanor apologized. "I haven't, you know, all across the country." The more they insisted, the thinner her politeness stretched. "No please. No. No interviews. If you please!" Hick "plucked" at Eleanor's sleeve, one reporter noticed, and the two women began to twine their way through the crowd. The throng followed them to their breakfast table at the Clift Hotel.

A photographer squatted down on the other side of the table as they ate, snapping exposure after exposure. Every crackling *whoosh* and flare of white light from the igniting flash powder stirred up Hick's age-old fear of bright flashes and sudden noises. It also filled the room with billows of smoke. The resulting photographs captured Hick hunched over her toast and coffee, looking very much as though she were trying to smash the camera through sheer force of will.

Hick and Eleanor tried to sneak out the back, but of course another photographer found them and another pan of flash powder popped in their faces. "You won't mind if I don't talk to you anymore?" Eleanor said to him, as if it were a suggestion. "You may follow us, but I wish you wouldn't."

Naturally, the reporters and photographers attached themselves like leeches, drawing more curiosity seekers. Herds of onlookers trailed them to Fisherman's Wharf, to Sausalito, and finally to dinner at the Fairmont Hotel. The endless attention was a horror to Hick. Bad enough that the entire city of San Francisco was trampling all over their vacation, but did they have to scrutinize her, too? The reporters' descriptions were as unflattering as the photographs—"the plump, ruddy, and hatless Lorena Hickok," one article said, calling her "guardian in chief to the First Lady," as if she were a bulldog or a hired grunt.

The next day only got worse. Nothing but dashing and elbowing from one place to another. Even Eleanor's patience was getting rubbed raw.

"Please, please," she begged, shouldering her way back into the Worth's small lobby. "No interviews at this time. I really haven't anything to say. I'm just here as a private citizen, trying to see your lovely city." Piles of notes, orchids, and gardenias had accumulated in their absence.

That night, she and Hick gave up and decided to leave the city a day early. The public and the press were not going to let them enjoy anything. With the exception of that first lovely evening, it had been "a pretty dreadful time," Hick remembered.

A final parting gesture awaited. When the valet fetched Hick's car from the garage the next morning, the inside was bare, right down to the glove compartment. Souvenir hunters had stripped it clean. Hick's cigarette lighter was gone. No maps, sunglasses, suntan lotion, or chocolate bars remained. Even her St. Christopher medal had been pilfered. Hick marveled that the plunderers had done her the courtesy of leaving her hubcaps in place.

Thoroughly exasperated, Hick put the top down and pointed the car toward Portland.

⁕

Unscheduled side trips to Muir Woods and Crater Lake helped salvage the end of their holiday. Standing alone in a grove of 250-foot-tall redwoods, Hick and Eleanor reveled in the silent awe they'd craved at Yosemite. After being hounded and harried at every turn, they found it soothing to be dwarfed by the immense majesty of nature.

The moment they checked into their hotel in Bend, Oregon, all the hullabaloo started right back up again. By the time they'd changed out of their dusty clothes and fixed their windblown hair to go downstairs for dinner, the whole town knew that the president's wife had arrived. Eleanor wearily declined the manager's request to greet the people who were so eager to see her. She and Hick managed to have a pleasant supper together, watching the last pink rays of sun slide over the snowcapped peaks of the Cascade Range.

Entering the lobby after dinner was like stepping backward into San Francisco. A brand-new swarm of people crammed the space, with the mayor of Bend front and center.

Eleanor handed Hick the key to their room without a word. "I was apt not to behave well under such circumstances, as she had learned," Hick wryly recalled. "And I went upstairs and left her."

Sharing Eleanor with her husband and children was one thing. Sharing her with the entire country was quite another. After all Hick's waiting, counting down the days until they could simply be together, this was her reward.

Half an hour passed before Eleanor came in, slamming the door behind her. That sound was more shocking than the cameras' flashes. Eleanor Roosevelt simply did not relinquish her self-control. Ever. That night, though, Hick saw the red spots on Eleanor's cheeks that signaled her exasperation.

"Franklin said I'd never get away with it, and he was right!" she huffed, and then deflated with a sigh. "From now on I shall travel as I'm supposed to travel, as the President's wife, and try to do what is expected of me."

⁂

Even with all the mishaps and thwarted plans, Hick treasured her time with Eleanor and mourned when it was over. "I hope you are having a happy, restful time at camp—a happier, more peaceful time than you had with me," she wrote after they'd parted in Oregon. Now that the frustrations were behind her, Hick could apologize for the moments when her temper had gotten the better of her. "Oh, I'm bad, my dear, but I love you so, at times life becomes just one long, dreary ache for you."

CHAPTER 61

WITNESSING THE DEVASTATION OF THE GREAT DEPRESSION CONtinued to yank Hick's mood under like a riptide as the months rolled by. Almost every night she sat down to write to Eleanor, filling pages of hotel stationery with Americans' misery and her own frustration and despair. Hick needed a safe place to unburden herself, to turn her feelings loose so they'd stop running circles in her head.

Eleanor tried to offer advice, but the way she dealt with melancholy didn't do Hick a bit of good. Eleanor's solution was to shuck it off as quickly as possible, usually by throwing herself into work, "for it is just a passing mood with me & it never tears me the way it does you!" Hick couldn't do that. Her work *was* the problem.

"Oh, I know you all think this is temperamental with me—that it's impossible for me to see anything but the dark side," Hick wrote. "But, God, I wish some of the rest of you had to listen to this, day in and day out. I bet you'd all feel gloomy, too."

Eleanor had frustrations of her own to wrangle during the spring of 1935. "I've been ready to chew everyone's head off!" she exclaimed to Hick after a careless remark from FDR's mother stung Eleanor badly enough to ignite a rare eruption of fury. The day after that, FDR's callous treatment of their son James set Eleanor off all over again. The anger she felt toward her husband seemed to reach all the way back into the deepest wound of her marriage, shocking Hick with its intensity. Hick's replies have not survived, but Eleanor's side of the conversation indicates that Hick wondered if Eleanor might go so far as to leave FDR.

"I'm sorry I worried you so much," Eleanor answered. "I know I've got to stick." Divorce was out of the question. "I never tell F.D.R. how I feel," she explained. "I blow off to you but never to F!"

～

Delving so far into their emotions put both women in a philosophical mood. They contemplated and debated the meaning of happiness and its relationship to love—a conversation that helps illuminate the inner workings of their own relationship.

"One thing I differ with you on," Eleanor wrote, "the thing which counts in the long run is never any one person's happiness." She believed in the greater good firmly enough to punctuate her conviction with an uncharacteristic expletive. "If you pick up happiness by the way well & good but remember always you are damned unimportant!"

Eleanor's view of love went hand in hand with happiness. Happiness came from love given and received, she believed. "Over the years the type of love felt on either side may change but if the fundamental love is there, I believe in the end the relationship adjusts to something deep & satisfying to both people." Their own relationship proved it, she told Hick. "I know you often have a feeling for me which for one reason or another I may not return in kind but I feel I love you just the same." For Eleanor, all love was both unique and equal. "One cannot compare them." Yet for Hick, Eleanor's love was itself without comparison.

The rockiest moments in their relationship would always trace their roots back to this intrinsic difference in outlook. Eleanor, who'd been brought up in material plenty, had learned as a child to gather up scraps of contentment until they made a meal large enough to sustain her. Hick's reaction to the material and emotional wants of her early years was just the opposite. She'd lived through enough scarcity to last a lifetime, thank you very much, and found little fulfillment in settling for crumbs. Especially when it came to Eleanor's affection, Hick craved a banquet.

⪻⪼

Over the course of 1935 and 1936, Hick continued to ping-pong from one side of the country to the other, conducting FERA investigations in California, Nevada, Utah, Wyoming, Kansas, Maryland, Indiana, Illinois, and New Jersey.

Hick's boundless empathy pricked her conscience at every turn. The fact that she couldn't reach into her own pocket and help the folks she met just about maddened her to tears on occasion. People needed help, and they couldn't afford to wait for the wheels of the government to turn. "I feel a good deal as though I were shouting into space!" she lamented to Eleanor.

Hick rarely got the chance to see the impact her reports were making on people's lives. Only occasionally did Mr. Hopkins ask her to revisit a community to learn if anything had changed for the better. Her boss didn't realize just how badly Hick needed to see those improvements for herself. She needed more opportunities to feel the value of her work, and to replenish the strength it took to continue chronicling the nation's woes.

⪻⪼

A white mongrel dog named Missy finally put Hick over the edge. At a homestead in Red House, West Virginia, a farmer's son took Hick out to the barn to show off a new litter of puppies. Right away Hick could see that the pups weren't thriving.

"We ain't got nothin' to feed her," the boy admitted, "and so she ain't got no milk for the pups."

Small boys and dogs could tug at Hick's heart like little else. She wanted to cry, and she wanted to *do* something for that dog.

When Hick told the director of the state department of public welfare about Missy as they drove away, he stomped so hard on the brakes that Hick lurched dangerously toward the windshield.

"By God, I'll send that kid a case of dog food!" he exclaimed. Hick volunteered to pay half.

"Pardon me, dear, but—GOD DAMN these government bureaucracies," Hick railed in her letter to Eleanor that night. "It seems to me that every day I work for the government I get madder." Submitting her reports and hoping they would eventually generate change didn't satisfy her anymore. Hick wanted to take action, to see it happen before her eyes. "We may have the best intentions in the world, but, God, how inefficient we are."

～

Hick witnessed the most galling example of that inefficiency in Iron Mountain, a small town in Michigan's Upper Peninsula. On the bitter December day she visited, a crew of two hundred men were working on a road that wound up the side of a hill, where a park would eventually be built. Most of them were grouped around bonfires for warmth. A few men scratched at the earth with picks and shovels without much enthusiasm.

"Lady, I can't push 'em," the foreman told her. It wasn't just the cold, which bit down to the bone on that hilltop. "I want to show you something," the foreman said, and led her among the crew.

One worker after another opened up his basket or pail to show what he had for dinner. Onions. Again and again, nothing but raw onions. And those who had onions were the lucky ones. Thirty of them had no dinner pails at all. There was nothing at home to put into one.

Thanks to some kind of bureaucratic snafu, the men's weekly relief checks were late—deplorably, unforgivably late. They had not received a penny for over three weeks. And still they worked, "plodding along," Hick wrote Eleanor that night, "patient, dumb."

"I had had a big hot breakfast," Hick remembered. "I was very warmly dressed. They didn't, any of them, have overcoats and their clothes were ragged." Here she was, a representative of FDR's administration, watching these half-starved men try to build a road they intended to call the Franklin D. Roosevelt Parkway.

Hick couldn't stand it. She and Mr. Sweet, the Works Progress Administration official who'd driven her up to the worksite, raised a ruckus the instant they set foot in the disbursing office. Paychecks would go out that afternoon and the next morning, they were promised.

Even that didn't satisfy Hick. Tomorrow's paychecks wouldn't do those cold, hungry men any good today.

"Aw, hell, let's send some food out there," Mr. Sweet said.

"You bet," Hick replied. They offered up $10 between them, and Mr. Sweet threatened their deliveryman not to tell a soul where the coffee and sandwiches had come from.

Two days later Hick dug into her pocket once again, consequences be damned. This time it was a tiny old widow, "a wisp of a thing," not so different from Hick's own Aunt Ella. "Such a dark, dismal, ramshackle little hole," Hick marveled of her house, "but, oh, so clean!" The glass chimneys on her kerosene lamps sparkled, and her bath towel was both ironed and starched. The lady lived on $6.71 a month—or tried to. It didn't always stretch. When it didn't, she sometimes had to last as long as four days without food. Her eyes, Hick wrote Eleanor, were "almost unbearably wistful" as she bent over her supper of milk and dry bread.

All evening, that woman's diminished existence haunted Hick. Finally, just before she got on the train that night, Hick peeled off a $5 bill and gave it to the relief administrator with instructions "to do something about Christmas for the old lady."

CHAPTER 62

ELEANOR TRIED HER BEST TO HELP HICK COPE, BUT THE THINGS that saw her through difficult times ran contrary to Hick's nature. Eleanor had schooled herself to muscle through the duties she dreaded. "I have lived so much of my life 'going thro' & being relieved when certain periods are over," she explained, "& yet I don't really mind."

Instead of raging or complaining, Eleanor burrowed within herself, expressing as little as possible until the offending emotion was smothered into submission. She called these still and silent fits of temper her Griselda moods. It wasn't a choice she made, but rather an unconscious reflex that baffled her as much as it maddened her friends and family. The difference between Eleanor and Griselda was so plain, everyone knew *something* was wrong, but Eleanor would not—could not—acknowledge her unhappiness, much less its cause. She just turned to stone.

Hick had no such defenses. She felt what she felt, and she minded every throbbing second of it.

"Darling, I wish I could give you emotional security," Eleanor told her, "but I guess that is one thing we have to get for ourselves!"

⁓

Fortunately, Eleanor was not Hick's only source of emotional sustenance. Hick's high school Latin teacher, Alicent Holt, was also keeping up an intimate correspondence with her former student.

Fifty-seven of Alicent Holt's letters to Hick survive, primarily spanning February through September of 1936. Just as in Eleanor's case, an unknown number of letters have been lost or destroyed, including the entirety of Hick's side of the conversation.

A playful mother-and-child dynamic colors Alicent's letters, though she was the older of the pair by only five years. She called Hick Rena, as she must have back in their Battle Creek days, and signed herself Alix. Alix doted on Hick, showering her with endearments like *cara mia* and *carissima* (Italian for "my dear" and "dearest") and refusing to allow Hick to berate herself. "You will please not call my dear child names," Alix chided in one letter. "She is neither selfish nor irresponsible, nor any of the other things you said about her—but my very dearest dear!" She also loved to baby Hick, so much so that Hick sometimes wriggled against it. They even had their own French saying, just as Hick and Eleanor did: *Toujours et toujours! Always and always!*

Hick trusted Alix enough to send Alix copies of her FERA reports. Judging by Alix's replies, Hick also must have written of the emotional wear and tear she experienced during her travels among the down-trodden. Here, Alix's kindness shone.

Alix, whose temperament was more similar to Hick's than Eleanor's, lingered with Hick over her woes. She understood about things like loneliness, and how it felt to see yourself as an irksome trial for others. Having known Hick as a teenager, Alix might also have had a more in-stinctual understanding of Hick's vulnerabilities. Her earliest surviving letter to Hick, in fact, broached that very topic. "When your letter was late this week, I hoped it was because you were merely busy, and not depressed, nor worried. I am sorry—very, very sorry—that you have been down in the depths again." Alix had no difficulty seeing why, either. "People naturally tell you their troubles, dear, for you seem strong and sure, at least on the surface," she wrote in another letter. "I judge all your friends repose their woes on your (seemingly) broad shoulders."

Although Alix's existing letters to Hick lack the passion of Eleanor's, Alix's deeply rooted tenderness is impossible to overlook. Without ques-tion, Alix and Hick loved each other. "If you were here," Alix wrote after

Hick had received some bad news, "I would smooth your hair and put your head on my shoulder and try to tell you how dear you are to me." Was theirs a romance? Or were the childless Alix and the motherless Hick building a kind of family together? No one can say for sure.

Just how much Alix understood about Hick's relationship with Eleanor and vice versa isn't clear, either. Eleanor clearly knew that Alix was one of Hick's dearest friends, for Hick freely mentioned letters and visits both to and from Alix in her correspondence with Eleanor. If Hick and Alix's closeness bothered Eleanor, she gave no sign of it.

Alix was not quite so blithe about Hick's affection toward Eleanor, however. A hint of jealousy surfaced after Alix met the first lady in March of 1936, when Alix apparently tried to probe Hick a little too deeply about Eleanor's place in Hick's heart. "Dear, I'm so sorry about my tactless and selfish questions," she wrote. "Truly, it bore no meaning except just what it said, and certainly I didn't intend to question your loyalty and your affection." Neither those touchy questions nor Hick's "gentle, forbearing" response to them have survived, but Alix's penitent tone leaves no room for doubt that she realized she'd overstepped her bounds.

Disappointed though she might have been, Alix valued Hick's friendship too much to insist upon being Hick's one and only. "Indeed I *do* need you—and more than 'a little'—and, dear, I'm truly glad that *you* need *me*," she wrote. "So, we will do all we can for each other, and be happy in this good friendship of ours—and we'll 'stay'—for keeps."

CHAPTER 63

ALICENT WAS A BALM, BUT HER DEVOTION COULD NOT CURE what ailed Hick's heart deep down. No one's love mattered as much to her as Eleanor's, but Eleanor's growing renown as a woman of action and principle, a woman who wielded her influence as first lady for the benefit of the social causes close to her heart, ate such great gouges into her schedule that Hick struggled to *feel* loved.

True to form, Eleanor was willing to be satisfied with very little time with Hick. "If you steal a day or two away here & there & two weeks in summer we'll be having more than our share of good times!" she declared with an enthusiasm Hick almost certainly didn't share. But if that was how it had to be, Hick was determined to make a feast out of each and every morsel—so determined that she sometimes undermined their pleasure.

After pinning her hopes for weeks or months on a holiday or a meal or even a chat with Eleanor, Hick was crushed if things didn't go perfectly. When she got frustrated, the way she had in Yosemite, she gave herself hell for tainting their precious hours with her own irritation.

None of this seemed to faze Eleanor. "I'm afraid you & I are always going to have times when we ache for each other & yet we are not always going to be happy when we are to-gether," she wrote. "Somehow we must find the things which we can do & do them so that what time we have to-gether is as happy as it can be in an imperfect world!"

~

No wonder, then, that *someday* had become a recurring theme in Eleanor's letters. "Someday," she'd said in 1934, "perhaps fate will be kind &

let us arrange a life more to our liking." Someday she would not be the president's wife anymore, and they would have all the time and privacy in the world to "lead a leisurely life . . . & do all the things we want to do." All they needed was patience.

When that magical someday came, the two of them could travel to the places they'd visited by themselves and enjoy them together. "That's a tall order," Eleanor said, "for I have a great many places abroad I want to show you." Someday, Eleanor mused, they would settle down together in a little place all their own. "I've thought of you so much & wished you could be happy here but you and I will have to build a cabin together somewhere else sometime!" The mere sight of a cunning piece of furniture could send her into flights of fancy, picturing how it would fit into their imaginary home.

～～

In 1936, that faraway someday receded further yet when FDR ran for reelection.

Hick found herself caught between her own desires and the greater good of the nation. On the one hand, there was Eleanor. If FDR lost, Hick and Eleanor could revel in privacy and bring their dreams to life.

But the thought of FDR being voted out of office, and what it would mean for the thousands of people she'd met over her two years with FERA, terrified Hick. "Oh, I know that, so far as your personal life is concerned—and that does matter to me, a very great deal—you'd probably be relieved. Things might be simpler, easier for you, as a person," she wrote to Eleanor that summer. "But—my dear, my dear, if he is defeated, what is going to happen to these people?" Compared to what she was seeing, "somehow, personal happiness doesn't seem to matter very much."

Hick was physically exhausted, and so discouraged that her ragged emotions often left her feeling shaky and unstable. "I'm holding on tight, trying to remember all the nice things I've had this Summer and all the beautiful places I've seen," she continued. "But I'm having a hard time to keep from getting panicky, just the same."

"I feel, as usual, completely objective & oh! Lord so indifferent!" Eleanor replied.

Eleanor's apathy unsettled Hick so much that she administered a rare scolding. "I'm wondering if you or I—or any other enlightened person really has any right to be as indifferent about the outcome of this election as you are," she wrote. "Oh, I know—you hate it all. The 'position.' And so do I when I'm with you. I can't even be polite about it. You can." If anyone knew how much Eleanor craved freedom, it was Hick. "All your personal inclinations would be to rejoice in defeat," she conceded. But, she admonished, it was almost impossible to understand the situation from Washington, DC, with all its "pomp and fuss and adulation."

Hick saw the possibility of FDR's defeat as "a terrible calamity for millions of people in this country. The kind of people *you,* of all people, are supposed to care about. The poor and the lowly. Forgive me if I have offended you."

Eleanor wasn't offended, only resigned. Her old habit of heading off disappointment by refusing to hope for anything she wanted had surfaced again. "I'm afraid my reasons for thinking I will probably never be much happier than I am are different than yours dear," she replied. "You think some one thing could make you happy I know it never does!" Happiness was elusive, unpredictable, Eleanor believed. There was no use in chasing after it, because the things you dreamed of didn't always satisfy in reality. Happiness came from within.

"I truly don't think that what I do or say makes much difference, someone else could do equally well what I do," Eleanor added. Hick was different, she insisted. "You have gifts & can really get somewhere."

Hick had a hard time believing that lately. Her own work felt futile. "I don't believe a soul except you ever reads my reports anymore."

CHAPTER 64

HICK'S WORK WITH FERA CAME TO AN END JUST AS FRANKLIN Roosevelt won reelection in the fall of 1936.

Every bit of her—mind, heart, and body—needed a break from travel and scenes of strife. "And yet—as I'm about to give it up—I realize what a fascinating job this has been," she told Eleanor.

For the umpteenth time in her life, Hick had to figure out what to do with herself. Her old dream of becoming a war correspondent had flared up again, thanks to an insurrection in Spain. "I wonder if that Spanish business *is* going to lead to a European war!" Hick wrote of the failed coup that was boiling over into a civil war. "Boy, if it happens, I'll be tempted to drop everything and go to New York and try to land a job!"

Eleanor had a tamer idea: the World's Fair. The mammoth international exposition, set to open in April 1939, had already begun construction in New York. Dozens of pavilions showcasing the culture and technology of nations around the globe were under way, along with a massive amusement park, restaurants, fountains, and commercial exhibits from a host of industries. In the meantime, the fair's publicity department needed to produce guidebooks, leaflets, brochures, advertisements, and other promotional materials that would convince people to come visit when the gates opened. Hick seemed like a natural choice to Eleanor. She was even willing to use her personal connections to put in a good word for Hick with the man in charge of it all, Grover Whalen.

Hick hemmed and hawed. She was also giving serious thought to writing a book about her journeys for FERA. After all, Harry Hopkins had said that her reports "would be the best history of the depression in future years." Hick met with Eleanor's literary agent and got enough encouragement to start sifting through her reports in search of "the color stuff about people. *Individuals*."

To help her refresh the details, Eleanor lent Hick the whole stockpile of letters Hick had written to her. Reading the ones from her FERA travels mortified Hick. "Most of them are *awful!*" she declared. Somehow, Hick had already managed to forget how much she'd written about herself. "Meanderings of a damned idiot living on her emotions," she bemoaned. "'Emoting' all over the place." Experiencing her letters as Eleanor had experienced them shone fresh light on just how precarious her state of mind had been for the past two years. "I'll try not to gag over these letters, dear," she promised. "But—oh God!"

Other letters, the earliest ones she'd written while she was still on the Associated Press payroll, steeped Hick in fond memories. "Dear, whatever may have happened since—whatever may happen in the future— I was certainly happy those days," she wrote Eleanor in December, "much happier, I believe, than many people ever are in their whole lives. You gave me that, and I'm deeply grateful." That whole year, she realized with the evidence spread before her, had been a rare and beautiful thing.

By now Hick and Eleanor's relationship had mellowed from a passionate, sparking blaze to a cozy hearth fire fed by tenderness and mutual understanding—the kind where each *I love you* carries with it the unspoken echo of the thousands that have gone before. But though the dazzle of the flames between her and Eleanor had dimmed, their fundamental warmth remained, impossible to extinguish. "You have been swell to me these last four years," Hick added, "and I love you—now and always."

※

In the end, Hick pursued the most practical option. She submitted a résumé to the president of the New York World's Fair, hoping to work "in publicity or in some sort of 'contact' job" that would give her the opportunity to travel to small towns and "sell the fair" directly to potential ticket buyers.

Hick got the job. Or rather, she got hired, but not for the type of position she wanted. She ended up in an office in the Empire State Building, with a secretary and an influx of mail that would have made anyone but Eleanor Roosevelt herself cower. After she'd sized the place up and submitted "a kind of a survey of the whole organization," much as she'd done for Harry Hopkins at FERA, Mr. Whalen put her in charge of promoting the fair to children.

Graphs, conferences, school boards, and printers dominated Hick's waking hours. Once, she'd interviewed accused murderers and shipwreck survivors. Now she was running a poster contest for schoolkids.

Hick felt like an impostor. As far as she was concerned, she was "absolutely unfit, by temperament, by experience, or by any other standard, to be an executive." She'd told Mr. Whalen outright that she wasn't interested in such a position. Yet there she was, behind a desk.

The effort of "trying to control my impatience, my natural irascibility, my loathing of friction and disorder" sometimes made her grit her teeth until they ached. "I want to be interested in my job, dammit, and do it as well as I possibly can," she told Eleanor. "But much of the time that only means being irritated."

Hick evidently complained to her former editor back in Minneapolis, "Old Man" Tom Dillon. Dillon saw Hick's trouble plainly: "ingrained newspaper habits." Outside of the newsroom, he warned, she'd better not judge the quantity or quality of her writing by newspaper standards. Journalism's breakneck pace and stringent demand for facts didn't apply to other kinds of writing. "That's a fact you should repeat to yourself," he advised, "until you cease to quarrel with it."

Anyone who could make something as insignificant as a kids' dogsled derby sound like the Minneapolis sporting event of the year would be able to write about the fair, he insisted—once it actually existed, anyway. Until then it was all going to feel like a lot of imaginary nonsense. "You know this as well as I," Dillon said. "In fact, you'd be writing almost an identical letter to a friend in this position. Why don't you write a letter to yourself?"

But even the Old Man's encouragement couldn't convince her. Hick couldn't imagine that the shortcomings staring her in the face weren't painfully obvious to the rest of the office. "It's the whispering that goes on about me and those sidelong glances that are so hard to bear," she wrote to Eleanor in an echo of the days when Hick's schoolmates gossiped about her father and the housekeeper.

"I doubt if the whisperings & side long glances are all that you imagine," Eleanor soothed, "but when one is sensitive one suffers doubly." Sensitivity like Hick's largely baffled Eleanor. She didn't care in the least what people thought about her. "No matter what you do," Eleanor's aunt had taught her, "some people will criticize you." Eleanor used her aunt's simple test to banish disapproval from her consciousness: "If you are entirely sure that you would not be ashamed to explain your action to someone whom you loved and who loved you," she had counseled, there was no need to fear anyone's criticism.

Letting off steam was also something Eleanor rarely indulged in. If something was wrong, she wanted to fix it, and there was no fixing this. Hick just had to stick it out.

※

Hick's most reliable solace was a weekend cottage on the southern shore of Long Island, part of a larger estate near Mastic owned by the very same Bill and Ella Dana that Hick and Eleanor had visited in Nevada in 1934.

She and a pal from her Minneapolis newspaper days, Howard Haycraft, teamed up to split the rent. From the outside they seemed an unlikely pair (Howard was twelve years younger than Hick and built like a toothpick), but he enjoyed football and opera as much as Hick did. He also had a passion for detective stories, and a knack for keeping on Hick's good side. Their arguments about politics, Hick reported to Eleanor, were "perfectly joyous."

Every weekend the office and all its nuisances melted away the moment Hick and Prinz arrived at their own little wedge of beachfront. The woods, the ocean, and especially the garden soothed Hick's soul.

Ella Dana thought the place should be called "Hicky's Hole." Hick treated herself to stationery that read *Little House on Top of Dana Place*.

At the Little House, Hick swapped her tailored suits and blouses for a bathing suit and white sailor pants (or checkered shirts, corduroy breeches, and hunting boots, depending on the season). In the fall, she and Prinz took long rambles through the woods, then came back to read or listen to the radio beside the fire with Howard. Summer meant swimming and beachcombing during the day, followed by singing in harmony under the moon on Saturday nights. Most of the time, Hick got herself "so sunburned that I looked like a half-skinned tomato," and she didn't care one bit. There was always sand in the beds, and what cooking she and Howard could do on the little kerosene stove wasn't exactly gourmet. Sometimes, if the tide ran high, the outhouse threatened to float away.

Hick loved the place and every rustic, beautiful thing about it. The way her spirits lifted and her mind settled at the Little House made the eighty-one-mile drive from New York City worth enduring. "This place has the most marvelous effect on me," Hick wrote Eleanor. "I feel so much happier here and so much more contented than anywhere else."

Prinz loved it, too. After five days in a kennel, he delighted in splashing through the waves, sniffing out the trails of foxes and deer, and luxuriating before one of the three fireplaces. Best of all, Hick was at his side all day long. "Poor Prinz—how he hates Monday mornings," Hick wrote to Eleanor. "His tail was so far between his legs when I put him in his kennel this morning that the tip of it was practically tickling his chin!"

True bliss for Hick lay in her garden. "You get so fond of things you plant and raise yourself," she explained to Eleanor. "It's like a child, I suppose, or a dog—the more you do for it, the more you love it!" And for all that she'd loathed the drudgery of housework as a teenager, Hick found that puttering about her own place was different. Fussing over the little tasks that kept her haven neat and pretty was nothing like scrubbing other people's floors in exchange for food and shelter.

Hick treated a steady stream of friends and coworkers to weekends at the Little House. Some of the women found it a bit too rustic, while others returned again and again. One night on the beach, Howard and his fraternity brothers unofficially inducted Hick into Kappa Sigma, anointing her head with gin.

That place, more than any other, came to mean *home* to Hick.

CHAPTER 65

"I GET SO GOD DAMNED TIRED OF HEARING PEOPLE SAY, 'IF I had your connections . . . ,'" Hick complained. Everyone at the World's Fair knew about her friendship with Eleanor. Hick might have been back at the Associated Press, the way her coworkers constantly brought up her link to the White House.

Hick, however, wondered if her connection was thinning. The intensity had continued to fade incrementally from their correspondence, shifting its tone from ardent love letters to convivial chats. That in itself was no cause for alarm. Love evolves, after all, and no particular incident appears to have dampened the warmth between them.

Nevertheless, doubts came creeping into Hick's heart during the summer of 1937. She tried not to mind all the time Eleanor was spending in Hyde Park, converting her Val-Kill furniture factory into a cottage retreat of her own, tried to read Eleanor's letters about Ping-Pong games and poolside luncheons with good humor, but it didn't help. She did mind being left out, and pretending otherwise only dragged her feelings lower. Even long visits from Ellie Morse Dickinson and Alicent Holt did her no good. Hick wasn't just too tired to entertain anyone—she couldn't even summon the energy to care about the people she loved most. "I'm all dried up inside, I guess," she wrote Eleanor.

Deep down, of course, Eleanor was the person Hick wanted. Eleanor, who seemed to be having herself a jolly summer, had still never even come to see Hick's Little House. Hick had long ago dismissed the idea of compromising by inviting Eleanor's secretary along to Long Island so that Eleanor wouldn't fall behind on her mail. "When you are together you can never forget for more than fifteen minutes at a time your darned jobs," Hick told Eleanor. "That shuts me out, and I get bored and miserable." Those "half-time" vacations were no good.

From where Hick stood, it looked as if she were the one doing most of the trying. And if Eleanor wasn't making an effort, Hick figured, what else could it mean except that Eleanor didn't really want to see her?

It wasn't until September that they managed to straighten things out.

"I'm glad we had a chance to talk, last night and this morning, dear," Hick wrote after a long-awaited weekend together. "Not that we got anywhere much. But somehow we seemed closer. It's this drifting—or seeming to drift—apart that bothers me so."

Eleanor was grateful for Hick's honesty, for she had not perceived any extra distance between them. "I didn't realize you felt we were drifting apart," she replied. "I just take it for granted that it can't happen!" Knowing how busy she was in Hyde Park, knowing how neglected Hick felt when other people and duties took up the majority of Eleanor's time, Eleanor saw "no use in you coming here to be miserable." The lack of invitations was meant to spare Hick extra misery, not cause more of it. That was pure Eleanor. Always, she placed absolute trust in the under-lying bedrock of their friendship.

Hick, on the other hand, had grown up not only being beaten, but getting scolded for the beatings—as if she were responsible for the abuse. The blows and recriminations pounded a two-pronged message into Hick's psyche that lingered for the rest of her life: *You are unlovable, and it is your own fault.* "How you can even like me is beyond me," she'd once admitted to Eleanor. "I think that is one reason why I have had such bad times. I can't for the life of me understand why a person like you would care anything for a person like me, and therefore it has been hard for me to have any confidence in you." For Hick, assuming that anyone who loved her was somehow mistaken—and would eventually realize their mistake and flee—was easier than altering her fundamental beliefs about herself.

Even after their heart-to-heart, it was hard for Hick to wrap her head around the possibility that she had misread the situation all summer long. "Perhaps I was right. I may have been wrong. I don't know any of the answers," she wrote. "I guess the only thing I really do know is that I love you, with all my heart. And that it's a Hell of a lot harder to see you unhappy or listless than to be unhappy myself. All of which sounds like perfect twaddle."

༺༻

It was true, though—Eleanor and Prinz and the Little House were about the only things Hick could manage to care about anymore. By 1938, she showed every sign of being mired in a depression. Life wearied her, left her with a sense of futility. "It isn't worth the bother. I'll get through this mess and then there will be another—maybe worse," she lamented to Eleanor. "Well—I'll try not to talk about it any more. You shouldn't be such a good listener."

But Hick couldn't get through it. Sitting behind that desk at the World's Fair headquarters all day made her fairly itch. Twenty-two years she'd spent out in the world, talking to people about things that really mattered. The fair didn't matter one iota to Hick in the grand scheme of things. The work didn't engage her mind or her emotions—aside from irritation, anyway. All the fair meant to her was a regular paycheck. "This bores me to extinction," she wrote Eleanor.

CHAPTER 66

WHILE HICK LANGUISHED FIVE DAYS A WEEK, ELEANOR THRIVED.
But if Hick ever resented it, not a peep of envy leaked out. She celebrated
Eleanor's every success, even when those successes mirrored the career
Hick missed so desperately.

Eleanor's relationship with the press had burgeoned. Not only had
her regular press conferences turned her into "God's gift to newspaper
women," but Eleanor was also becoming something of a journalist
herself, with articles appearing in prominent national magazines like
McCall's, Ladies Home Companion, and *Reader's Digest.* Eleanor sent
Hick drafts of her articles and Hick read them, offering nothing but encouragement, praise, and advice to strengthen them.

On December 31, 1935, Eleanor had launched her own newspaper
career with a syndicated column called My Day. Six days a week for the
next twenty-six years, readers across the country contemplated and debated the first lady's daily thoughts. Even Republican papers carried Eleanor's column. "Those who read it and like it ought not to be deprived
of it," one right-leaning Massachusetts newspaper declared. "Those who
do read it now and then for the sheer joy of getting good and mad at it—
and there are those who do—likewise ought not to be deprived of it."
Often the column was no more than a mundane account of Eleanor's
comings and goings, but as time went by, My Day became a place where
Eleanor could air her forward-thinking views on controversial social issues like segregation, which FDR steered clear of for fear of alienating
voters and legislators alike.

It's hard to imagine that some small fragment of Hick wasn't galled
by the success of My Day. Here was Eleanor, making a name for herself

in the papers with apparent ease. Not only that, but the whole idea of Eleanor chronicling her daily life had evolved from her diary-style letters to Hick. Yet Hick read and collected Eleanor's columns avidly, offering congratulations anytime she thought Eleanor expressed her views especially well.

Nor did Hick express any dismay when Eleanor published the first volume of her autobiography, *This Is My Story*. In fact, she cheered it every step of the way, reading in installments as Eleanor wrote. "I think I'm prouder of 'This Is My Story' than I am of anything else you've ever done," Hick told her when she read the finished copy. The final chapter, which had put Eleanor in "a hellish state of mind" as she'd tried to write it, turned out to be Hick's favorite.

In spite of the wounds her parents, aunts, uncles, and grandmother had inflicted upon her childhood, in that chapter Eleanor found the grace to lay her pain aside, painting them not as villains, but as very human people, each of whom deserved recognition for contributing something valuable to her character.

Although she intended her book "to give as truthful a picture as possible of a human being," she glided silently past Franklin's affair. Those who knew the closely guarded truth, like Hick, could sense hints here and there, as well as a quiet acknowledgment of the debt Eleanor owed to the people who had seen her through her worst moments.

Eleanor's generosity toward those who'd hurt her touched Hick. She knew how mightily Eleanor had struggled with herself as she searched for a way to be truthful without reopening her most private scars. "Somehow it brings back and very near the you that I love," Hick wrote to Eleanor after finishing the book. "A very big person."

※

The emotions Eleanor had evoked put Hick in a mood to reminisce about their own relationship's ups and downs. "There is nothing mean or petty or selfish about you," she praised Eleanor. "You are one of the most forgiving people I know—even though you'd never admit it." Yes, Hick conceded, there were times when Eleanor had hurt her, like the 1933 Christmas blunder that had stung Hick to the bone. "But you have also done a thousand things to make life easier and happier for me. And I'm deeply grateful. So don't, please, feel—as you seem to feel sometimes— that you have failed in your relationship with me."

For Hick, Eleanor's love was the furthest thing from a failure. It was and would forever be the brightest light in her life. "As I look back over these last five years—I don't think anyone ever tried harder to make another human being happy and contented than you have tried with me," Hick reassured her.

Hick's praise meant the world to Eleanor, especially in light of the pain she'd inadvertently caused. "Of course dear, I never meant to hurt you in any way but that is no excuse for having done it. It won't help you any but I'll never do to anyone else what I did to you. I'm pulling myself back in all my contacts now," she explained. Better to take a step away, she reasoned, than to risk repeating that mistake with someone else. "Such cruelty & stupidity is unpardonable when you reach my age. Heaven knows I hope in some small & unimportant ways I have made life a little easier for you but that doesn't compensate."

For all that Eleanor could absolve others for wounding her, the ability to forgive herself for hurting Hick remained just out of reach.

CHAPTER 67

Eleanor came to spend an entire week at the Little House.

"I'll be awfully glad to see you, dear, *when*ever and *how*ever you come, and if you like it here one tenth as much as I do, I'll be satisfied," Hick wrote.

Eleanor did love it. Until her deluge of mail caught up with her, she could relax and read for pleasure. She still had her column to turn in every day, which she typed on Hick's sunporch. To her great gratification, that was the week she finally mastered the art of keeping her "inept fingers" from inserting spaces into every word.

"This is a beautiful place which gives you a feeling of remoteness, for you are buried deep in the woods," Eleanor told her readers. "They are dark and mysterious at dusk and when the sun is filtering through they make you think of Robin Hood."

It was just the kind of vacation they both needed—beautiful weather, saturated with peace and quiet. Not even a telephone to disturb them. "We hear only the drowsy insects hum and the usual farm noises, punctuated now and then by the dog's bark as an occasional car goes by," Eleanor wrote.

Only the mosquitoes intruded on their time together, clouds of them thick enough to pester even the stalwart Eleanor into voicing a mild complaint or two. The mosquitoes were a trifling distraction, though. Hick's small paradise was a picture-perfect setting for all the simple things they most loved to do in each other's company. They read aloud to each other, as they always did on their private retreats, and motored through the countryside to see a craft fair that featured the work of Arthurdale residents. In the chest-deep water of the bay, Hick and her neighbors taught Eleanor to rake clams, which they ate at a picnic supper on Fire Island. All of it lulled Eleanor into setting aside the problems of the world for once to simply knit and "vegetate."

It was "a grand week," Eleanor wrote Hick when it was all over. "The chief thing however was my great pleasure in seeing you in the place where you are happy."

Thankfully Eleanor had seen it when she did, for in a matter of weeks, Hick's narrow stretch of Long Island's shore would never be quite the same again.

<hr />

On September 21, a hurricane fast and furious enough to earn the nickname the "Long Island Express" came barreling toward New England. The storm struck Bellport, just a few miles west of the Little House, at 2:45 p.m., lashing the coast with gusts up to 186 miles per hour. Hick listened to the same winds shrieking through New York City's streets at 60 to 70 miles per hour and wondered what was happening to her precious haven.

By the next afternoon, Hick was practically writhing with worry. No word had come from the Dana estate. Phone and electrical lines all over New England were down—twenty thousand miles' worth of them. The instant her boss turned her loose from work, Hick leapt into her car and rocketed toward Mastic.

Dark had just fallen when Hick finally reached the entrance to the Dana place. Branches brushed the roof of her car as she steered through the ravaged woods. After the length of a football field, Hick had to grind the car to a stop. A fallen pine lay splayed across the entire road.

"I can hardly describe to you my sensations," she wrote to Eleanor of that moment. Hick had no flashlight. An eerie quiet as dense as the darkness thoroughly unnerved her. Even the insects were silent. "And that tree lying there, the branches so green and fresh," she remembered. "It was like looking at a person who had just died."

Frantic and stymied, Hick doubled back to the post office in Mastic in search of news. Nobody there had gotten word of anyone killed or hurt at the Dana place. But what about Prinz in his kennel, Hick wondered, and the property itself? No one knew.

Hick had no choice but to climb, stumble, and crawl across the mile and a half of debris that barred the way to the Dana house. "I had never seen anything like it in my whole life before," she told Eleanor. "And I went through quite a few disasters of one sort and another, both in the newspaper business and while I was with the Government." Fallen trees blocked the route so densely, it was more like climbing the rungs of a giant ladder than traversing a road. "That trip in, in the darkness, with the growing realization of what had happened, was all horror," Hick recalled afterward.

Over an hour and a half into the ordeal, Hick saw a light and heard a motor. It was the Danas' generator.

The Danas had been unspeakably lucky. Upward of four hundred people died that day and tens of thousands of homes were destroyed, but the couple's lives and property were spared. Even Prinz was cozied up safely in the Danas' kitchen after a nightmarish escape. He owed his life to a neighbor who had swum down to the kennel in search of him. Chained to his run, Prinz had paddled and paddled to keep his head above the rising water. By the time his rescuer arrived, Prinz was clinging to the kennel door, howling for help with the last of his strength.

The Little House suffered a flooded cellar and a single broken window. Hick's generator and pump looked like her only financial casualties.

All the luck and relief in the world couldn't stop Hick from grieving for the trees, though. The Dana property looked like a brand-new housing development, with the buildings sticking up out of the landscape like misplaced teeth. "The beauty of the place is just about ruined," Hick mourned to Eleanor. "And it will never be the same again—not in our time."

⚬⚬⚬

On top of reconciling herself to the hurricane's destruction, Hick also had to face the fact that she'd gotten herself into one doozy of a financial mess. By January of 1939, she could ignore it no longer. Rent on the apartment in the city and the Little House made up the bulk of it, with her car running a close third. Prinz's kennel and dog walkers ran up a respectable bill. Then there were her maid's wages. Her teeth were giving her hell, too, and the dentist needed hundreds of dollars to fix them. She even owed Eleanor $100.

Hick finally had to admit that her salary wasn't enough to keep paying them all. Something would have to go.

The Little House, Prinz, and the car Hick deemed absolutely essential. "Now of course it would be perfectly reasonable to say that it was silly—insane, really—for a woman of 45, almost 46, without a cent in the world except her salary, without any very promising prospects for a well paid job in the future, etc, etc, to try to hang on to these three luxuries," she wrote Eleanor. But logic had no part in this equation. Without Prinz's companionship and the soul-soothing magic of the Little House, daily life held no appeal whatsoever.

"Living—just going on living—doesn't mean a God damned thing to me, dear," Hick confessed. "I'm being perfectly honest when I say I'll be relieved when it's over, provided the actual ending isn't too painful. You are always horrified when I say that I wish it had happened when I had that automobile accident out in Arizona. But I still do." She wasn't capable of ending her life herself, Hick quickly assured Eleanor, any more than she was capable of giving up the Little House. Plain old cowardice would keep her from that, along with the knowledge that her death would shatter those she loved—especially Ellie, with her enormous, fragile heart. Hick would not, could not, put Ellie or anyone else she cherished through that.

"I'll wiggle through somehow," she vowed.

Hick made a plan. She tallied everything up and charted a way to rein in her spending and pay off her bills in monthly increments. If it meant subletting her apartment, doing the cleaning and laundry she'd abhorred since her teenage years, and accepting another loan from Eleanor, so be it.

CHAPTER 68

THE 1939 NEW YORK WORLD'S FAIR OPENED ON A SUNSHINY April day full of fanfare, and still Hick had no use for it. Opening day "was a nightmare for me, more or less," she told Eleanor. To Hick, the whole grand and glorious 1,216-acre exhibition amounted to no more than crowds pushing and shoving—"the most disorganized mess I ever saw." Every time a kid wound up lost, Hick got a call in her office to go deal with it. And with every lost kid and frantic parent, her real work piled up higher. "This job is getting to be simply impossible," she vented. "My days are beyond description."

Mostly, the fair's opening was another reminder of the fact that before long, she'd need to find a new job. Exhibitions like this were always temporary, lasting a season or two, and every day that passed helped convince Hick that she was getting too old to expect anyone to hire her.

～

More than her finances were dragging Hick down. Her sister Ruby was in a fix, too. Ruby's husband had lost his job. Hick didn't like Ruby much, but worries over their situation still bedeviled Hick so much that she reluctantly asked Eleanor to help her brother-in-law get a job. Then Bill Dana died unexpectedly, leaving his widow in a precarious state both emotionally and financially. Suddenly, Hick couldn't be sure she'd be welcome at the Little House even if she did manage to get her rent payments back on track.

As if in protest of all her work and worry, her joints took to aching when it rained, sometimes with such insistence that it cost her a whole string of sick days.

World news darkened her outlook, too. In Germany, Hitler and his Nazi Party were making the political situation in Europe ever more volatile. He'd "gobbled up" Czechoslovakia in March and then headed for Lithuania, a situation Hick, who wanted the United States to keep its nose out of any foreign entanglements that might lead to war, found increasingly ominous.

And then at the end of May, Hick wrecked her car. The insurance payment for a new one added another $175 to the pile of debt she was already trying so hard to shrink.

The accident just about put Hick over the edge. Even writing to Eleanor demanded more of her than she could muster. "I don't know—somehow, when I feel so low as I have this week, I just don't want to talk to anyone," she apologized. "Just want to be let alone, I guess. Which is a hell of a thing to do to you when you are so sweet to me."

Eleanor wanted to do whatever lay in her power to ease Hick's woes. "You know, of course, that I'm so thankful you weren't hurt in the car smash-up that I just hate to have you cast down!" she'd written. "Please wipe that feeling of a debt off your books & out of your consciousness," she offered. Money meant nothing to her compared to Hick's well-being.

Hick couldn't bring herself to accept. This whole mess was her own doing, and she'd been taking care of herself since she was fourteen. She didn't want help. Or maybe it's more accurate to say that Hick didn't want to *need* help. She'd already fended off Eleanor's offer to rub out $100 of her debt as a birthday gift.

Hick couldn't begin to repay Eleanor for all the material comforts Eleanor already showered on her—to say nothing of Bluette, Stepchild, and the job at FERA. Eleanor also had fresh flowers from the White House delivered to Hick's desk throughout the winter, and always sent a Thanksgiving turkey from Arthurdale. Then there were the custom-made suits and hand-me-down dresses far finer than Hick could afford on her own, and all sorts of thoughtful treats, like baskets of grapefruit direct from Texas, for no reason whatsoever. If Hick so much as mentioned that she was thinking of replacing her raincoat, Eleanor would swoop in and buy one for her.

It was just another way of saying *I love you* as far as Eleanor was concerned, but the one-way flow of presents and favors left Hick feeling uneven somehow, as though she were forever taking more—at least when it came to tangible things—than she could give. Hick craved balance in a way Eleanor did not. As much as Hick appreciated the little luxuries and the care and thought that Eleanor put into them, what Hick wanted most was Eleanor's time and presence. And that was the one thing Eleanor Roosevelt could not give freely.

⁓

While Hick juggled everyday irritations like insurance policies and inept coworkers, Eleanor had her hands more than full preparing for a state visit from King George VI and Queen Elizabeth of England. After all the official engagements in Washington, the Roosevelts planned to treat the royal couple to an overnight at Hyde Park, culminating in a very American picnic complete with hot dogs.

Hick had no intention of attending. "As for me—the only reason in God's world why I'd ever go up there would be to see you, my dear, you and no one else," she wrote in response to Eleanor's invitation. "As you know, even as you devil me about it, I'd run a mile to get away from meeting their Royal Highnesses."

Hick always harbored a lopsided attitude toward Eleanor's celebrity. The fact that Eleanor was the president's wife didn't faze Hick in the least. It was the dignitaries who rubbed elbows with the first lady who intimidated her. Friends who saw Hick at the White House came away amused by her manners there. "Most of the time Hick looks like a royal Bengal tiger that has been mussed up a bit," as Bill Dana said.

~~~

Three months later, when the Nazi army invaded Poland, and the United Kingdom promptly declared war on Germany, Hick found herself flooded with sympathy for the royal couple. Hearing the news that Europe was once again at war, only twenty-one years after the War to End All Wars, she and Howard wept together before their radio.

CHAPTER 69

THE WORLD'S FAIR WAS NEVER PERMANENT. HICK KNEW THAT, but as her time there dwindled, the thought of finding herself yet another job seemed more daunting than it ever had. "I don't worry particularly about holding a job, once I get it," she told Eleanor in November of 1939. "Getting them is what's tough."

Hick's coworkers were concerned, too. On New Year's Eve, one of her greatest allies at the fair, the executive vice president, pulled her into his office for a chat that ended up feeling more like a scolding to Hick.

"You never do anything except sit around that apartment evenings and go off to the country with that damned dog of yours," he said. She had to make connections, he lectured—go to cocktail parties and *talk* to people. How else would she ever find a job after the fair closed down for good? Worst of all, he accused Hick of sitting back and letting Mrs. Roosevelt find a job for her.

"It was bad because it brought to the surface things that I've been secretly worrying about for weeks and weeks," Hick admitted to Eleanor.

The thought of cocktail parties and teas filled Hick with plain old revulsion—"those huge, God-awful affairs where you stand around on tired feet, your back aching, trying to manage a cigaret, a cup of tea, a sandwich, and your gloves, plus a paper napkin, and shout inanities at the top of your lungs over the noise at someone you never saw before and never expect to see again." It was all so superficial, so at odds with the kind of conversations Hick truly valued.

Hick knew perfectly well how to talk with people. Between her newspaper days and her investigations for FERA, she'd made two solid careers out of gathering people's stories. "But, oh, Lord, how does one go about using people and selling oneself?" she lamented.

~≈~

Hick need not have worried. At the first lady's urging, the publicity director of the Democratic Party hired her just as the World's Fair was petering out. He tasked Hick with traveling through the heart of the country to see what people thought of FDR and the Democrats. Specifically, did it look like FDR could possibly win another election?

Since 1796, presidents had followed the example set by George Washington of voluntarily stepping down after serving two terms of office. That was merely a time-honored tradition. No law yet barred a president from seeking a third term. With Europe at war, the Democratic Party was especially loath to imagine a Republican at the helm of the government at such a critical time in world politics. If it meant breaking a 144-year-old tradition to stay in power, the Democrats were willing to risk it and back FDR for an unprecedented third term. Hick's job was to figure out whether the liberal-leaning voters' loyalty lay with the Democratic Party in general, or with the man in the Oval Office in particular.

It was as if the door of a cage had been thrown open. Finally, Hick was back out in the world, talking to people about something that actually mattered. It was like working for Harry Hopkins and FERA all over again, minus the soul-crushing poverty and hopelessness. "I was so bitterly unhappy and emotionally unstable all through that period, or most of it," Hick admitted. But this—this was different.

"It's a strenuous job alright, but don't feel sorry for me," she wrote Eleanor. For the first time since her AP days, Hick felt content and fulfilled. "This way of living, completely wrapped up in my work, is something I've been hungry for—for a long time."

The job also came with an invitation from Eleanor to bunk at the

White House again. "I'd like to very much, because it gives me at least a few glimpses of you," Hick replied carefully. "But I'm NOT going to hang around the place the way I used to," she vowed. "That business of moping around the W.H.—never again." Fixing all her happiness on how much time she got to spend with Eleanor only led to heartache. "Now you are either laughing like Hell or a little bit hurt inside," Hick added. "I hope—and believe—you are laughing, dear."

"I roared over your letter," Eleanor wrote back. "You would be foolish to stay here if you had to live here," she acknowledged, "but if you are just in & out I'm sure it's quite ok for you." Hick accepted the invitation and moved into a corner sitting room adjoining the Lincoln Bedroom at the east end of the hall—the mirror twin to Eleanor's small bedroom at the west end.

Within just a few weeks on the job, Hick could see plainly that FDR was indeed the Democrats' best chance at holding the White House for another four years. Great swaths of the country wanted the United States to keep its nose firmly out of foreign entanglements, and as the Nazi army continued to infest Europe, Franklin Roosevelt was the man they trusted to steer the country clear of the conflict.

Women, Hick believed, might well be the key to winning the 1940 election. "Whoever can convince the women of this country that he will keep us out of war can win their votes—almost solidly, regardless of party lines and how their husbands vote," she reported in February. If ever women's votes were going to swing one way, this would be the year, and the issue, she predicted. "It's the first really definite thing I've encountered."

The sentiments about a third Roosevelt term were just as definitive. "The President is going to be under terrific pressure to run again," Hick reported to Eleanor in March. In Ohio, for instance, everyone Hick encountered told her that the only chance the Democrats had to carry the state in November was with FDR on the ticket. "Darling, I'm sorry, but it's all Third-Term," she repeated just days later.

Eleanor, who'd dared to look forward to quietly slipping out of the public eye at long last, deflated at the news. "I groan," she replied.

~~~

Come November, Franklin Delano Roosevelt did indeed win that election.

"And so how do you feel, now that it's over?" Hick wrote Eleanor after the votes were counted. Since 1932, Eleanor had consoled herself with the implicit assumption that the White House gates would swing open in eight years, returning her to the real world. Instead, they had slammed shut. "I hope, dear, that you won't mind these next four years too much," Hick soothed.

"No, I don't look forward to the next four years," Eleanor wrote back, "for I will probably be too old for a new job at the end & I dread getting accustomed to 4 more years of easy living but perhaps I can keep from being too dependent on it."

"I don't know anyone in the world who works harder than you do!" Hick exclaimed in reply. As for Eleanor's age, Hick considered that irrelevant. "If you were going to get old, you'd be showing signs of it by now," she insisted. "As a matter of fact, I'd never have believed it possible for a woman to develop after 50 as you have in these last six years. My God, you've learned to do, surpassingly well, two of the most difficult things in the world—to write and to speak."

Eleanor might have been insensible to her own significance, but Hick certainly was not. She could foresee what Eleanor was still incapable of recognizing—that Eleanor was already forging a permanent place for herself in the world that no one else could fill. As long as Eleanor Roosevelt wanted to devote her energy to the betterment of others, there would always be good, satisfying work for her to do.

Hick also mentioned that she'd been reading the recent biography of Eleanor by newspaperwoman Ruby Black. The chapters on the first lady's White House career, she admitted, were better than anything she herself could hope to write about Eleanor. "My trouble, I suspect, is that I've been so much more interested in the *person* than in the *personage,*" Hick reflected. "I resented the personage and fought for years an anguished and losing fight against the development of the *person* into the *personage.*"

That last sentence was pure nonsense. Somehow Hick had remained oblivious to her own impact on Eleanor's life, while simultaneously fostering and enabling Eleanor's growth into a public figure. "I still prefer the *person,*" Hick confided, "but I admire and respect the *personage* with all my heart!"

CHAPTER 70

HICK'S JOB ENDED WITH THE CAMPAIGN. FORTUNATELY, THE Democratic National Committee needed a new leader for its women's division, and Eleanor saw Hick, with her political savvy and skill with the written word, as a natural fit for the position. Eleanor's friend and fellow Democratic activist Molly Dewson wasn't so sure. The two of them had devoted years to nurturing the women's division into an organization of real backbone, and Molly wanted to be certain Hick was willing to give her all in areas that weren't so well suited to her personality.

"[Molly] worries as to whether you will have patience to answer endless letters constructively and help endless 'little' women to move up one step at a time in [the] organization," Eleanor wrote to Hick. "Also meet the endless visitors & stand constant entertaining & hounding me to entertain those I should."

Hick swore up, down, and sideways that this job would be different from her stint at the fair. "I honestly don't think you and Molly have any real cause for worry about my getting bored, restless, or impatient with the ladies," she wrote. "What neither of you seems to realize is how desperate my plight is—and how little I can afford to be choosy! I am 47 years old, my dear, and have reached an age where it is very, very difficult for a woman to get a job." A salary that would let her keep the Little House meant "the difference between getting some joy out of life and just merely working to keep on existing," she told Eleanor.

Hick also offered a solution—hire a "front woman to make most of the speeches and pose for photographs," so that Hick could put her own formidable skills to use behind the scenes. The Democratic National Committee ended up doing just that, pairing her up with Mrs. Gladys

Tillett, an attractive, pedigreed society lady known for her eloquence before a crowd.

"Oh, damn it—what have I ever done to deserve a friend like you!" Hick wrote Eleanor shortly after learning she was about to become the executive secretary of the women's division. "I love you more than I love anyone else in the world except Prinz."

⁓

Hick called her colleagues the "Democratic 'WIMMIN,'" and though they aggravated her now and again with "the usual quarrels and jealousies," the Democratic National Committee was no frivolous fantasyland. Daily, Hick was expected to lend a hand in strengthening the muscle of the Democratic Party, from the national level down to the smallest local precinct. The biggest job facing women Democrats was to ensure that ordinary people understood and supported the defenses that were being built up in response to Hitler's aggression.

Hick's workload included attending meetings of Democratic women, recruiting volunteers, organizing conventions, attending receptions, facilitating invitations to White House teas, writing speeches, and composing articles for the committee's newsletter, the *Democratic Digest*. "I love the way all these women consult me about their speeches," she wrote Eleanor, "—I who know less about speaking than my dog Prinz does!" Hick also had a knack for orchestrating fundraising luncheons to maximize donations—who would make an irresistible hostess, which hoity-toity club should serve as the venue, and which well-to-do, Democratic-leaning society ladies "would get a big kick out of being invited."

Watching Mrs. Tillett speak to the press awakened the newspaperwoman in Hick and gave her fits. "The trouble is that, when I sit in on those interviews, I want to ask the questions and answer them, too!" she told Eleanor. Watching inexperienced reporters "flounder about" pushed her patience to its limits.

～⁓

All the while, Hick kept her address—1600 Pennsylvania Avenue—as quiet as she could. Eleanor had invited her to stay on in her little southwest-corner nook during the week to keep her expenses as manageable as possible. There was no concealing her connection with the Roosevelts, but if her coworkers knew Hick lived just down the hall from the president—near enough to place a letter on FDR's desk—she'd be inundated with requests for impossible favors. Hiding that fact complicated Hick's life in all kinds of ways, but it also enabled her to pay the rent on her Long Island weekend haven, a trade she considered well worth the charade. "I doubt if anyone ever lived at the White House less conspicuously than I did," Hick wrote years afterward with some satisfaction.

Anytime someone offered to give Hick a lift home, she told them she lived at the Mayflower Hotel on Connecticut Avenue. Hick would say her goodbyes in the lobby and make for the elevator, sidling into a phone booth to wait until the coast was clear so she could hail a cab to the White House.

Accompanying delegations from the women's division to Eleanor's table for political teas and luncheons was just as tricky. Hick enlisted the White House doormen and ushers in her ruse, ensuring that they always greeted her as though she were a formal guest. "In residence today? Or just a visitor?" one of them murmured as he took her coat one day.

Eleanor played along, too. "Why, how nice to see you!" she would exclaim, as if they hadn't breakfasted together upstairs that very morning.

Evenings, Hick always poked her head into Eleanor's sitting room to say good night. If Eleanor was out, or occupied with visitors, Hick could usually count on her appearing later, when she'd perch at the foot of Hick's bed and talk for a little while.

Living at Washington's most exclusive address also meant occasionally sharing a roof with the exiled royals of Europe. Crown Princess Märtha of Norway and Crown Princess Juliana of the Netherlands had fled the invading Nazi army to avoid capture, and both found temporary shelter at the White House.

Hick mostly tried to melt into the woodwork, drawing as little attention to herself as possible. Now and then she did get herself into a pickle, such as the summer day she took a notion to do some sunbathing up on the roof. She donned a bathing suit and basked until noon. As she passed the skylight on her way back to her room, Hick heard an unusual number of voices wafting up from below. As far as Hick knew, Eleanor and the president were in Hyde Park for the weekend. Peering down to the second floor stopped her cold.

The secretary of state and his undersecretary were there, along with a passel of navy men decked out in dress uniform. Their gold braiding glittered up at her like a taunt. Hick hadn't thought to bring a bathrobe, and she could not sneak back to her room without scurrying through the hallway where the men were gathered. Hick was stranded until she caught the notice of a servant, who smuggled up some clothes.

The only nagging problem with the whole arrangement was Prinz. Hick missed him all week long, and hated the weekends when she couldn't make it back to Long Island to see him and the Little House. "Poor old fellow—he is failing rapidly—and I find it terribly hard to face," she told Eleanor. "Thirteen years. We've been through so much together—and he's always been the same loving companion, no matter what happened."

CHAPTER 71

ON SUNDAY, DECEMBER 7, 1941, HICK WAS SITTING IN THE LIT-
tle House with her weekend guests, lingering over a late lunch, when
the neighbors came running. "Turn on your radio!" they shouted. "The
damned old [Japanese] are bombing the Hawaiian Islands!"

The news, the sheer enormity of it, left the entire country reeling.
The Empire of Japan had executed a surprise strike on the United States
naval base at Pearl Harbor, killing or wounding more than thirty-five
hundred servicemen and civilians in just over an hour. The next day,
Congress declared war on Imperial Japan; before the week was over,
Nazi Germany and Fascist Italy both declared war on the United States.

On Monday, Hick headed straight for the White House, where she
promptly landed in bed with the flu. Eleanor and the president were both
away, but precautions for their safety were already in progress. "I never
saw a place change so abruptly as the White House did after Pearl Harbor," Hick remembered. "The house was chill and silent, as though it
had died." Even Fala, the Roosevelts' newest little Scottish terrier, kept
quiet.

Outside, though, the sound of a steam shovel digging a bomb shelter
in the front lawn kept Hick company all day and into the night. Machine
guns soon appeared on the office roof outside her window, each manned
by a pair of soldiers. Blackout curtains, designed to keep enemy bomber
pilots from spotting any telltale light from the ground, blotted out every
one of the mansion's enormous windows.

The mood inside the White House changed as well.

"In the early days when the President laughed you could hear him all over the house—a great, ringing, musical laugh, so joyous and infectious that you involuntarily laughed, too," Hick recalled. The sound of that laugh had become rarer and rarer as Hitler's grip on Europe tightened.

Now that the United States had joined the fight, Hick decided that the kindest thing she could do for FDR was to make sure she didn't add a single ounce to the load the president was already carrying. "I could be the one person he did not have to talk to, did not have to 'give out' to," as she put it. If the big machine gun outside her window was manned, Hick knew the president was in residence, and she slunk around as stealthily as a spy.

"Franklin says he never knows when you are in the house!" Eleanor told her, pleasing Hick immensely.

~

Midafternoon on December 23, the night of her private Christmas celebration with Eleanor, Hick got a call from Tommy. "Mrs. Roosevelt would like you to get home early if you can," Eleanor's secretary said. "By 6 if possible. The president has some plans which will involve her in the evening."

Hick did as she was told. Since the 1933 Christmas fiasco, when an interruption had nearly ruined the whole holiday for both of them, the yearly ritual of dining quietly together had become something sacred to Hick and Eleanor. Hick could hardly fathom what might cause Eleanor to alter their long-standing tradition.

A puzzling sight greeted Hick as she approached her bedroom. A tea service sat untouched at the west end of the hall. There were liquor bottles and ice as well—a rarity at the White House.

"Hick, I'm afraid our party is ruined," a ruffled Eleanor declared when she entered Hick's room a few minutes later. "Winston Churchill is arriving. Franklin has gone to meet him—they'll be here any minute."

"I stared at her for a second," Hick remembered, "then threw back my head and howled with laughter." What else but a surprise visit from the prime minister of England could be important enough to upend their Christmas plans?

Hick's amusement was not contagious. Thoroughly annoyed, Eleanor hustled Hick into her sitting room. Hick snapped on the radio and caught the announcement of Churchill's arrival at almost the same moment the prime minister's voice sounded in the hallway.

～～

Eleanor, who had been scarce before, became scarcer still. Now more than ever, FDR needed her to travel to places he could not because of both his workload and his disability.

In the autumn of 1942, Eleanor visited England, staying in Buckingham Palace as the guest of the king and queen. Trips like these left Hick stewing in a mix of pride and anxiety. "They told me in the usher's office a few minutes ago that you had arrived safely," she wrote after learning that Eleanor's plane had touched down on British soil. "So I feel very much relieved, although no public announcement has been made. I hated to go to sleep thinking of you and Tommy away out over the Atlantic somewhere last night—and didn't until late."

This was the closest Hick came to experiencing what so many other women were going through. Husbands, sons, fathers, sweethearts, and brothers across the nation were enlisting in droves. "My staff has been on the verge of tears for three days," she told Eleanor in that same letter. Now Hick's beloved was far across the sea, in a country being pummeled by the Nazis' blitzkrieg campaign. Even the palace itself had suffered a hit from a Luftwaffe bomber, which meant Eleanor was potentially in the line of fire.

"Darling, I hope you are comfortable and contented tonight—in Buckingham Palace—and not too weary," Hick wrote. "Goodnight, dearest. Do a good job. I know you will!"

Hick was right. The newspaper stories Hick read about Eleanor's British tour confirmed that she was fulfilling her duties as only Eleanor Roosevelt could. "I'm awfully happy about it and so proud of you," Hick told her.

❧

April of 1943 took Eleanor to the Gila River War Relocation Center in Arizona, a concentration camp where over thirteen thousand Japanese Americans were imprisoned for the duration of the war, thanks to FDR's infamous Executive Order 9066. The order had wrested residents and citizens of Japanese descent from their West Coast homes and warehoused them in government-guarded barracks, for fear they might sabotage the war effort.

"I hope you will get a lot out of your trip and that it won't be too tough," Hick said. "Don't take any chances that you don't have to take, will you?"

Though Eleanor wasn't in a combat zone, and though she publicly opposed Executive Order 9066, the trip was not without risks. What would thousands of unjustly imprisoned people do at the sight of the first lady—the wife of the man whose racist paranoia had cost them their freedom?

To Hick's relief, the visit passed without incident. But Eleanor still wasn't done. Just a few months later, she embarked on a grueling twenty-five-thousand-mile tour of the Pacific front, visiting Australia, New Zealand, Hawaii, Guadalcanal, New Guinea, and fifteen other islands.

This was by far the most nerve-racking of Eleanor's absences Hick would endure. For the first time, she was traveling through an active combat zone. The combination of security precautions and her relentless schedule meant that Hick received only five letters during the five weeks Eleanor was away.

"I didn't take the trip for pleasure & I haven't enjoyed it," Eleanor confided to Hick midway through her journey, but that was of no consequence. Anything she could do to cheer the recruits even for a moment justified her own small sacrifices and inconveniences as she zigzagged from island to island, visiting thousands upon thousands of men in endless mess halls and hospital wards. "My love to you dear. I think of you & your love for travel & wonder if you would have enjoyed it."

⁓

At 2:00 p.m. on September 24, Hick's office phone rang. "I talked to her," Tommy's joyful voice cried out when Hick picked up. "I talked to her. I was crying, and I couldn't think of anything to say." Eleanor was back on American soil, safe at last. Hick wasn't one to cry, but the wash of relief nearly wrung tears out of her, too.

CHAPTER 72

MEANWHILE, HICK SOLDIERED ON FOR THE GOOD OF THE DEMO-
cratic Party.

When talk of disbanding the women's division for financial reasons surfaced in 1942, Hick blew her top. After all the pontificating men had done about how vital women were to the war effort—now this? When women were the very people charged with "hold[ing] the party together"?

"I get so mad I can hardly contain myself," she sounded off to Eleanor. The way men ran things, the party ended up burdened with "a lot of damned nonsense and outworn ideas." Hick wanted to see a Democratic Party motivated by ideals and convictions, "not the kind the men believe in, the kind that makes the word 'politics' stink in the nostrils of the public."

Peace in the world *was* possible, Hick insisted. It had to happen. "And if our system is to survive, we've got to be at least as sincere in working for our political ideas as the Nazis are!"

❧

Working toward these ideals deepened Hick's broad network of friends, providing her with unexpected support and affection in Eleanor's frequent absences.

One was Mary Norton, a New Jersey congresswoman known as "Fighting Mary." In many ways, Hick and Mary were two of a kind—both of them warm, bold, and fierce champions of underdogs. Mary had lost her only child under tragic circumstances, and Hick had never truly felt mothered. The two of them linked up as naturally as a pair of magnets.

"I love her, too," Hick told Eleanor, "—more than I ever loved my own mother." It turned out that Hick and Mary shared a birthday, and starting with Hick's fiftieth, they celebrated with a joint party hosted by Eleanor.

⁓

Another was Marion Harron, the only woman on the bench of the United States Tax Court. How exactly they met is lost to history, but intentionally or unintentionally, Hick captured Marion's heart, and a romance bloomed.

Like Hick, Marion had found success in a traditionally male field: law. She'd been breaking new ground for women since her college days back in San Francisco, where she'd integrated the prestigious all-male national debate society, Delta Sigma Rho, and made headlines such as "Girls Assert Right to Yell Just Like Boys."

The only remnants of Marion and Hick's romance are letters—207 of them, all written by Marion. None of Hick's replies are known to exist. Nevertheless, there can be no mistaking the significance of the relationship, for Marion presents herself quite clearly as a woman in love.

She began her letters to Hick with endearments like "Dearest Madame Queene" and "Hello my little Piccallilli." From the beginning, she showed a determination to make Hick appreciate herself, to see herself as her many friends did. "You don't have a faint notion of how magnificent a person you are," Marion wrote in 1942. "But I shall try to introduce you to yourself and make your heart feel very proud."

At a time when Hick was battling to make ends meet, Marion encouraged Hick to remember that her true worth lay in her intangible, unquantifiable qualities. "People are greatly in your debt," she wrote, "—the score on your side is very high in your devotion to people, in your friendships to people, in your capacity to give to others companionship and comfort and warmth." To Marion, it was completely obvious that Hick lived "more for others than for yourself."

Marion herself was a meditative sort of person who'd muse about the personalities of flowers—how the fat-cheeked daffodils jerked their heads to say good morning, while the poppies bowed low. Like Alicent Holt, Marion had patience for Hick when her mood faltered.

Hick's everlasting frustration with Eleanor—the perpetual competition for even a sliver of the first lady's time—had no parallel in her relationship with Marion. Hick didn't have to share Marion with anyone but Marion's elderly mother. Though Marion traveled from state to state to hear cases, when she was in Washington, the two of them could indulge in dinners, long drives, and late-night chats to their hearts' content, without the added bother of dodging newspaper reporters or photographers. The White House guards soon came to know Marion well enough to wave her through the gate without asking for identification.

Most of all, Marion opened her life and her home to Hick in a way Eleanor simply could not. Marion was as devoted to Hick as a puppy, and she knew it. "My name is Butch—or Bo—and I always come when you whistle—lie flat when you say 'flat'—and lick your cheek as well and as much as either of those four-footed furry dogs," she wrote to Hick.

Marion also shared Hick's love of gardening, and took special pleasure in bringing new plants to the Little House, a place she referred to as "an acre of peace." Marion dug right in as Eleanor never had, and never would. She planted nasturtiums and pansies, transplanted violets from the woods, and bought lilacs and peonies. "You see, a day will come, I feel all too certain, when I may not be in your garden myself—and I will be pleased if a peony or two is there in my place," she told Hick.

Perhaps because she sensed that her place in Hick's life was temporary, Marion threw herself wholly into the time she had. "I thought often while I was there—'This must be my real home,'" she wrote after a visit to the Little House. "May I think so?" Marion was just as eager to have Hick consider her Washington apartment a second home. She encouraged Hick to leave some of her things there, and gave her a key. Little pleased Marion more than the sight of Hick's razor, tobacco, or type-writer among her own belongings.

It was just the kind of devotion Hick longed for from Eleanor, and yet the fact that anyone could adore her so completely baffled Hick on occasion. "You ask—Do you make me happy?" Marion wrote in 1944. "Yes—Sometimes you make me the reverse—That is because I love you—There ain't no such thing as perpetual happiness—any more than there is such a thing as perpetual motion."

Their relationship included fussing and grousing, but, as Marion said, "I don't care how much fussing is thrown in. It is all part of it." Eleanor found hurting others so abhorrent that she would rather end a friendship than risk repeatedly causing anyone pain. But Marion understood that upsets between partners were inevitable, and accepted them as part of loving someone. "All my love," she wrote, "—come stormy weather or fair."

Yet no matter how gently and constantly Marion loved her, Hick's heart always belonged most of all to Eleanor.

⁂

And what of Eleanor herself—where did she stand in this maze of intimacies? Eleanor believed love could not be measured. She had told Hick so herself. Years earlier she'd written that love comes in many forms, which could not and should not be compared to one another. Love in all its shapes (with the notable exception of Franklin's affair with Lucy Mercer) was something she revered. Her father's death and Franklin's infidelity had also shown her the perils of entrusting your whole heart to just one person. And so if Hick had a chance to experience another facet of love, Eleanor Roosevelt was not the kind of person to stand in her way. She seems to have understood that Hick and Marion's affection for each other would not shrink her own place in Hick's heart.

It's difficult to say just when Marion faded from Hick's life—or indeed, if she ever did. Hick apparently stopped saving Marion's letters sometime in the summer of 1945, yet Hick's correspondence with Eleanor mentions both news and visits from Marion as late as the mid-1950s.

⁓

June 30, 1943, brought Hick news she had long dreaded. Prinz's hind legs had given out, leaving him paralyzed. There was nothing the vet could do. Hick was in Washington, with no chance of getting to Long Island in time to say goodbye.

Hick's neighbors wrapped Prinz's body in her old raincoat and buried him in the west lot on the Dana estate, "a place he loved above all others," Hick told Eleanor, "because we used to start our walks there."

She consoled herself with the knowledge that Prinz had "lived a long and honorable life." Her only regret was that she hadn't been able to spend as much time with him near the end as he deserved.

"Of course I knew it had to happen—and before very long," she wrote. "And when so many women are suffering so much greater losses these days, I probably have no right to mourn over the death of a dog. But you can't lose an old, loyal, and very dear friend, like Prinz, without feeling lonely and a bit desolate. I think I shall miss him all the rest of my life."

⁓

Not long after Prinz's death, a delivery arrived at the White House for Hick—a caramel-colored English setter puppy, from Eleanor. Hick named him Mr. Choate and promptly set out with him for the Little House.

Hick would rarely be without a dog, but never would there be one equal to Prinz.

CHAPTER 73

ANOTHER ELECTION YEAR ARRIVED IN 1944, AND THE DEMO-cratic Party saw reason for FDR to make a precedent-shattering fourth run for the presidency. With a world war still raging in Europe and the Pacific, the Democrats were willing to bet that most Americans wouldn't be interested in swapping the commander in chief for a new man. Hick agreed with them, in spite of what it meant for Eleanor.

"For your sake and his, I hate to see him do it," she wrote Eleanor that summer. "I'm not a Fourth-Termer, under normal conditions. But there's no one else I'd trust now. But it's awfully tough on you—and him."

Like Abraham Lincoln before him, the strain of war had begun shaving pounds from FDR's frame, and carving ever-deepening lines into his face. Even his supporters wondered if he was physically up to another four years at the helm.

Once FDR's doctors gave him the green light, the race was on. Hick and her fellow Democratic women threw themselves into the campaign, helping Franklin Delano Roosevelt wallop his opponent, Thomas Dewey, in what Hick called "the meanest campaign since 1928."

❧

"Well—are you glad the darned old campaign is over?" Hick wrote Eleanor after FDR's win. "I'll bet you are. And so am I!"

The election had nearly done Hick in. Even before the votes were tallied, she'd realized that she couldn't keep on at such a pace much longer. Fatigue had been saturating her bit by bit for at least two years. The only sensible thing to do was retreat to the Little House and take it easy. "Six months, anyway," she decided. "Longer if I can swing it financially."

Eleanor agreed wholeheartedly. She also pushed Hick to see a doctor for a thorough checkup while she was at it, even offering to go with her.

"It isn't good for people to know all about their blood pressure all the time," Hick protested. "And it's damned depressing." But she went anyway.

"Were you ever right!" Hick reported back. Her blood sugar was stratospheric, an infection had been plaguing her for who knew how long, and her heart, the doctor said, sounded like "a tired old man."

Lucky for Hick, the damage could still be undone. If she ate carefully and didn't skimp on rest, she could expect a full recovery. "Darling— thanks for making me go to the doctor," she wrote Eleanor. "He says you probably saved my life."

Hick obeyed the doctor's orders to the letter. She even forbade herself to make lists, to ensure that her mind rested, too. Hick felt the results almost immediately. Within days, the lines and bags under her eyes were disappearing. Nevertheless, her doctor believed it was best if she didn't return to an office routine—ever.

Hick resigned from the women's division in March of 1945, just two weeks after her fifty-second birthday. "The goodbyes have all been said, and presently I shall be on my way out of Washington with two orchids pinned to my shoulder—and wishing that I could live up to the nice things that have been said to me these last few days," she wrote to Eleanor. "I shall miss you. Yet I shall feel that you are near. After all these years, we could never drift very far apart. You are a wonderful friend, my dear."

❧

Hick indulged in much-needed peace and quiet for three weeks—until April 12, when she answered the door of the Little House and found three of her neighbors, grim-faced. Howard had phoned from the city with terrible news he'd heard on the radio and asked them to relay it to Hick. President Franklin Delano Roosevelt was dead, felled by a cerebral hemorrhage at his Warm Springs, Georgia, retreat.

Hick was stunned, overcome with "bewilderment and *terror.*" It didn't seem possible. The president had aged visibly, even alarmingly, over the course of the war, and yet the idea of his life blinking out in an instant defied comprehension. Hick, like many Americans, still pictured him as the strong and vital warrior who had vanquished polio and the Great Depression alike, and was on the verge of victory in Europe. "I'll never forget his warm, fierce handclasp—the hand shake he had, not for the receiving line, but for his *friends,*" she wrote the next day.

As soon as she could think, Hick's thoughts flew to Eleanor; Hick was ready to drop everything and race to her beloved's side.

But Eleanor didn't need Hick—not yet. "Hick, I don't want you to come," she said. "You know what it will be like." Hick knew exactly what she meant. Eleanor hated elaborate funerals, and now she would have to stand like a national monument in the center of FDR's final rites while managing her own impossibly complicated grief for the man who had both loved her and betrayed her. "And you, of all people, must realize what a load I am carrying now," she went on. "If you came, at this time, you'd just be another worry."

Ten years earlier, words like that might have crushed Hick. Not anymore. "I was terribly proud of her confidence in me," Hick confided to a mutual friend, "—the simple fact that she had known that, in time of stress, she could tell me how she really felt, what she really wanted, and that I would understand." Hick resolved to wait patiently and faithfully, ready to give the former first lady a safe place to collapse when all the pomp and rituals had passed. "And from then on—and as long as we both shall live—I shall be yours to command," she vowed to Eleanor.

"For you and your future I have no worries at all," Hick reassured the newly widowed first lady. "You will find your place—a very active and important place, I feel sure—and fill it superbly."

Their correspondence had naturally tapered off during the years Hick had lived in the White House, but now she decided to write every day. "It's one of the very few little things I can do at this time, and it somehow makes me feel closer to you."

"It's 5 o'clock, and the ceremonies in the East Room must be over by now," she wrote the day of the president's funeral. "I spent most of the time working in the garden—to make things live and grow."

Hick's letters had just the effect she'd hoped for. Eleanor was weary, "too weary to do more than say I love you," she said, but Hick's words made a terrible ordeal more bearable. In addition to burying her husband with the entire world watching, Eleanor had to pack up her family's personal belongings and bid goodbye to the White House staff that had served the Roosevelts for thirteen years. "I've felt you near in thought every day," Eleanor added. "When these busy weeks are over, the business settled & the children are all busy with their own lives again you will come & be with me a while. Won't you?"

There was nowhere else on earth Hick would rather be. When an exhausted Eleanor returned to her Greenwich Village apartment, Hick would be there waiting for her.

PART FOUR

ALONE

CHAPTER 74

were so accurate, she might have been peering into the future with a
telescope. Within twenty-four hours of FDR's funeral, Eleanor had received two job offers, though "job" is something of an understatement.
The offer she accepted was an appointment by President Truman to
serve as a United States delegate to the United Nations.

Eleanor set out for England aboard the *Queen Elizabeth* on New Year's
Eve of 1945. For the next three years, she would channel every ounce
of her bottomless energy and innate diplomacy into passing the Universal Declaration of Human Rights, a document that would affirm
the fundamental dignity and equality of all human beings and serve
internationally as "the foundation of freedom, justice and peace in the
world."

While Eleanor was off making the world a more humane place, Hick
tried to figure out how to cobble together a living that wouldn't jeopar-
dize her health. Her diabetes had given her quite a scare at the end of
1945; from now on, she'd need daily injections of insulin. The doctor's
decree against any sort of office routine made job hunting that much
harder.

Congresswoman Mary Norton came to Hick's rescue. She refused to
let Hick overwork herself again, or subject herself to the mental anxiety
of financial worries. "You must take as long as necessary to regain your
health so that you will be able to use the gifts God gave you," Mary

insisted. "He was so good to you." Mary knew how well Hick could write, and how well she could analyze news. With her congressional duties, Mary explained, she never had enough time to stay as informed as she wanted to be. In exchange for speechwriting and helping Mary keep ahead of political developments, Mary offered to pay Hick $1,200 a year.

Hick accepted. The idea of living off her friends rubbed uncomfortably against her pride, but her pay from Mary and a few other freelance jobs let her scrape up enough funds to take a cross-country vacation in 1947. Hick visited eighty-eight-year-old Aunt Ella; her Minneapolis mentor and editor, "Old Man" Tom Dillon; and her first love, Ellie Morse Dickinson. The finances might have pinched, but Hick couldn't bring herself to regret the expense—within months, both Ellie and Dillon would be dead.

Eleanor always had a safety net ready to unfurl beneath Hick. After the Universal Declaration of Human Rights passed in December 1948, Eleanor invited Hick and her new cocker spaniel, Muffin, to her cottage at Val-Kill for the winter so that Hick wouldn't have to heat the Little House. While Eleanor worked on the second volume of her autobiography, Hick tried her hand at writing her own life story, churning out four chapters and an outline before she stalled. She could compose vivid descriptions of anyone from a dirt farmer to a prime minister, but when it came to her own life, Hick wrote from a peculiar distance. Little emotion infiltrated the most wrenching moments, as though she could not bear to relive them, and so the publisher said, No, thank you. Eleanor helped fill in the financial gaps, paying Hick for the same kind of research and reading she did for Mary Norton.

Hick even tried her hand at transcribing Eleanor's letters into typewritten copies—filtering out the vast majority of endearments and private longing for each other, of course. She envisioned donating one copy to the Franklin Delano Roosevelt Presidential Library's archives and keeping another for herself and Tommy, "if we ever get around to writing Mrs. R.'s biography, which we have promised to do if we survive her," she told an old Minneapolis friend. But nobody was going to pay her for that, and Hick fizzled out after running only about 130 of the letters through her typewriter.

❧

Luckily, Eleanor came up with yet another job for her in 1952. "Mrs. R. and I are co-authoring a book, for Putnam's, on Women in politics (Go ahead and have a good laugh!) and we want you in it!" Hick wrote to their mutual friend, Congresswoman Helen Gahagan Douglas, that September.

The project was supposed to have been solely Eleanor's. "I can't do it alone," Eleanor admitted to Hick when her publisher proposed the idea. "Please consider it," she asked, "it's needed, but I can't give the time." Eleanor's triumph at the United Nations had earned her the title of First Lady of the World; her schedule now was even more packed than it had been during her years in the White House. Of course Hick accepted.

The book, *Ladies of Courage,* profiled an array of women—including Eleanor—who had made an impact in politics in every role from grassroots organizer to mayor, congresswoman, and governor. It also included a chapter of practical advice for getting involved in politics, tailored specifically to women.

Putting Eleanor's name on the cover was a bit of a ruse. Eleanor wrote the introduction and very little else. The bulk of the book was Hick's doing. But Eleanor understood how much her name was worth, and how much higher the sales figures were likely to be if she was billed as coauthor. Hick needed money much more than she did, and Eleanor was happy to turn the advance and 60 percent of the royalties over to her.

Hick had a grand time. "It's fun," she said, "and the people at Putnam's appear to be quite excited about it." Eleanor was equally pleased with Hick's efforts. "It's simply swell, I think. Much more interesting than I thought it could possibly be made."

CHAPTER 75

JUST WHEN HICK WAS FINALLY MAKING SOME MONEY AGAIN, her eyesight betrayed her. The first inklings of trouble had started in 1950. Thanks to her diabetes, she found herself prone to eye hemorrhages—burst blood vessels in the retina that cause streaky, spiderwebby vision and floating blind spots. A particularly nasty one in her left eye in 1953 took six weeks to clear. For those six weeks, Hick could distinguish nothing but light and shadow with that eye. Each time a hemorrhage cleared, Hick noticed, it took a little bit of her sight with it forever.

By 1955, Hick didn't trust her eyes enough to drive anymore. It was hard, giving up her car, but that was better than the anxiety that overtook her every time she got behind the wheel. Better to relinquish her license than risk hurting anyone.

❧

Hick bade goodbye to her beloved Little House on Long Island that same summer. Ella Dana wanted to sell, and Hick had no choice but to move out. On August 1, Eleanor sent a car, and Hick and Muffin were whisked off to Hyde Park, where Hick moved in with Eleanor at Val-Kill.

It ought to have been a dream come true for both of them. There they were, in a cottage together at last, and yet the reality didn't quite match the "someday" they'd imagined. Eleanor's children and friends— "the usual mob," as Hick called them—were always coming and going. Eleanor's friends, who probably didn't know the true depth of her relationship with Hick, found Hick's presence at Val-Kill mystifying and irritating in equal measure. When Hick's resonant voice called out

"Darling!" to Eleanor from across the living room, they could barely conceal their horror at what appeared to be a blatant breach of propriety.

The disdain was often mutual. "I have a special distaste for rich, arrogant old women," Hick wrote in later years. And even those who enjoyed her company had to admit that Hick was "a massive presence." There was also the matter of Hick's essentially solitary nature. Where Eleanor thrived on bustle and constant activity, the big gatherings she so loved to host drained Hick. And without enough time to herself, Hick was prone to wearing out and getting testy.

Hick's Val-Kill sojourn lasted a year. Muffin apparently didn't get along with Eleanor's Scottish terriers any better than Hick got on with Eleanor's guests. The threat of violence between the dogs became the final straw. Hick and Eleanor still loved each other, but that did not change the fact that they led very different kinds of lives.

Lakeview Motor Court was supposed to be a temporary solution. It was a motel, really, but Hick ended up liking it well enough to make a home of the place. She had her own little log-style cabin with a screened porch overlooking the lake, just as the sign out front promised. Arthritis had begun to torment her, and the compact room with its kitchenette and bath accommodated her dwindling mobility. Lakeview gave her the privacy and seclusion she needed to work, all within three miles of Eleanor.

Hick had a new vocation now. It turned out that all those years of writing newspaper articles—laying out facts clearly and getting straight to the point—had trained her well for writing biographies for children.

First came *The Story of Franklin D. Roosevelt*. "No politics," the publisher demanded, so Hick wrote an uncomplicated account of FDR's life that hopscotched clean over the 1932 election and plunked him down into the White House.

Hick dedicated it to "the two bravest people I ever knew, the President and his 'Missis.'" A foreword by Eleanor announced to the world that she was "very glad that this short book about the life of my husband for young people has been written by my friend, Miss Lorena Hickok."

Hick's publisher was so pleased, they offered her another contract—a similar biography of Helen Keller, an international celebrity and the first deafblind person to earn a college degree. Hick didn't exactly jump at the chance. She'd be ashamed to admit it later, but the idea bored her.

"In my innocence I didn't think there was enough drama in Helen Keller's life to interest a child," Hick confessed to a friend. Despite her close ties with FDR, she'd fallen prey to some of the worst stereotypes about disabled people. "I'd thought of her vaguely as a combination of trained seal and do-gooder," Hick said. "Was I ever wrong! Never in my life have I met a human being who had quite the effect on me she has."

Thanks to Eleanor, who counted Helen Keller among her many friends, Hick got the opportunity to interview Miss Keller in person. That meeting changed Hick's perspective entirely. Miss Keller's intellect and zest for life were enough to overturn anyone's notions of physical disability. The encounter left Hick fired with a desire to get "enough of the real Helen Keller" into her book as possible. It wasn't easy, but to Hick's gratification it was *fun*. "I'm loving it!" Hick said. "I'm enjoying the writing of this book more than I've enjoyed any writing I've done in years—if ever."

The Story of Helen Keller became "a hit, as much as juveniles ever are," Hick hastened to add. Children devoured it. Teachers adored it. Scholastic put it in their book fairs, and the Doubleday bookstore in New York City kept it constantly in stock. That one little book would keep Hick afloat financially for years to come. The next year she even managed to turn out a children's biography of Eleanor, as a companion to her volume on FDR. "My books, bless 'em," Hick boasted with fondness, "provide me with a fairly good living."

CHAPTER 76

AFTER HICK HAD BEEN AT LAKEVIEW A YEAR OR SO, ELEANOR arranged for her to take a downstairs apartment in what had been the rectory of an Episcopal church in Hyde Park.

Hick no longer had a damn left to give about what anyone thought of her. She settled comfortably into herself in Hyde Park, where she consigned her girdle and skirts to the closet, favoring white duck pants and men's T-shirts. But if Eleanor invited her to Val-Kill and the guests were important enough, she'd put on a dress.

"She WAS a 'character,' but a kind and interesting one," Hick's upstairs neighbor recalled. And when Eleanor was around, that same neighbor noticed, Hick could act "a little 'kittenish.'"

Most days, Hick worked. Gardening was well beyond her now, with her worsening arthritis. Even on Sunday afternoons Hick sat at her typewriter with a cigarette in her mouth, though if she spotted a neighbor passing by the window, she'd often wave them in for a chat.

⁓

Hick also found another, unexpected companion in her work. While she was writing a biography of Anne Sullivan Macy, Helen Keller's teacher, an intangible bond formed between author and subject. No matter that Mrs. Macy had died twenty-some years earlier. Hick felt an undeniable kinship with this woman who had been orphaned as a child, was herself partially blind, and had devoted her entire life to her famous pupil. Hick's own dimming sight made it impossible to type for more than an hour at a stretch, and her arthritis would spare her only one hand at a time.

Nevertheless, she worked day after day to bring Annie Sullivan to life for her young readers.

"No author ever finished a book with greater regret," Hick wrote in the foreword of *The Touch of Magic*. "During the months I worked on this book she became as real to me as a living person—a warm, very human, greatly loved friend. I miss her. Not as Miss Keller must miss her always. But nevertheless I miss her."

⁓

Hick's next project was closer to her heart than anything she'd done before—a biography of Eleanor herself.

Plenty of people had been salivating for years at the idea of writing about Eleanor Roosevelt's life. There had already been one biography, back in 1940. Eleanor herself had written a three-volume autobiography over the course of the previous two decades. And there was Hick's children's book. But anytime someone had approached Eleanor with the possibility of another book, she'd sent them to Hick to fend them off for her. Now that Eleanor was getting on in years, these prospective biographers—including some of Eleanor's friends—thrummed with a new sense of urgency.

Hick bristled at watching what she called "the way the ghouls are gathering round." As she'd bluntly put it to a mutual friend in 1957, "Mrs. R. will be 73 next month. You can see how their minds are working. One of these days Mrs. R. will go. And then they'll be ready, with manuscripts in their hot little hands, ready to cash in."

Hick was not about to give any of them that chance. After almost thirty years, Hick at last sat down at her typewriter to portray Eleanor Roosevelt as only she could. She had a unique trove of thousands of letters to draw upon, recounting the minutiae of Eleanor's daily life from her first night in the White House. In the end, she used almost none of that. Hick instead focused on a narrow slice of Eleanor's life, from the time she first made Eleanor's acquaintance in New York until their be-leaguered trip to California in 1934. Outwardly a chronicle of Eleanor's "transition from a private individual to First Lady of the land," as the book's dust jacket would describe it, the narrative also coincided with the budding and blossoming of Eleanor and Hick's romance. Could that choice have been mere coincidence? Or did Hick intend all along to write a camouflaged account of their love story?

"Of one thing I'm sure," Hick told a mutual friend after *Reluctant First Lady* was published, "—no other book like it has been ever been written about Mrs. R." Whether Hick realized it or not, that was a colossal understatement.

Hick and her publisher classified *Reluctant First Lady* as a biography. In reality, it might be most properly called a tribute. Hick imbued that book with her love and admiration for Eleanor from the first page to the last. "The story in this book is a very personal one," Hick said in the book's opening line. "It had to be." She could not tell the truth about their relationship, but the truth is there nonetheless. It's there in the intimacy of her knowledge of Eleanor's thoughts and feelings. It's there in the descriptions that bring out the very human *person* Hick cherished, rather than the idealized *personage* venerated by the public.

In spite of—or perhaps because of—Hick's love, *Reluctant First Lady* "never got off the ground in sales." Part of its trouble lay in the fact that Hick couldn't tell the full truth of Eleanor's reluctance to become first lady. It was all wrapped up in Franklin's infidelity, and how Eleanor had bandaged those wounds with her work. Without that truth, her reluctance would always ring a little hollow.

But her biggest mistake, Hick later decided, was writing in the first person. The narrator of a biography shouldn't be an actual person who had also played a role in the events as they unfolded. Things could get fuzzy when you used that pronoun, "I," in a book that readers expected to be purely objective.

"I was horrified when I read it in print," Hick would confess to Anna

Roosevelt in 1968. Hick was thankful that the book had gone out of print by then; she'd blame its failure on the publisher for not editing it sufficiently. It was an odd place to lay the responsibility. *Reluctant First Lady* certainly wasn't too long, or sloppily written. Perhaps what Hick really meant was that in retrospect, seeing how her feelings saturated so many of its pages was mortifying. If her editor had slashed those parts with a blue pencil, Hick and the publisher both might have been better off in the long run.

CHAPTER 77

ELEANOR ROOSEVELT HAD BECOME AN ICON. SHE WAS DE-mocracy's beloved grandmother, and the living embodiment of the nation's moral conscience. After decades of indefatigable work and travel, it was hard to fathom that she was just as mortal as any other human being. She came from a family that was synonymous with robust health and physical triumph—first her uncle Ted, the great outdoorsman, and then her husband, who, as far as the public knew, had beaten polio. Eleanor herself had been renowned for her unparalleled stamina since the 1920s. But as she neared her ninth decade, Eleanor's mortality became all too apparent.

A persistent case of anemia that flummoxed her doctors landed Eleanor in and out of the hospital during the early 1960s. No matter what they tried, they couldn't keep enough iron in her blood to deliver oxygen to her body. The slightest exertion left her panting, and a fever dogged her nearly every day. Each time, the medical team ran tests and boosted her numbers as best they could, then sent her home with instructions to take it easy—an order harder for Eleanor Roosevelt to swallow than any medicine. Despite her fundamental benevolence, she could be diabolically stubborn, and almost no one on earth had the mettle to oppose her.

In August of 1962, Eleanor insisted upon traveling to the Roosevelt family retreat on Campobello Island, in part to attend the dedication ceremonies for the newly completed Franklin Delano Roosevelt Memorial Bridge joining the Canadian island to Maine. But her recurring fever and shortness of breath fatigued her so that she could not help christen the bridge after all. Yet on the way back to Hyde Park, she summoned an otherworldly, almost frightening determination to pay overnight visits to two of her oldest friends, Molly Dewson and Esther Lape. "How she garnered her strength for these undertakings was a marvel," her doctor's wife recalled.

The very day after returning from her trip to Campobello, Eleanor appeared unannounced in Hick's kitchen before Hick had even finished her breakfast. She'd tried to call the night before, Eleanor explained, but got no answer. Probably Hick had missed the telephone while she was busy with the dinner dishes and the radio.

"I know how you hate to talk about being ill," Hick said, "so let's not."

"Well, I've been pretty sick," Eleanor admitted, "but I'm getting better, although it's taking me a long time to get my strength back." The simple fact that she would acknowledge her weakness signaled to Hick how serious the matter had become.

The next morning, Hick did hear the phone ring. "If you are going to be at home this afternoon, I might come over," Eleanor said. The day was bright, teetering on the edge of summer and autumn. Hick asked a neighbor to put a pair of garden chairs under the maple in the yard. Eleanor stayed for an hour that day, enjoying what Hick would remember as "a long, quiet, relaxed, intimate talk." Even after thirty years it was still rare for them to have these private moments, and Hick cherished every minute of that visit.

 ✺

Eleanor's doctors wrestled her back into the hospital once again in late September for a stay that would last three weeks. Hick did not go to see her. She knew how Eleanor felt about being incapacitated, and her own difficulties in navigating New York City with her walker made the whole prospect thoroughly unappealing.

Instead, Hick wrote, just as they'd done decades ago when circumstances had kept them apart—"little chatty, cheerful notes and letting her know that I was thinking about her and loving her." Hick's own health had stabilized, and she was grateful for the chance to take the weight of that worry off Eleanor's mind. It was her turn now to encourage Eleanor.

"When you are feeling a little stronger, I suggest you get out a copy of your own book, *You Learn by Living,* and read the chapter you wrote on making adjustments. In that book you paid me a wonderful compliment on the adjustments I've had to make. Well—if I could make them, you can. You have a much stronger character than I have," Hick wrote. "And, remember, you'll always be surrounded by your friends, who love you. Loneliness—the lack of companionship with my contemporaries and with people who have the same interests—has been the hardest thing for me. You won't have that."

Hick's last known message to Eleanor closed with a jaunty "I loves yer very much, Missis Roosevelt!"

Eleanor's final letter came on October 10—the day before her seventy-eighth birthday. Writing was beyond her now, but her new secretary, Maureen Corr, had faithfully typed as Eleanor spoke, thanking Hick for her letters and her love. "I'm still horribly weak, but as soon as I'm able to hold the phone I'll call you," she promised. Even as Hick read those words, she understood that she would not pick up the phone and hear her darling's voice again.

⁓

The discouraging news began running together. There was the day a message came from Maureen, gently asking Hick not to send any more notes. They were "no use." In the middle of October came another call. There would be no more tests, Maureen told Hick. They were taking Eleanor back to her apartment in Manhattan. "I think you will know what that means," Maureen said. Right after that came a letter from one of Eleanor's grandchildren, saying that her grandmother was "slipping away." Likely only days remained, perhaps a week or two.

Eleanor herself welcomed the inevitable. If she could not live a useful life, fulfilled by the humanitarian work she loved, she would rather surrender it entirely. Her body was not so complaisant; her old iron constitution held out nearly three weeks—until 6:15 p.m. on November 7, 1962.

✦

The following day brought Hick a telegram from the Roosevelt family, formally inviting her to the funeral service at St. James Episcopal Church and the interment that would follow in the rose garden at the Roosevelt estate.

Hick carefully laid the telegram away with her letters, but she did not attend. The great majority of guests would be there to mourn the First Lady of the World. Hick's grief was for someone else—not for the personage, but for the person, as she'd said so many years ago.

She and Eleanor had both disliked funerals, anyway. "All that show and fuss made over the shell that is left behind," Hick called them. Eleanor thought memorial services "cruel to those who really love you & miss you." To everyone else in the pews, a funeral was nothing more than "an obligation fulfilled."

Hick agreed. "Anyway, I shall be nowhere around," she'd said once when the topic of Eleanor's funeral had come up.

"I'd much rather you weren't, my dear," Eleanor had replied.

Hick also knew that the service would reflect not Eleanor herself, but rather the world's feelings for her. Eleanor had craved the plainest of arrangements: a pine coffin, pillows to rest on, and a sheet to cover her. No embalming. Instead of grand floral tributes, she'd requested a blanket of fir boughs. That much she'd receive, but all the rest of the trappings would be nothing but pomp and majesty. Hick wanted no part of it.

✦

Eleanor's granddaughter Sisty came the morning of the funeral and sat with Hick. At noon, Hick drove out to the Catskills and spent the afternoon reminiscing quietly with Mary Margaret McBride, a journalist who had also known and admired Eleanor. When it was all over at last, Eleanor's daughter, Anna, dropped in with her husband. Those private remembrances did Hick more good than any public sermons or speeches. There was something about Sisty's presence in particular. Hick couldn't help feeling that Eleanor would have been pleased to see them drawing together—"as though [she] wanted some member of her family to be close to me after she had gone."

"Through it all," Hick wrote afterward, "I tried to do what I knew she would have wanted me to do—to keep my emotions strictly under control and to try to comfort other people who needed it. I managed fairly well—I'm not a weeper."

That night, though, Hick made a pilgrimage of her own. After midnight, a car pulled up to her apartment. The tall, white-haired minister who had officiated over Eleanor's funeral stepped out. Reverend Kidd helped Hick into the passenger seat and drove the few miles to the Roosevelt estate. Hick held a bouquet of dried wildflowers like those that grew at Val-Kill—a heartfelt offering she knew would mean more to Eleanor than the veritable hedge of hothouse blooms sent by dignitaries the world over.

Reverend Kidd remembered how "spooky" it was, driving up to the uninhabited Roosevelt estate at that hour. But Hick had been quite clear: she did not want to be seen, did not want another soul in the vicinity. After all the years of waiting on the sidelines for those rare and precious times alone together, Hick refused to share her last moment with Eleanor with anyone but Reverend Kidd, and then only by necessity.

A guard stopped them briefly, then recognized the reverend and waved the car through. Reverend Kidd parked as near to the rose garden as he could. This far from the road, the darkness was like fabric, so close and intense you could almost feel it. Neither of them could see the Roosevelt plot. A line of hemlock bushes bordered the garden, walling it off from the surrounding landscape. If she wanted to stand at Eleanor's graveside, Hick had to make her way around the entire perimeter to the gap at the south end.

Hick couldn't do it. Between her arthritis and her ever-dimming eyesight, those few hundred yards were too much for her. Reverend Kidd gallantly took the fragile bouquet and felt his way into the garden, barking his shin as he advanced toward his only guide—the barely perceptible outline of FDR's white marble monument. A few feet before the monument, where the earth had been recently cut, Reverend Kidd gently laid Hick's small tribute.

CHAPTER 78

"MRS. R. SHOULD HAVE MANY MORE YEARS," HICK HAD WRIT-
ten to a mutual friend at FDR's death in 1945, "—when *she* goes, if she
goes before I do, I shall *want* to die." Simply wanting it wouldn't make
it happen, though. Hick lasted six more years without Eleanor, years in
which she battled loneliness and occasionally won.

"If you go before I do, my dear," she'd said, never expecting to outlast
the indomitable Eleanor Roosevelt, "I'll not drape myself around the
shoulders of your children." That wasn't hard—she'd never liked them
much, anyway. Of the five, Hick only had any fondness for Anna. "After
your Mother left," she wrote Anna, "I decided to look about and make
new friends who never knew your Mother or any of the Roosevelts." It
was easier that way, without the sting of memories, or the petty jealousies that still flew like arrows among Eleanor's circle.

Very few members of Eleanor's inner circle liked her, either. "I never
resented any of her friends," Hick insisted, "even though some of them
I did not like." What she thought of them didn't matter so long as they
made Eleanor happy. "I never criticized them to her and tried always to
be polite to them." For all Hick claimed to have tried, her disdain likely
leaked through her polite façade. "She was outspoken, all right," Reverend Kidd acknowledged of her.

There were still old friends she could write to, people from Washington and Minneapolis, but no one she could count on seeing face to face
anymore. Her reliance on canes and walkers made Hick reluctant to go
out under her own steam. "I can't help feeling terribly self-conscious and
humiliated by my awkwardness," she confessed.

On the first anniversary of Eleanor's funeral, Hick made an exception and attended a regular Sunday service at St. James Episcopal Church. "There was something very healing about the experience," she recalled, "—it was all so quiet, serene, and, well, normal." That church was the last public place she'd ever been with Eleanor. After the hymns and prayers ended, Hick stood for a long time beside the roped-off Roosevelt family pew, remembering. "The church was empty when I finally blew her a kiss and left. Yes, a terrific emotional impact—but the right kind, quiet, intimate."

Hick would always keep her Eleanor—her beloved Mrs. Joe Doaks of Olewein, Iowa—separate, and sacred, from the public figure revered around the globe. "It's the difference between the Chandor portrait, a very handsome portrait of 'the First Lady of the World,' and a simple photograph which I have here in my apartment," she explained in a letter to Anna. "In the photograph she is smiling slightly—she could smile, as you know, without showing all her teeth—and the expression around her eyes is thoughtful, a little wistful, a little sad, but warm and understanding. That was the Eleanor Roosevelt I knew and loved, for herself."

At Christmas, she saw to it that the plot of grass above Eleanor's final resting place was bedecked with "a nice, shaggy wreath of the greens she loved. No red bow, no card. Just a little thank-you for all the lovely things she used to do for me at this time of year."

And each year on Eleanor's birthday, Hick would leave a single yellow rose—Eleanor's favorite—at her darling's grave.

※

About a year before Eleanor's death, when Hick began to realize that Eleanor's health was failing, she'd come to a decision. "I made up my mind that I'd have to reorganize my life and accept the fact that I'd no longer have the warm, close companionship I used to have with people of my generation or older."

What happened next was like something out of a storybook. "Maybe there really is a God—without the long white whiskers," Hick wrote to one of her old friends, for no sooner had she made that resolution than two new families moved in nearby. One, the O'Learys, had eight children, seven of them boys. Another, a family of recent immigrants from Holland, added three more boys and two girls to the mix.

Before the year was out, Hick had employed every last boy in the neighborhood in one way or another. It took her longer to befriend their sisters—"I'm inclined to be shy and ill-at-ease with little girls," she once explained to Anna—but eventually she hired them, too.

Morning, noon, and night Hick's kitchen door banged open and shut as the kids arrived to walk her dog, wash her windows, rake her leaves, defrost her icebox, fix her plumbing, and even help her put drops in her eyes. "And do I love it?"

Hick kept her refrigerator stocked with king-sized bottles of Coca-Cola to treat her young helpers, even as she groused good-naturedly about the expense of buying a dozen every week.

The Friday before Christmas, Hick invited twenty-two kids for a party at her place. On Christmas Eve, the three oldest boys found brand-new hockey sticks and pucks waiting for them when they came to do the dog walking. There were toys for their younger siblings, too, plus whole crates of oranges for her two favorite families. She'd overspent and she knew it, but the whoops of delight when those boys saw their gifts was worth it.

Hick found herself welcomed into their holiday celebrations, spending Christmas Eve with the O'Learys and then joining her Dutch neighbors for Christmas dinner. In her own small corner of the world, she had become an auxiliary grandmother.

The Christmas after Eleanor's death, however, Hick fled. Though the neighbors brought Hick kindness by the bucketful, no one could fill the hole Eleanor had left behind. That cavern was simply too large, too hallowed for anyone else to occupy. "I love them of course," she said of her young pals, "but I do long for adult conversation."

"My life right now is pretty dull," Hick wrote to Anna. "Just work, work, work." Her latest project was a biography of Detroit labor leader Walter P. Reuther, but these days the spark of enthusiasm was lacking. "There are mornings when I sit on the edge of my bed, staring at a picture of your Mother on the opposite wall, wondering if I couldn't simply drop the whole thing."

Her eyes and her arthritis shrank her world in increasingly larger increments. The radio, at least, brought her some excitement through baseball games, and she rooted passionately for the Dodgers. But "the long black evenings" bored her so much that she occasionally defied the doctor's orders and read in "great gulps." Then she had to pay the price with eye fatigue.

"I'll probably live for years and years," she half complained in a letter to another old friend. "There is apparently nothing wrong with me that might carry me out of this messy existence. My doctor says I have the heart and blood pressure of a woman ten years younger than I am. The things I have never kill you—they're just damned inconvenient."

⁓

But that wasn't entirely true. Diabetes was slowly consuming her. She'd relinquished most of her sight, and in 1968 Hick's doctor said she'd have to give up at least one of her legs. Without proper circulation, they were destined to die gradually from the toes up. The fact that her toes were already numb did not bode well. The only solution was to amputate before gangrene had a chance to creep any higher.

Hick entered the hospital in April to undergo the first of what would likely be two amputations. The second operation never happened. Two weeks into her recovery, her chronic bronchitis, a consequence of decades of smoking, turned into pneumonia. Late on the night of May 1, 1968, Hick succumbed. She was seventy-five years old.

~⚬~

"I hope there is no purgatory, no Hell—no Heaven," Hick had written to Eleanor thirty years earlier. "Just nothingness." Her final wishes reflected that hope. Hick wanted her remains "disposed of as soon as possible" via cremation, and without any fuss whatsoever. No embalming, no casket, and especially no funeral ceremony. The closest thing to a religious service that she'd tolerate was "a brief prayer" at the crematory chapel, and only if it was recited by Reverend Kidd. As for what to do with the ashes themselves, that was "immaterial" as far as Hick was concerned. The location made no difference to her. "Although," she added, "if it can be done, I should like to have them dug into the soil around growing trees, which may benefit from whatever chemicals the ashes contain."

Nearly all of Hick's wishes were fulfilled. After a prayer by Reverend Kidd, she was duly cremated. And then her ashes were placed on a shelf in a Hyde Park funeral home, where they would sit unclaimed for the next twenty years.

EPILOGUE
COMING OUT

CHAPTER 79

Hickok, if not for something she'd done a decade earlier. Back in 1958, Hick had begun quietly donating boxes of her papers to the Franklin Delano Roosevelt Presidential Library. Among them were over thirty-five hundred of the letters she and Eleanor had exchanged. Not the edited versions she had typed out in the 1940s, but the handwritten originals, complete with every "dearest" and "darling," every longed-for kiss and embrace.

Hick, a self-described "stickler for clarity" with "a very great respect for the libel laws," knew what was in those letters. She had to have understood what people might think of them. Eleanor Roosevelt also knew what her correspondence with Hick contained, and according to Hick, Eleanor herself had wanted their letters to become part of the library's collection. So Hick had donated them, she explained to Anna Roosevelt, "because [your mother] thought I should."

Hick did admit to keeping back fifteen from 1932. "I know that those letters were intended for my eyes only," she told Anna.

A number of reasons could have compelled Hick to withhold them. As she put it to Anna in the 1960s, "Your mother wasn't always so very discreet in her letters to me." Exactly what form those indiscretions took is not perfectly clear. Eleanor could very well have expressed her love more intimately than Hick was willing to share. Given the tenor of their surviving correspondence, that seems the most plausible answer. It's also possible that Eleanor aired frustrations and complaints about family and friends whom Hick did not want to see hurt. There could have been politically sensitive material as well.

"The people at the Library are going to have conniptions when they found—or find out what I've done to some of your mother's letters," she confessed. "Years ago I started to copy them on the typewriter, carefully omitting anything personal, everything about the family. But I only started. Never had the time or the eyesight to finish. You know her writing!"

"So—to Hell with history!" Hick exclaimed, and entrusted the most sensitive fifteen letters to Esther Lape.

Lape was an intriguing choice. She had known Eleanor for forty years and had spent her life romantically partnered with Elizabeth Read, another of Eleanor's longtime friends. She, of all the people Hick might have tasked as caretaker, was the most likely to have understood the particular intricacies of these letters' significance—both what they meant to Hick and what they might mean to Eleanor Roosevelt's legacy. "Esther will burn them some evening in her fireplace," Hick reported.

Why not destroy them herself? Perhaps she couldn't bear to watch them go up in flames. Hick still held great affection for the things Eleanor had given her, and would take infinite care to find worthy homes for those most precious possessions in her will. The handling of Eleanor's letters mattered just as much. "I'll be damned if he's going to get his hot little hands onto my papers," Hick said of Joseph P. Lash, another of Eleanor's most intimate friends, who had by then already published a memoir of his own and would eventually make a literary career out of his relationship with the former first lady.

Hick's donation included one telling condition: her papers were not to be opened until ten years after her death. She'd also included her correspondence with Alicent Holt and Marion Harron, making it crystal clear that she'd had long-lasting emotionally and perhaps physically intimate relationships with women. Anyone who might be harmed by that revelation would likely be gone by the time the contents were made public. In effect, Lorena Hickok had engineered her own posthumous coming-out with as much precision as she could. Ten years after her death, the world would know the truth.

CHAPTER 80

MERE DAYS AFTER THE TENTH ANNIVERSARY OF HICK'S DEATH, children's biographer and former *New York Times* reporter Doris Faber happened to be at the FDR Presidential Library, researching a book on Eleanor Roosevelt. The library director offered her first access to the newly opened Lorena Hickok Papers. No one, other than the archivist who had cataloged and organized them, had looked inside the eighteen cartons in the years since Hick had donated them.

Faber opened the first box and began to read.

"Probably about an hour later, in something like a classic state of shock," she recalled, "I left my seat in the serene research room where four or five other people were poring over documents, and, in a voice that sounded very strange to my own ears, I asked the library aide on duty if she would call the library's director for me."

By her own admission, what Faber had seen gave her "the connip-tions." Those letters were "fraught with an electrifying emotional im-pact," she thought. It was 1978, a time when same-sex relationships were still almost universally viewed with disgust.

Faber told director William R. Emerson that she wanted the letters resealed, removed—anything to keep them from the public eye. " 'Bury them!' I decreed like an Alice-in-Wonderland despot." The scandal of Eleanor's longings for Hick splashed across a tabloid newspaper repre-sented a horror Faber recoiled from imagining. "Eleanor Roosevelt was a great woman," she argued, as though Eleanor's love for Hick would somehow negate her achievements.

Emerson refused. For one thing, he "could not believe that there were valid grounds for suppressing the letters." Besides, it couldn't be done without a significant breach of the protocol of the National Archives and Records Administration, which oversees the country's presidential libraries. Once a document has been viewed by one researcher, a library cannot deny access to someone else. In her desperation, Faber even promised never to divulge what she'd seen, if only the most sensitive letters could be hidden away again. That wouldn't work, either. National Archives protocol demands that every document removed from a box be replaced by a pink slip noting its absence. Dozens, if not hundreds, of such slips in the Hickok collection would quickly raise researchers' eyebrows, leading to unwelcome questions and speculation about the suppressed material.

"It's going to come out," a library staffer advised Faber as she struggled to accept Emerson's decision.

Faber's solution, which she embarked upon with "very mixed emotions," was to write her own biography of Lorena Hickok—to recount Hick and Eleanor's relationship before anyone else could come to what she perceived as the wrong conclusions. To Faber, it was unthinkable that Eleanor Roosevelt could have been in love with a woman. The words Hick and Eleanor had written to each other *had* to mean something other than what they so plainly said.

The result was an impeccably researched yet ultimately flawed biography. "I have chosen not to speculate about feelings alluded to only cryptically by either woman," Faber wrote in the introduction to *The Life of Lorena Hickok*—a promise she failed to keep.

～

As knowledge of Hick and Eleanor's correspondence spread, members of Eleanor's inner circle also scrambled to alter the meaning of what the two women had written to each other. Joseph Lash, another of Eleanor's dearest friends, published two fat volumes of selections from her correspondence with an array of friends in an effort to prove that the intimacy the first lady used with Hick was simply her style. In the introduction to Lash's first volume, Eleanor's son Franklin Jr. "urged that my mother's letters be read in the context of those written to other close friends." Her endearments and expressions of affection were "customary and conventional" during her lifetime, Franklin Jr. declared.

⚬⚬⚬

Two things happened simultaneously over the next twenty years. More people read Hick and Eleanor's letters for themselves, and attitudes toward queer relationships began shifting in the public at large. Slowly but surely, the gay rights movement and the AIDS epidemic forced Americans to confront their prejudices toward same-sex couples, and more and more Americans learned to accept and affirm queer relationships.

Meanwhile, articles on Hick appeared in journals and magazines, and a one-woman play about her debuted in Provincetown, Massachusetts. Producer Linda Boyd Kavars saw that play in 1997 and immediately realized it deserved a larger audience. She decided to take it on the road.

Patsy Costello, president of the Hyde Park Historical Society, saw *Eleanor Roosevelt and Lorena Hickok: A Love Story* when Kavars brought it to Kingston, New York, and became interested in locating Hick's grave. When she called the Dapson Funeral Home, Costello learned that after twenty years on a shelf, Hick's ashes had been buried in a section of the Rhinebeck Cemetery set aside for unclaimed remains.

The information galvanized Kavars. "Just the thought of being forgotten on a shelf and written out of history got me very angry," she recalled. She plunged herself into research at the FDR Library, assembled a group of like-minded women (including Blanche Wiesen Cook, Eleanor Roosevelt's most eminent biographer), and formed the Lorena Hickok Memorial and Scholarship Fund. Concerts and sailing excursions soon earned enough money to properly mark Hick's grave.

On May 10, 2000, Kavars and Costello's small band of activists gathered in the southwest corner of the Rhinebeck Cemetery to pay tribute to Hick. They laid a plaque in her honor and installed a bluestone bench beside it. Recalling Hick's wish that her ashes be spread beneath a tree, the women also planted a dogwood to shade the memorial. There were no trees in that corner, "so we brought the tree to her," Kavars said simply. The plaque reads:

Lorena Hickok
"Hick"
Mar. 1893 East Troy, WI—May 1968, Hyde Park, NY
A.P. Reporter
Author
Activist
and
Friend of E.R.
Dedicated May 10, 2000

Sometime in the winter of 2022–2023, a Pride flag appeared beneath Hick's dogwood—an offering from an unknown admirer.

～

The Lorena Hickok Memorial and Scholarship Fund continues to provide funding to young women's social justice projects via the Eleanor Roosevelt Center at Val-Kill in Hyde Park, New York.

AUTHOR'S NOTE

Over thirty-five hundred letters between Lorena Hickok and Eleanor Roosevelt reside in the Franklin Delano Roosevelt Presidential Library, chronicling an extraordinary relationship. And yet so much is missing. Despite the tremendous volume of correspondence—ten archival boxes filled to the brim—hundreds, if not thousands, of letters are absent. Great gaps of weeks or even months pass by without a peep from Hick in the early 1930s, for example, although it's clear from Eleanor's side of the conversation that Hick was writing almost daily. Again and again in later years, Eleanor references letters from Hick that no longer exist. Hick herself admitted to holding back just over a dozen. What happened to the rest, and why, is anyone's guess. Whether the missing letters would substantially change our understanding of Hick and Eleanor's relationship is also a mystery.

I quickly learned that reading the Hickok-Roosevelt correspondence in full is a wholly different experience from reading the selected excerpts that have been published in articles and anthologies. Context is vital. On the rare occasions when Hick or Eleanor expressed anger or irritation with each other, for instance, the overall tone of the letter remains cheerful and friendly. What I might otherwise have taken for dramatic outbursts are hardly as momentous in context as they appear in isolation. Rather, Hick and Eleanor simply aired their grievances and then got on with the rest of the day's happenings. And so reading every letter—from the most deeply intimate to the most numbingly mundane—became essential to my research.

Perhaps the greatest challenge of reading these letters is resisting the urge to project one's own feelings on them. The fact that I grew weary of reading about interoffice politics at the 1939 World's Fair, for example, does not necessarily mean Eleanor Roosevelt also found that information tedious. Hick aired all sorts of frustrations frequently; it's not difficult to come away from the Hickok-Roosevelt correspondence feeling that she was tiresome in some way or another and to conclude that Eleanor must have felt the same. But no matter how strongly we may react to Hick's professional, financial, or emotional struggles, it is often impossible to know whether Eleanor Roosevelt (who was infinitely more likely to offer advice or concern than to complain) would have agreed with us. Because of that, and because of the multitude of missing letters, I've tried to avoid making assumptions about their feelings toward each other. Any emotions I attribute to Lorena Hickok or Eleanor Roosevelt are documented, usually in their own words. (Likewise, no dialogue in this book is invented. Everything in quotation marks is taken verbatim from print, audio, or film sources.)

⁓

Several authors and scholars argue that Hick and Eleanor's relationship cooled over the years. I'm not so sure. It's true that the tone of their letters shifts across the decades. The circumstances of their lives also shifted over those thirty years in ways that potentially affected their correspondence. In 1933 and 1934, while their relationship was still new, Hick and Eleanor were separated for painful stretches of weeks and months. Both women were also navigating pivotal changes in their lives. Personally and professionally, their days were filled with vast, complex emotions—enough to fill ten or twelve pages. Later, when they had settled into their relationship and their jobs, and could see each other more regularly, their letters shrank to three or four pages.

It's also tempting to draw conclusions about the intensity of their relationship based on the way the letters taper off over the years. That, too, is a risky assumption. At a glance, the written record gives the impression that Hick and Eleanor were hardly in contact from 1942 to 1945. (A total of 257 letters exists for those four years, in contrast to the 257 from 1934 alone.) In reality, Hick was living at the White House during the war, and saw Eleanor frequently enough that letters weren't so essential to keeping in touch. The same is true of the mid-1950s, when Hick lived in Hyde Park, just three miles from Eleanor's cottage at Val-Kill.

Changes in technology further affected the way Hick and Eleanor maintained contact. Just as we today send fewer emails now that texting and instant messaging are prevalent, Hick and Eleanor's letters dwindled as telephone calls became more affordable. Perhaps it's only coincidence—then again, Eleanor wrote over and over in the mid-1930s how much it meant to her to hear Hick's voice on the phone when they were apart.

All of these factors have made me cautious about reading anything into the gradually diminishing length and frequency of Hick and Eleanor's letters.

The fact that the Hickok-Roosevelt correspondence exists at all is itself extraordinary, particularly in light of how Eleanor Roosevelt had been stricken by the discovery of Lucy Mercer's love letters to FDR. In her anger and sorrow at her husband's betrayal, Eleanor destroyed her own early correspondence with him. And yet Hick tells us that Eleanor wanted her letters to Hick preserved in the FDR Presidential Library, knowing that they would one day be visible to the public. Eleanor Roosevelt, it seems, was not ashamed of what the Lorena Hickok Papers contained.

The precise nature of Lorena Hickok and Eleanor Roosevelt's relationship is still debated today, forty years after the Lorena Hickok Papers were opened to the public. It will probably still be debated years from now. In the end, only one indisputable fact matters: Eleanor Roosevelt and Lorena Hickok loved each other until the day Eleanor died.

ACKNOWLEDGMENTS

Many thanks to:

Kirsten Carter, Virginia Lewick, Christian Belena, and especially Patrick Fahy of the Franklin D. Roosevelt Library and Museum for granting me access to the Lorena Hickok Papers, fetching endless carts full of materials, digging up photos, and suggesting resources I might otherwise have overlooked. And a special thank-you to Luciano Lacen ("Security Lou"), who makes entering and leaving the FDRL a delight every time I visit.

J. A. Pryse, Senior Archivist III at the Carl Albert Congressional Research and Studies Center; Melissa Shriver at the Milwaukee Public Library; and Lewis Wyman at the Library of Congress for retrieving obscure articles and letters, often with lightning speed.

Clare McCarthy, for her insightful read—gratias tibi ago.

Christopher Elias Pritchett, for mulling over the intricacies of LGBTQIA+ terminology at a moment's notice.

Wendy Schmalz: agent, research assistant, and friend.

The Random House Studio team, especially:

My editor, Annie Kelley, who always knows how to make a book better, even if I have to pout over heaping helpings of mac and cheese and ice cream before implementing her advice.

Alison Kolani, Barbara Perris, Amy Schroeder, and Christine Ma for catching all of my silliest mistakes and ironing out the stubbornest wrinkles.

Angela Carlino and Cathy Bobak, who made *Hick* shine inside and out.

SOURCES

Archival

The principal source is, of course, the Lorena Hickok Papers in the Franklin D. Roosevelt Presidential Library and Museum in Hyde Park, New York. While at the library, I also collected information from the papers of Maureen Corr, Doris Faber, Robert Graff, Henry T. and John Hackett, Harry L. Hopkins, Esther Lape, Anna Roosevelt Halsted, Eleanor Roosevelt, and the Women's Division of the Democratic National Committee.

The Bess Furman Papers at the Library of Congress and the Helen Gahagan Douglas Collection at the University of Oklahoma provided vital information as well.

Books

Bauman, John F., and Thomas H. Coode. *In the Eye of the Great Depression: New Deal Reporters and the Agony of the American People.* Northern Illinois University Press, 1988.

Beasley, Maurine H. *Eleanor Roosevelt and the Media: A Public Quest for Self-Fulfillment.* University of Illinois Press, 1987.

Bird, S. Elizabeth. *For Enquiring Minds: A Cultural Study of Supermarket Tabloids.* University of Tennessee Press, 1992.

Black, Ruby. *Eleanor Roosevelt: A Biography.* Duell, Sloan, and Pearce, 1940.

Cook, Blanche Wiesen. *Eleanor Roosevelt, Volume One: 1884–1933. The Early Years.* Penguin, 1992.

Cook, Blanche Wiesen. *Eleanor Roosevelt, Volume Two: 1933–1938. The Defining Years.* Penguin, 1999.

Cook, Blanche Wiesen. *Eleanor Roosevelt, Volume Three: 1939–1962. The War Years and After.* Penguin, 2016.

Davis, Kenneth S. *Invincible Summer: An Intimate Portrait of the Roosevelts Based on the Recollections of Marion Dickerman.* Atheneum, 1974.

Douglas, Helen Gahagan. *The Eleanor Roosevelt We Remember.* Hill and Wang, 1963.

Faber, Doris. *The Life of Lorena Hickok, E.R.'s Friend.* William Morrow, 1980.

Ferber, Edna. *A Peculiar Treasure.* Doubleday, Doran, 1938.

Ferentinos, Susan. *Courage to Love: Gender and Sexuality in the Life of Eleanor Roosevelt.* National Park Service, 2023.

Freidel, Frank Burt. *Franklin D. Roosevelt: Launching the New Deal.* Little, Brown, 1973.

Furman, Bess. *Washington By-Line.* Alfred A. Knopf, 1949.

Golay, Michael. *America 1933: The Great Depression, Lorena Hickok, Eleanor Roosevelt, and the Shaping of the New Deal.* Free Press, 2013.

Gurewitsch, Edna P. *Kindred Souls: The Friendship of Eleanor Roosevelt and David Gurewitsch.* St. Martin's Press, 2002.

Hickok, Lorena A. *Reluctant First Lady.* Dodd, Mead, 1962.

Hickok, Lorena A. *The Story of Franklin D. Roosevelt.* Dodd, Mead, 1956.

Hickok, Lorena A. *The Touch of Magic.* Dodd, Mead, 1961.

Hyde, Grant Milnor. *Newspaper Editing: A Manual for Editors, Copyreaders, and Students of Newspaper Desk Work.* D. Appleton, 1915.

Lash, Joseph P. *Love, Eleanor: Eleanor Roosevelt and Her Friends.* Doubleday, 1982.

Lash, Joseph P. *A World of Love: Eleanor Roosevelt and Her Friends, 1943–62.* Doubleday, 1984.

Levy, William Turner, and Cynthia Eagle Russett. *The Extraordinary Mrs. R: A Friend Remembers Eleanor Roosevelt.* John Wiley & Sons, 1999.

Lowitt, Richard, and Maurine Beasley, eds. *One Third of a Nation: Lorena Hickok Reports on the Great Depression.* University of Illinois Press, 1981.

Lukas, J. Anthony. *Big Trouble: A Murder in a Small Western Town Sets Off a Struggle for the Soul of America.* Simon & Schuster, 1997.

Lutes, Jean Marie. *Front-Page Girls: Women Journalists in American Culture and Fiction, 1880–1930.* Cornell University Press, 2006.

Michaelis, David. *Eleanor.* Simon & Schuster, 2020.

Morison, Bradley L. *Sunlight on Your Doorstep: The Minneapolis Tribune's First Hundred Years.* Ross & Haines, 1966.

Parks, Lillian Rogers, with Frances Spatz Leighton. *The Roosevelts: A Family in Turmoil.* Prentice Hall, 1981.

Perkins, Frances. *The Roosevelt I Knew.* Viking, 1946.

Pompeo, Joe. *Blood and Ink: The Scandalous Jazz Age Double Murder That Hooked America on True Crime.* William Morrow, 2022.

Quinn, Susan. *Eleanor and Hick: The Love Affair That Shaped a First Lady.* Penguin, 2016.

Roosevelt, Eleanor. *On My Own.* Harper and Brothers, 1958.

Roosevelt, Eleanor. *This I Remember.* Harper and Brothers, 1949.

Roosevelt, Eleanor. *This Is My Story.* Garden City Publishing, 1939.

Roosevelt, Eleanor. *You Learn by Living.* Harper and Brothers, 1960.

Roosevelt, Eleanor, and Lorena Hickok. *Ladies of Courage.* Putnam, 1954.

Roosevelt, James, with Bill Libby. *My Parents: A Differing View.* Playboy Press, 1976.

Ross, Ishbel. *Ladies of the Press.* Harper and Brothers, 1936.

Russell, Jan Jarboe. *Eleanor in the Village.* Scribner, 2021.

Sandifer, Irene Reiterman. *Mrs. Roosevelt as We Knew Her.* Privately printed, 1975.

Strachey, Dorothy. *Olivia.* Hogarth Press, 1949.

Ward, Geoffrey C. *Before the Trumpet: Young Franklin Roosevelt, 1882–1905.* Harper, 1985.

Wilson, Emily Herring. *The Three Graces of Val-Kill: Eleanor Roosevelt, Marion Dickerman, and Nancy Cook in the Place They Made Their Own.* University of North Carolina Press, 2017.

Articles

Beasley, Maurine H. "A 'Front Page Girl' Covers the Lindbergh Kidnapping: An Ethical Dilemma." *American Journalism,* Summer 1983.

Beasley, Maurine H. "Life as a Hired Girl in South Dakota, 1907–1908: A Woman Journalist Reflects." *South Dakota History,* Spring 1982.

Beasley, Maurine H. "Lorena Hickok to Harry Hopkins, 1933: A Woman Reporter Views Prairie Towns." *Montana: The Magazine of Western History,* Spring 1982.

Beasley, Maurine H. "Lorena A. Hickok: Woman Journalist." *Journalism History,* Autumn–Winter 1980.

Kaszuba, David. " 'Auntie Gopher': Lorena Hickok Tackles College Football." *Minnesota History,* Fall 2006.

Martinelli, Diana Knott, and Shannon A. Bowen. "The Public Relations Work of Journalism Trailblazer and First Lady Confidante Lorena Hickok, 1937–45." *Journalism History,* Fall 2009.

Audio

Dickerman, Marion, and Mary Belle Starr. *Reminiscences of Marion Dickerman, 1971.* Columbia Center for Oral History, Columbia University, dlc.library.columbia.edu/time_based_media/10.7916/d8-2zxs-fs15.

Roosevelt, Eleanor. *My Husband and I: Eleanor Roosevelt Recalls Her Years with FDR.* Columbia Records, 1965.

NOTES

Abbreviations

ER: Eleanor Roosevelt
FDRL: Franklin Delano Roosevelt Library
LAH: Lorena A. Hickok
LHP: Lorena Hickok Papers

Epigraph

I love you & you've made of me: ER to
LAH, undated (possibly 1934), LHP, box 2,
FDRL.

Prologue

"Franklin is tied up" and "Would you mind
coming over": Hickok, *Reluctant First Lady*,
94.
"I was just about the top gal reporter in the
country": Lorena A. Hickok to Malvina
Thompson, July 23, 1947, LHP, box 17, FDRL
(dated as 1949).
"Anything could happen" through "That night":
Hickok, *Reluctant First Lady*, 95–96.

Chapter 1

"warm and yellow" and "Ever since I can
remember": Lorena A. Hickok, unpublished
autobiography, ch. 1, p. 1, LHP, box 14, FDRL.
"In the memory pictures of my very early life":
Lorena A. Hickok, unpublished autobiography,
ch. 1, p. 2, LHP, box 14, FDRL.
"wide-spreading trees": Lorena A. Hickok,
unpublished autobiography, ch. 1, p. 3, LHP,
box 14, FDRL.
"a sizzling flash" through "I do not remember
what my grandfather looked like": Lorena A.
Hickok, unpublished autobiography, ch. 1, p. 2,
LHP, box 14, FDRL.
"When I was hardly more than a baby": Lorena
A. Hickok, unpublished autobiography, ch. 1,
pp. 3–4, LHP, box 14, FDRL.
"A doll was just a doll": Lorena A. Hickok,
unpublished autobiography, ch. 1, p. 14, LHP,
box 14, FDRL.

Chapter 2

"the other world—the world in which I was
actually going to have to live": Lorena A.
Hickok, unpublished autobiography, ch. 1, p. 5,
LHP, box 14, FDRL.
"There must have been times when he was
not angry": Lorena A. Hickok, unpublished
autobiography, ch. 1, p. 6, LHP, box 14, FDRL.
"My childhood was a confusing, kaleidoscopic
series": Lorena A. Hickok, unpublished
autobiography, ch. 1, p. 12, LHP, box 14, FDRL.
"I kept wondering, all through those childhood
years": Lorena A. Hickok, unpublished
autobiography, ch. 1, p. 6, LHP, box 14, FDRL.
"a kind of resentful bewilderment": Lorena A.
Hickok, unpublished autobiography, ch. 1, p. 8,
LHP, box 14, FDRL.
"get along" through "Sometimes it would make
me sick": Lorena A. Hickok, unpublished
autobiography, ch. 1, p. 16, LHP, box 14, FDRL.
"Nobody ever called me pretty" through "a
kind of hiding place": Lorena A. Hickok,
unpublished autobiography, ch. 1, p. 13, LHP,
box 14, FDRL.
"became thickly populated and richly furnished":
Lorena A. Hickok, unpublished autobiography,
ch. 1, p. 14, LHP, box 14, FDRL.
"happy and contented enough" through "a queer,
surly, unpromising youngster": Lorena A.
Hickok, unpublished autobiography, ch. 1,
p. 16, LHP, box 14, FDRL.
"Everything about her was exquisite" and "She
was the first person who ever made me feel":
Lorena A. Hickok, unpublished autobiography,
ch. 1, p. 10, LHP, box 14, FDRL.

Chapter 3

"round and flat, like an empty plate": Lorena A.
Hickok, unpublished autobiography, ch. 1,
p. 17, LHP, box 14, FDRL.
"infinite and intoxicating freedom" and "You
could run all the way to the rim of the world":

Lorena A. Hickok, unpublished autobiography, ch. 1, p. 18, LHP, box 14, FDRL.

"a succession of dusty little prairie towns": Lorena A. Hickok, unpublished autobiography, ch. 1, p. 17, LHP, box 14, FDRL.

"must have fitted to perfection my mother's idea of hell": Lorena A. Hickok, unpublished autobiography, ch. 1, p. 18, LHP, box 14, FDRL.

"huddled together": Lorena A. Hickok, unpublished autobiography, ch. 1, p. 17, LHP, box 14, FDRL.

"Sitting there in the surrey": Lorena A. Hickok, unpublished autobiography, ch. 1, p. 19, LHP, box 14, FDRL.

"the dustiest and dreariest of the little Dakota towns": Lorena A. Hickok, unpublished autobiography, ch. 1, p. 20, LHP, box 14, FDRL.

"frozen in horror": Lorena A. Hickok, unpublished autobiography, ch. 2, p. 4, LHP, box 14, FDRL.

"a bitter hatred": Lorena A. Hickok, unpublished autobiography, ch. 1, p. 6, LHP, box 14, FDRL.

"Do you want to kill the child?": Lorena A. Hickok, unpublished autobiography, ch. 1, p. 7, LHP, box 14, FDRL.

"Never once did he whip me": Lorena A. Hickok, unpublished autobiography, ch. 1, p. 6, LHP, box 14, FDRL.

"hopelessly ugly" and "a terrible ordeal": Lorena A. Hickok, unpublished autobiography, ch. 1, p. 16, LHP, box 14, FDRL.

"violently ill": Faber, *The Life of Lorena Hickok*, 13.

"in a peculiarly sympathetic way" and "One Sunday": Lorena A. Hickok, unpublished autobiography, ch. 2, p. 2, LHP, box 14, FDRL.

"boasting and strutting" and "We were at the age": Lorena A. Hickok, unpublished autobiography, ch. 2, p. 3, LHP, box 14, FDRL.

Chapter 4

"breaking up housekeeping" through "Perhaps I should have been dismayed": Lorena A. Hickok, unpublished autobiography, ch. 2, p. 2, LHP, box 14, FDRL.

"Feeling grown up and important" through "She showed no surprise, asked no questions": Lorena A. Hickok, unpublished autobiography, ch. 2, p. 4, LHP, box 14, FDRL.

"a suspicion that amounted to obsession" through "rather cheerful and cozy": Lorena A. Hickok, unpublished autobiography, ch. 2, p. 5, LHP, box 14, FDRL.

"What they got in return for their generosity": Lorena A. Hickok, unpublished autobiography, ch. 2, p. 6, LHP, box 14, FDRL.

"be natural": Lorena A. Hickok, unpublished autobiography, ch. 2, p. 7, LHP, box 14, FDRL.

"In her warm, careless way": Lorena A. Hickok, unpublished autobiography, ch. 2, p. 6, LHP, box 14, FDRL.

"Everyone in our small circle" and "Fatty": Lorena Hickok, "The Reward of Stuffing," *The Laurentian*, no. 19, 1913.

His eyes are green, his hair is white: Lorena A. Hickok, unpublished autobiography, ch. 2, p. 18, LHP, box 14, FDRL.

"One bleak afternoon": Lorena A. Hickok, unpublished autobiography, ch. 2, p. 17, LHP, box 14, FDRL.

"sugary scenes": Lorena A. Hickok, unpublished autobiography, ch. 2, p. 6, LHP, box 14, FDRL.

"The plate might be a shield": Lorena A. Hickok, unpublished autobiography, ch. 2, p. 7, LHP, box 14, FDRL.

Chapter 5

"bright interlude" and "I lived at the kitchen sink": Lorena A. Hickok, unpublished autobiography, ch. 2, p. 7, LHP, box 14, FDRL.

"House cleaning in the institution was most casual" and "kindly and courteous": Lorena A. Hickok, unpublished autobiography, ch. 2, p. 8, LHP, box 14, FDRL.

"an exceedingly shabby, grimy spectacle" through "surly, sloppy savage": Lorena A. Hickok, unpublished autobiography, ch. 2, p. 9, LHP, box 14, FDRL.

"sooty premises": Lorena A. Hickok, unpublished autobiography, ch. 2, p. 10, LHP, box 14, FDRL.

"scrawny and dirty" and "medicine": Lorena A. Hickok, unpublished autobiography, ch. 2, p. 11, LHP, box 14, FDRL.

"the houses": Lorena A. Hickok, unpublished autobiography, ch. 2, p. 10, LHP, box 14, FDRL.

"Whether by imagination or experience": Lorena A. Hickok, unpublished autobiography, ch. 2, pp. 10–11, LHP, box 14, FDRL.

"What Mrs. Hagedorn did not know" through "I can still feel the warm glow": Lorena A. Hickok, unpublished autobiography, ch. 2, p. 11, LHP, box 14, FDRL.

"the house of discord" through "a pallid, nervous, fretful little thing": Lorena A. Hickok, unpublished autobiography, ch. 2, p. 12, LHP, box 14, FDRL.

"really tried" through "I drudged along, hopeless, weary": Lorena A. Hickok, unpublished autobiography, ch. 2, p. 13, LHP, box 14, FDRL.

Chapter 6

"She even praised me when I did things right!" through "It would be a good home for the right girl": Lorena A. Hickok, unpublished autobiography, ch. 2, p. 14, LHP, box 14, FDRL.

"vast, round, golden plate" through "The paper burned, and the flames licked": Lorena A. Hickok, unpublished autobiography, ch. 2, p. 15, LHP, box 14, FDRL.

"I was a squirrel in a sweltering cage": Lorena A. Hickok, unpublished autobiography, ch. 2, pp. 15–16, LHP, box 14, FDRL.

"an ungrateful daughter" through "That change in his attitude": Lorena A. Hickok, unpublished autobiography, ch. 2, p. 16, LHP, box 14, FDRL.

Chapter 7

"I could not have put it into words at that time": Lorena A. Hickok, unpublished autobiography, ch. 2, p. 16, LHP, box 14, FDRL.

"What I needed, I decided, was a better education" through "read, write, 'n' figger": Lorena A. Hickok, unpublished autobiography, ch. 2, p. 17, LHP, box 14, FDRL.

"who gave me my first glimpses": Lorena A. Hickok, unpublished autobiography, ch. 2, p. 18, LHP, box 14, FDRL.

"the stature of a hero": Lorena A. Hickok, unpublished autobiography, ch. 2, p. 17, LHP, box 14, FDRL.

"After resolving that I was no longer": Lorena A. Hickok, unpublished autobiography, ch. 2, p. 20, LHP, box 14, FDRL.

"belonged": Lorena A. Hickok, unpublished autobiography, ch. 2, p. 19, LHP, box 14, FDRL.

"She would say things to me" through "seemed like awful drivel": Lorena A. Hickok, unpublished autobiography, ch. 2, p. 20, LHP, box 14, FDRL.

Chapter 8

"the 'nice' women of Bowdle" through "an elderly and somewhat frayed bird of paradise": Lorena A. Hickok, unpublished autobiography, ch. 2, p. 21, LHP, box 14, FDRL.

"Hunting for Tom's money" through "My wardrobe distressed her": Lorena A. Hickok, unpublished autobiography, ch. 2, p. 22, LHP, box 14, FDRL.

"Even I knew I looked funny": Lorena A. Hickok, unpublished autobiography, ch. 2, p. 23, LHP, box 14, FDRL.

"It was a nightmare": Lorena A. Hickok, unpublished autobiography, ch. 2, p. 22, LHP, box 14, FDRL.

"a very delightful reading": "First Place Goes to Selby," Aberdeen American, May 15, 1909.

"was cleverly done and won her much applause": "Aberdeen Girl in First Place," Aberdeen Daily News, May 15, 1909.

"I returned to Bowdle convinced that I had disgraced myself" and "The year was nearly over anyway": Lorena A. Hickok, unpublished autobiography, ch. 2, p. 22, LHP, box 14, FDRL.

Chapter 9

"Something ought to be done" through "Whereupon I slapped him, with all my might": Lorena A. Hickok, unpublished autobiography, ch. 2, p. 23, LHP, box 14, FDRL.

"Of Mrs. O'Malley's next move I took a dim view" and "I had a horror of family authority": Lorena A. Hickok, unpublished autobiography, ch. 2, p. 24, LHP, box 14, FDRL.

"The chances are I'd have been sent away somewhere": Lorena A. Hickok, unpublished autobiography, foreword, p. 5, LHP, box 14, FDRL.

"I still thought of Aunt Ella as the loveliest person" through "Gretchen style": Lorena A. Hickok, unpublished autobiography, ch. 2, p. 24, LHP, box 14, FDRL.

"With what I took to be perspiration": Lorena A. Hickok, unpublished autobiography, ch. 2, p. 25, LHP, box 14, FDRL.

Chapter 10

"Immaculate in a grey ensemble" and "The hands she held out in greeting": Lorena A. Hickok, unpublished autobiography, ch. 2, p. 25, LHP, box 14, FDRL.

"bare, bright, windy Dakota": Lorena A. Hickok, unpublished autobiography, ch. 1, p. 18, LHP, box 14, FDRL.

"sensitive": Leta Browning interview with Doris Faber, Doris Faber Papers, box 9, FDRL.

"a clever, lovely girl": Aleen Sleeper interview with Doris Faber, Doris Faber Papers, box 9, FDRL.

"awfully funny": Leta Browning interview with Doris Faber, Doris Faber Papers, box 9, FDRL.

"We always admired Lorena": Ruth Kelsey interview with Doris Faber, Doris Faber Papers, box 9, FDRL.

"The most gifted teacher I ever knew": Lorena A. Hickok, unpublished autobiography, outline, p. 1, LHP, box 14, FDRL.

"the best teacher I ever had": Hickok, *The Touch of Magic*, iv.

"remarkable" through "She spoke of the need for a fund": *Battle Creek Paean*, 1911, p. 96.

"She had the build for an opera singer" and "most unbecoming": Ruth Kelsey interview with Doris Faber, Doris Faber Papers, box 9, FDRL.

"Last night she gave one of the most fluent": "School Orators Score Big Hits," *Battle Creek Daily Moon*, April 11, 1912.

"I've got so many ideas that my head itches!": *Battle Creek Paean*, 1912, p. 137.

Chapter 11

"went sort of crazy": LAH to ER, April 10, 1940, LHP, box 7, FDRL.

"The 'unfortunate' women who had not found husbands": Lorena A. Hickok, unpublished autobiography, foreword, p. 2, LHP, box 14, FDRL.

"Well, I've decided to go away to college" through "Well, I've got sixty dollars": Leta Browning interview with Doris Faber, Doris Faber Papers, box 9, FDRL.

"sorority trouble": Lorena A. Hickok, unpublished autobiography, outline, p. 1, LHP, box 14, FDRL.

"At first my extravagant tales" through "For weeks I was subjected to all the torture": Lorena Hickok, "The Reward of Stuffing," *The Laurentian*, no. 19, 1913.

"other than sickness": Ella Ellis to Olin Mead, May 21, 1913, Doris Faber Papers, box 3, FDRL.

"Miss Hickok is a very bright girl" and "Now my dear girlie you know my faith in you": Ella Ellis to Lorena Hickok, June 1, 1913, LHP, box 13, FDRL.

Chapter 12

"Is the Newspaper Office the Place for a Girl?" through "In my eighteen years of experience": Edward Bok, "Is the Newspaper Office the Place for a Girl?," *Ladies' Home Journal*, February 1901.

"regarded as a threat to the peace": Ross, *Ladies of the Press*, 2.

"A woman—never!": W. T. Stead, "Young Women in Journalism," *Review of Reviews*, October 1892.

"In order to make any progress in her work" and "The editor calls out": Anne Eliot, "Experiences of a Woman Reporter," *Collier's*, August 21, 1909.

"would be *fine*": Ella Ellis to Lorena Hickok, June 1, 1913, LHP, box 13, FDRL.

"collecting 'personals'": Lorena A. Hickok, unpublished autobiography, outline, p. 1, LHP, box 14, FDRL.

"promptly raised hell": Ross, *Ladies of the Press*, 205.

"cordially disliked": Hyde, *Newspaper Editing*, 21.

Chapter 13

"People who knew her thought a great deal of her" through "I'm going out and make a name for myself in this world": Edna Browning interview with Doris Faber, November 9, 1978, Doris Faber Papers, box 9, FDRL.

"What in the world?" and "Look at the woman in man's clothing!": Leta Browning interview with Doris Faber, Doris Faber Papers, box 9, FDRL.

"Kind of a slovenly walk": Edna Browning interview with Doris Faber, November 9, 1978, Doris Faber Papers, box 9, FDRL.

Chapter 14

"complete misfit": Lorena A. Hickok, unpublished autobiography, outline, p. 1, LHP, box 14, FDRL.

"I was young then and full of hope": LAH to ER, November 9, 1936, LHP, box 3, FDRL.

"was as German as Germany": Ferber, *A Peculiar Treasure*, 132.

"fly-specked": Lorena A. Hickok, unpublished autobiography, ch. 2, p. 1, LHP, box 14, FDRL.

"The city editor—chivalrous soul": Ross, *Ladies of the Press*, 9.

"womanliness": Edward Bok, "Is the Newspaper Office the Place for a Girl?," *Ladies' Home Journal*, February 1901.

"Wisconsin has within her borders": Lorena A. Hickok, "African Princess Plain Miss Brown to College Girls," *Milwaukee Sentinel*, April 18, 1915.

"does not differ in many respects": Lorena Lawrence, "Restrictions Few at Girls' School," *Milwaukee Sentinel*, August 8, 1915.

"Girls! Here's Your Chance to Get a Husband!" and "I won't do": Lorena Lawrence, "Girls! Here's Your Chance to Get a Husband! Cupid Points the Way, Provided You Qualify," *Milwaukee Sentinel*, November 4, 1915.

Chapter 15

"Fundamentally, there is no better outlet": Ross, *Ladies of the Press*, 94.

"The most difficult assignment that can be

given": Anne Eliot, "Experiences of a Woman Reporter," *Collier's*, August 21, 1909.

"heroine of heroines" through "doubtfully": Lorena A. Hickok, "Farrar 'Goes to Bed' Early to Prove She's Still Prima Donna," *Minneapolis Tribune*, November 1, 1922.

"an Ethiopian gentleman" through "What, on the day when she is to sing?": Lorena Lawrence, "Geraldine Proves She's Prima Donna," *Milwaukee Sentinel*, November 19, 1915.

"Angry doesn't describe it at all": Lorena A. Hickok, "Farrar 'Goes to Bed' Early to Prove She's Still Prima Donna," *Minneapolis Tribune*, November 1, 1922.

"rippled with merriment" and "pounded a scorcher": Abe Altrowitz, "Memories of Her Abound," *Minneapolis Star*, May 16, 1968.

"After splashing through exactly 163 puddles of water" through "He also kissed me": Lorena Lawrence, "Geraldine Proves She's Prima Donna," *Milwaukee Sentinel*, November 19, 1915.

"Say, that's great stuff": Lorena A. Hickok, "Farrar 'Goes to Bed' Early to Prove She's Still Prima Donna," *Minneapolis Tribune*, November 1, 1922.

"stinger": Ross, *Ladies of the Press*, 206.

"a crackerjack" and "You tell Miss Farrar for me to go to hell!": Abe Altrowitz, "Memories of Her Abound," *Minneapolis Star*, May 16, 1968.

Chapter 16

"What I have to say to you won't mean much" through "'God bless the girl!'": Lorena Lawrence, "Melba Charms Large Audience at the Auditorium; Diva Plants a Kiss on Cheek of an Interviewer," *Milwaukee Sentinel*, December 4, 1915.

"I clasped the hand of the president of the United States" through "My heart gave a sudden bound": Lorena Lawrence, "First Lady of the Land Wins Way into Hearts of Thousands of Milwaukeeans by Personal Charm," *Milwaukee Sentinel*, February 1, 1916.

"funny yarns": Lorena A. Hickok, "Farrar 'Goes to Bed' Early to Prove She's Still Prima Donna," *Minneapolis Tribune*, November 1, 1922.

Chapter 17

"itching" through "dazzling": Ross, *Ladies of the Press*, 205–206.

"Whenever possible, they are steered into the quieter by-waters": Ross, *Ladies of the Press*, 3.

"Women's page stuff": Hickok, *Reluctant First Lady*, 16.

"Women began getting into all kinds of things": Lorena A. Hickok, unpublished autobiography, foreword, p. 2, LHP, box 14, FDRL.

"Yours truly, THE GIRL REPORTER": "Story of Girl Reporter at Circus, Two Horses, One Elephant and the Close of a Perfect Day," *Minneapolis Tribune*, July 17, 1917.

"an experienced and trusted": Ross, *Ladies of the Press*, 206.

"the well deserved tribute": James Gray to Harold Faber, undated, Doris Faber Papers, box 1, FDRL.

"Not, I *beg* of you, *Lorena*": Lorena A. Hickok to Bess Furman, undated (1933), Bess Furman Papers, box 27, Library of Congress.

"alternat[ing] 'hell' and 'damn' as punctuation marks": John P. Broderick, "An Interviewer Interviewed," LHP, box 14, FDRL.

"Many pecksniffs judged her by her pipe": Morison, *Sunlight on Your Doorstep*, 51.

Chapter 18

"Not from any altruistic motives": John P. Broderick, "An Interviewer Interviewed," LHP, box 14, FDRL.

"Overwhelmed": Lorena A. Hickok, unpublished autobiography, outline, p. 2, LHP, box 14, FDRL.

"Appalled" through "felt as if the sky had fallen": Ross, *Ladies of the Press*, 206.

"moral survey" and "separating girls from sailors": Lorena A. Hickok, unpublished autobiography, outline, p. 2, LHP, box 14, FDRL.

"uncontrollable habit of going after higher education" and "did not think that the post should go to a woman": Ross, *Ladies of the Press*, 207.

"deeply hurt": Bradley L. Morison to Doris Faber, October 17, 1978, Doris Faber Papers, box 1, FDRL.

"You write well" through "brilliant": Ross, *Ladies of the Press*, 207.

"Hundreds of people are reported missing": "EXTRA; Scores Dead in Up-State Forest Fires," *Minnesota Tribune*, October 13, 1918.

"the greater excitement of being on the spot": Ross, *Ladies of the Press*, 207.

Chapter 19

"the old man" and "at once the terror—and the idol—of the newsroom": Morison, *Sunlight on Your Doorstep*, 39.

"Writing is just like laying bricks": Morison, *Sunlight on Your Doorstep*, 40–41.

"taught me the newspaper business": Lorena A. Hickok, unpublished autobiography, outline, p. 1, LHP, box 14, FDRL.

"the cleverest interviewer in this section of the country": John P. Broderick, "An Interviewer Interviewed," LHP, box 14, FDRL.

"rather frowsy": Lorena A. Hickok, unpublished autobiography, outline, p. 2, LHP, box 14, FDRL.

"it was a great bore to submit to press interviews" through "submitted with the meekness of a lamb": Abe Altrowitz, "Memories of Her Abound," *Minneapolis Star,* May 16, 1968.

"The baby—I hated to see her go" and "And in the meantime": "Wife Dead, Baby Adopted, Man Fights to Keep Children," *Minneapolis Tribune,* December 24, 1922.

"May I be boiled in oil": "Juvenile Unbelievers Quick to Detect Fake Santa Claus," *Minneapolis Tribune,* December 21, 1921.

"It was one of those jobs" through "swell funny yarn": "She Dragged Her Weary Spats from Caffay to Cabbiray," *Minneapolis Tribune,* November 7, 1920.

Chapter 20

"Mrs. Peter Olesen May Have to Discard" and "none of her close friends in the capitol": "Mrs. Peter Olesen May Have to Discard Husband's Name on Ballot, Ruling Indicates," *Minneapolis Tribune,* April 19, 1922.

"special dispatch": "Ballot Ruling Against 'Mrs.' Checks Olesen Senate Race," *Evening Star,* April 20, 1922.

"Minnesota women are boiling over today" through "By next election day": Lorena A. Hickok, "Woman Politician Must Not Use Husband's Name," *Decatur Daily Review,* April 20, 1922.

"a general utility reporter": James Gray to Harold Faber, undated, Doris Faber Papers, box 1, FDRL.

"for the glory of it": Doris Faber Papers, box 9, notebook 1T, FDRL.

"I never heard her name spoken": James Gray to Harold Faber, undated, Doris Faber Papers, box 1, FDRL.

"a well-padded sofa": "Girl Reporter Tries Skating; But She'll Be Back at Work Next Week," *Minneapolis Tribune,* February 6, 1921.

"Hick always entered into this sort of nonsense with gusto" and Violent Study Club: Bradley L. Morison to Doris Faber, October 17, 1978, Doris Faber Papers, box 1, FDRL.

"self-improvement morally, socially, intellectually and spiritually": Hennepin County Library Special Collections: The Violet Study Club, archives.hclib.org/repositories/2/resources/107.

"frivolously devoted to get-togethers and good times": Bradley L. Morison to Doris Faber, October 17, 1978, Doris Faber Papers, box 1, FDRL.

"habitually amused, reassuring, and sisterly" and "starched blouses and sensible skirts": James Gray to Harold Faber, undated, Doris Faber Papers, box 1, FDRL.

"Dressing the part": "She Dragged Her Weary Spats from Caffay to Cabbiray," *Minnesota Tribune,* November 7, 1920.

"some damn woman bookkeeper" and "It was hotter than hell that day": John P. Broderick, "An Interviewer Interviewed," LHP, box 14, FDRL.

"The long moaning whistle around the bend": Lorena A. Hickok, "Iowa Village Waits All Night for Glimpse at Fleeting Train," *Minneapolis Tribune,* August 7, 1923.

Chapter 21

"short, dumpy, with wispy, hard-to-manage blonde hair": Lorena Hickok, "The Most Unforgettable Character I've Met," LHP, box 13, FDRL.

"Hickey Doodles": Ella Morse Dickinson to Lorena A. Hickok, July 15, 1938, and April 30, 1940, LHP, box 13, FDRL.

"On first meeting people were apt" through "a very great genius in the art of friendship": Lorena A. Hickok, "Memo on 'The Most Unforgettable Character I've Met,'" LHP, box 13, FDRL.

"swanky place": Doris Faber Papers, box 9, notebook 1T, FDRL.

"quite a gourmet": Jeannette Brice interview with Doris Faber, November 7, 1978, Doris Faber Papers, box 9, FDRL.

"looked askance": Nancy Elliott to Doris Faber, November 7, 1978, Doris Faber Papers, box 1, FDRL.

"roommate": "Yes Dearie, Whether Passenger's Male or Female, Elevator Operator Needs Sweet Disposition," *Minneapolis Tribune,* December 26, 1920.

"We did not even concede the existence of homosexuals": Morison, *Sunlight on Your Doorstep,* 41.

"You can believe it or not": Lorena A. Hickok,

"'On the Mishishippi, on the—,'" *Minneapolis Tribune*, May 25, 1924.

"Old Lady 501" through "a roaring, swaggering, joyous adventure": Lorena A. Hickok, "Reporter Crouches in Cab as 'Old Lady 501' Hits 55 Per," *Minneapolis Tribune*, March 7, 1926.

Chapter 22

"to deliver fawning 'feminine' perspectives": David Kaszuba, "'Auntie Gopher': Lorena Hickok Covers College Football," *Minnesota History*, Fall 2006, 104.

"Football must be a mighty interesting show" and "rehearsal": Lorena A. Hickok, "Gopher Secrets Perfectly Safe When Girl Writer Sees a Practice," *Minneapolis Tribune*, November 5, 1922.

"the Minnesota line fighting like wildcats": Alexander F. Jones, "Imported Runner Loses on Gopher 'Track,'" *Minneapolis Tribune*, November 16, 1925.

"a team with a fighting spirit": Lorena A. Hickok, "'Red' Grange Carried Home on His Shield," *Minneapolis Tribune*, November 16, 1925.

"And then the Minnesota prairie fire was off": Lorena A. Hickok, "Irish Greyhound Replaces Horsemen as Notre Dame Runs Down Gophers," *Minneapolis Tribune*, October 25, 1925.

"And then—An old hussy named Lady Luck got into the game": Lorena A. Hickok, "58,000 See Gophers Lose, 7-6," *Minneapolis Tribune*, November 21, 1926.

"To top the climax": "First on Sunday as Well as Daily," *Minneapolis Tribune*, November 13, 1925.

"Miss Hickok's rollicking sketch of the contest and crowds" and "The Supreme Thrill of the Football Season": "The Supreme Thrill of the Football Season," *Minneapolis Tribune*, November 20, 1925.

"Auntie Gopher": David Kaszuba, "'Auntie Gopher': Lorena Hickok Covers College Football," *Minnesota History*, Fall 2006, 101.

"dear nephews" and "the Gophers' poet laureate": Lorena A. Hickok, "Gophers Run and Run and Run Through Wabash in 67-7 Race," *Minneapolis Tribune*, October 24, 1926.

"Miss Goofer": Lorena A. Hickok, "Yost-men Frolic on Eve of Battle; Minnesota Grim," *Minneapolis Tribune*, October 16, 1926.

"[A] lot of folks are probably going to feel just a wee bit sad": Lorena A. Hickok, "Michigan Wins War, Jug, Title N'Everything Else," *Minneapolis Tribune*, November 22, 1925.

Chapter 23

"No go": Lorena A. Hickok, unpublished autobiography, outline, p. 2, LHP, box 14, FDRL.

"quite a crush": Nancy Elliott to Doris Faber, November 7, 1978, Doris Faber Papers, box 1, FDRL.

"took the tabloid formula and put it on full blast": Pompeo, *Blood and Ink*, 135.

"90 percent entertainment, 10 percent information": Bird, *For Enquiring Minds*, 19.

"by-line sobbie": "Chatter in New York," *Variety*, August 8, 1928.

"wild, boisterous, unmannerly crew": Lorena A. Hickok, unpublished autobiography, ch. 7, p. 4, LHP, box 14, FDRL.

"would sweep down on some defenseless little town": Lorena A. Hickok, unpublished autobiography, ch. 7, pp. 3–4, LHP, box 14, FDRL.

Chapter 24

"There are only two forces" and "great octopus": Lukas, *Big Trouble*, 632.

"an engine that causes 30,000,000 minds to have the same thought": Charles Edward Russell, "The Associated Press and Calumet," *Pearson's Magazine*, April 1914, 441.

"One noisy joint": Gardner Bridge to Harold Faber, November 9, 1978, Doris Faber Papers, box 1, FDRL.

"infuriating" through "something to remember": Hickok, *Reluctant First Lady*, 8.

"Sometimes, on particularly dull days" and "a rather forbidding New England exterior": Hickok, *Reluctant First Lady*, 9.

"you'd better get out of my way": Eleanor Lund, "Mamie," May 25, 1953, LHP, box 17, FDRL.

"my Boss": Hickok, *Reluctant First Lady*, 10.

"THE president": Hickok, *Reluctant First Lady*, 7.

"I got the impression that she didn't care very much": Hickok, *Reluctant First Lady*, 10.

"looked like a black straw pancake" and "You poor thing": Hickok, *Reluctant First Lady*, 11.

"To my amazement" through "I failed to get much news out of her": Hickok, *Reluctant First Lady*, 14.

"The new mistress of the Executive Mansion" and "Too editorial": Hickok, *Reluctant First Lady*, 15.

Chapter 25

"sumptuous breakfast": Gardner Bridge to Harold
Faber, November 9, 1978, Doris Faber Papers,
box 1, FDRL.
"two pluckiest people ever": "Rescue Ships
Bringing 206 Vestris Survivors to Port," *New
York Times,* November 14, 1928.
"by Paul A. Dana, as told to Lorena A. Hickok":
Lorena A. Hickok, "Drifted 22 Hours with
Woman in Sea," *New York Times,* November 15,
1928.
"Davies and myself walked along the railside of":
Carolos Quiros, "Survivor Tells of Disaster;
Had to Jump from Crowded Lifeboat," *New
York Times,* November 14, 1928.
"Toward sunset it began to cloud up": Lorena A.
Hickok, "Drifted 22 Hours with Woman in
Sea," *New York Times,* November 15, 1928.
"A Masterpiece of Reporting" and "she painted
a picture that will stand": "A Masterpiece
of Reporting," *Raleigh News and Observer,*
November 16, 1928.
"she could tackle anything": Ross, *Ladies of the
Press,* 208.
"The AP wouldn't let me handle a big story" and
"If only they'd let me be a reporter": Lorena
Hickok to Bess Furman, June 27, 1930, Bess
Furman Papers, box 27, Library of Congress.
"The idea seems to be": Lorena A. Hickok,
"Governor's Wife Finds Enough to Do
Although Past 45 Years," *Elmira Star-Gazette,*
October 31, 1930.
"I used to hope that we might at least get a little
bit sociable": Hickok, *Reluctant First Lady,* 23.

Chapter 26

"An excellent newsperson, a professional in every
way": Jane Griffing Bancroft to Harold Faber,
December 8, 1978, Doris Faber Papers, box 1,
FDRL.
"I'm going to teach you to play poker": Faber, *The
Life of Lorena Hickok,* 78.
"She'd open the door" and "thick huge steaks in
the oven": Jane Griffing Bancroft to Harold
Faber, December 8, 1978, Doris Faber Papers,
box 1, FDRL.
"trusted with straight news leads on big stories"
and "never hesitated to give her the best story
that came along": Ross, *Ladies of the Press,* 208;
see also Jane Griffing Bancroft to Harold Faber,
December 8, 1978, Doris Faber Papers, box 1,
FDRL.
"Al Smith had thrown up the sponge": C. E.

Butterfield, "Public Glimpses Drama of News
Gathering 'By the AP,'" *Chambersburg Public
Opinion,* March 8, 1931.
"six perfect examples of the successful front-page
girl": Ross, *Ladies of the Press,* 7.
"just about the top gal reporter in the country":
Lorena A. Hickok to Malvina Thompson,
July 23, 1947, LHP, box 17, FDRL (dated as
1949).
"The trouble is that, being a woman": Lorena
Hickok to Bess Furman, June 27, 1930, Bess
Furman Papers, box 27, Library of Congress.
"Every time I go out on a story I'm scared stiff"
and "The fascinating 'surprise' element": John
P. Broderick, "An Interviewer Interviewed,"
LHP, box 14, FDRL.
"If you're built as I am": Lorena Hickok to Bess
Furman, June 27, 1930, Bess Furman Papers,
box 27, Library of Congress.

Chapter 27

"Lindbergh Baby Kidnapped": "Lindbergh Baby
Kidnapped from Home of Parents on Farm
Near Princeton; Taken from His Crib; Wide
Search On," *New York Times,* March 2, 1932.
"Eaglet": James L. Kilgallen, "Famous 'We' a Trio
as Lindy Becomes Dad," *Detroit Times Extra,*
June 23, 1930.
"Every reporter in the country" and "cursing
under my breath all the way": Lorena A.
Hickok, unpublished autobiography, ch. 7, p. 3,
LHP, box 14, FDRL.
"expected and invariably got to work on": Jane
Griffing Bancroft to Harold Faber, December 8,
1978, Doris Faber Papers, box 1, FDRL.
"Never in my life did I see anything like
Hopewell": Lorena A. Hickok, unpublished
autobiography, ch. 7, p. 4, LHP, box 14, FDRL.
"Them's just moles!": Lorena A. Hickok,
unpublished autobiography, ch. 7, p. 2, LHP,
box 14, FDRL.
"The police were not interested": Lorena A.
Hickok, unpublished autobiography, ch. 7, p. 3,
LHP, box 14, FDRL.

Chapter 28

"Everybody quit driving around the countryside":
Lorena A. Hickok, unpublished autobiography,
ch. 7, p. 4, LHP, box 14, FDRL.
"There's a path up the mountain" through "The
cops had grown nervous": Lorena A. Hickok,
unpublished autobiography, ch. 7, p. 6, LHP,
box 14, FDRL.
"a grim and hopeless assignment": Lorena A.

Hickok, unpublished autobiography, ch. 7, p. 4, LHP, box 14, FDRL.

"an altogether gay and companionable time" through "The story was too big, the leads too few": Lorena A. Hickok, unpublished autobiography, ch. 7, p. 5, LHP, box 14, FDRL.

"The New York office": Lorena A. Hickok, unpublished autobiography, ch. 7, p. 10, LHP, box 14, FDRL.

"In all my twenty years in the business" through "Day after day there would be nothing": Lorena A. Hickok, unpublished autobiography, ch. 7, p. 5, LHP, box 14, FDRL.

"to get myself worked up to the proper pitch": Lorena A. Hickok, unpublished autobiography, ch. 7, p. 10, LHP, box 14, FDRL.

"It was heartbreaking, unrewarding, fantastic": Lorena A. Hickok, unpublished autobiography, ch. 7, p. 1, LHP, box 14, FDRL.

"Still Missing": Lorena A. Hickok, "Lindbergh Baby Still Missing; Search Goes On," *Charleston Evening Post*, March 3, 1932.

"Still No Clue": Lorena A. Hickok, "Still No Clue to Lindbergh Baby," *Washington Observer*, March 4, 1932.

"sounded positively hysterical": Lorena A. Hickok, unpublished autobiography, ch. 7, p. 7, LHP, box 14, FDRL.

Chapter 29

"I think I managed to fall down": Lorena A. Hickok, unpublished autobiography, ch. 7, p. 7, LHP, box 14, FDRL.

"the calm, unhurried motions of someone getting ready for bed": Lorena A. Hickok, unpublished autobiography, ch. 7, p. 8, LHP, box 14, FDRL.

"The man on the city desk": Lorena A. Hickok, unpublished autobiography, ch. 7, p. 7, LHP, box 14, FDRL.

". . . she made for me" through "didn't herself wish to surrender to these tendencies": Katherine Beebe Harris interview with Doris Faber, November 16, 1978, Doris Faber Papers, box 3, FDRL.

Chapter 30

"furiously" and "A week later, still whispering": Lorena A. Hickok, unpublished autobiography, ch. 7, p. 13, LHP, box 14, FDRL.

"A good, substantial tea": Lorena A. Hickok, "One of Mrs. Roosevelt's Friends Says Wife of President-Elect Is 'a Whirlwind,'" *Schenectady Daily Gazette*, November 12, 1932.

"I built that for my Missis" and "an impersonal way": Hickok, *Reluctant First Lady*, 30.

Chapter 31

"shut up inside herself" through "She's probably afraid her husband won't get it": Hickok, *Reluctant First Lady*, 32–33.

"Mrs. Roosevelt, aren't you *thrilled*": Hickok, *Reluctant First Lady*, xv.

"and went happily on my way": Hickok, *Reluctant First Lady*, 36.

Chapter 32

"did not try to be 'one of the boys'": Elton C. Fay to Harold Faber, November 12, 1978, Doris Faber Papers, box 1, FDRL.

"too good as a reporter" through "tender-hearted and, even, sometimes shy": W. B. Ragsdale to Harold Faber, December 13, 1978, Doris Faber Papers, box 1, FDRL.

"Boss": Hickok, *Reluctant First Lady*, 10.

"Tommy was so suspicious": Lash, *Love, Eleanor*, 311.

"as excited as I ever saw her" through "the feeling must have been mutual": W. B. Ragsdale to Harold Faber, December 13, 1978, Doris Faber Papers, box 1, FDRL.

"precious little" and "Puffing, panting, and perspiring": Hickok, *Reluctant First Lady*, 39.

"Were you frightened" and "If I had been frightened": Hickok, *Reluctant First Lady*, 41.

Chapter 33

"She's all yours now, Hickok": Hickok, *Reluctant First Lady*, 43.

"women's page stuff": Hickok, *Reluctant First Lady*, 16.

"While I had no occasion to write stories about her": Hickok, *Reluctant First Lady*, 17.

"It's good to be middle-aged": Hickok, *Reluctant First Lady*, 44.

"Send him to the glue factory": Jane Ely telephone interview with Harold Faber, January 14, 1979, Doris Faber Papers, box 2, FDRL.

"THE DAME HAS ENORMOUS DIGNITY": Lorena Hickok to Bill Chapin, LHP, box 14, FDRL.

"Stay with it, kid": Hickok, *Reluctant First Lady*, 47.

"I don't see many Democratic posters around": Hickok, *Reluctant First Lady*, 48.

Chapter 34

"I'm longer than you" through "Franklin used to tease me about you": Hickok, *Reluctant First Lady*, 49.

"She is such a funny child": Roosevelt, *This Is My Story*, 17–18.

"sink through the floor": Roosevelt, *This Is My Story*, 18.

"a curious barrier": Roosevelt, *This Is My Story*, 16.

"Attention and admiration were the things": Roosevelt, *This Is My Story*, 22.

"I slid down the banisters": Roosevelt, *This Is My Story*, 30.

"If people only realized what a war goes on": Roosevelt, *This Is My Story*, 17–18.

"Death meant nothing to me": Roosevelt, *This Is My Story*, 19.

"simply refused to believe it": Roosevelt, *This Is My Story*, 34.

"Every moment that they were there": Roosevelt, *This Is My Story*, 98.

"the ugly duckling": Roosevelt, *This Is My Story*, 89.

"I knew I was the first girl in my mother's family": Roosevelt, *This Is My Story*, 101.

"Poor little soul, she is very plain": Ward, *Before the Trumpet*, 293.

"I think I was a curious mixture": Roosevelt, *This Is My Story*, 109.

"May I write some of that?" and "If you like": Hickok, *Reluctant First Lady*, 49.

"I never talked to anyone": ER to LAH, April 8, 1933, LHP, box 1, FDRL.

Chapter 35

"You aren't going to be able to do that sort of thing": Hickok, *Reluctant First Lady*, 53.

"Want to bet?": Hickok, *Reluctant First Lady*, 54.

"I know what they'll be up against": Hickok, *Reluctant First Lady*, 56.

"I can either run the country": loc.gov/item/today-in-history/february-03.

"It's good to have you around tonight, Hick": Hickok, *Reluctant First Lady*, 58.

"I was reminded of a fox": Hickok, *Reluctant First Lady*, 59.

Chapter 36

"I know that some of you were heart and soul" through "But I'm not the wife of the President yet": Lorena A. Hickok, "Mrs. Roosevelt Back to Her Job," *Miami News-Record Sun*, November 13, 1932.

"But I haven't changed inside": Hickok, *Reluctant First Lady*, 4.

"I was not to quote her directly": Furman, *Washington By-Line*, 133.

"If I wanted to be selfish" through "And now—I shall have to work out": Lorena A. Hickok, "'If I Wanted to Be Selfish I Could Wish That He Had Not Been Elected,' Says New First Lady of the Land," *Schenectady Daily Gazette*, November 10, 1932.

"I loved it": Lorena A. Hickok, "Mrs. Roosevelt Had Odd Sort of Childhood; Is Brought Up by Her Mother's Mother," *Schenectady Daily Gazette*, November 11, 1932.

"I have a lot of fun doing things with money": Lorena A. Hickok, "One of Mrs. Roosevelt's Friends Says Wife of President-Elect Is 'a Whirlwind,'" *Schenectady Daily Gazette*, November 12, 1932.

"I hate to do it": Lorena A. Hickok, "'If I Wanted to Be Selfish I Could Wish That He Had Not Been Elected,' Says New First Lady of the Land," *Schenectady Daily Gazette*, November 10, 1932.

"She is, to use the expression of one of her friends": Lorena A. Hickok, "One of Mrs. Roosevelt's Friends Says Wife of President-Elect Is 'a Whirlwind,'" *Schenectady Daily Gazette*, November 12, 1932.

Chapter 37

"If you insist": Hickok, *Reluctant First Lady*, 65.

"very much perturbed" through "Nonsense!": Hickok, *Reluctant First Lady*, 67.

Chapter 38

"affectionately": ER to LAH, October 26, 1932, LHP, box 1, FDRL.

"Hicky" and "Mrs. Roosevelt": LAH to ER, undated (1932), LHP, box 1, FDRL.

"Miss Hickok": ER to LAH, October 26, 1932, LHP, box 1, FDRL.

"Hick my dearest": ER to LAH, March 5, 1933, LHP, box 1, FDRL.

"Hick darling": ER to LAH, March 6, 1933, LHP, box 1, FDRL.

"My Dear": LAH to ER, November 26, 1932, LHP, box 1, FDRL.

"little saying" and "Je t'aime et je t'adore": ER to LAH, March 6, 1933, LHP, box 1, FDRL.

"We continued to see a great deal of each other": Hickok, *Reluctant First Lady*, 78.

"warm friends": Roosevelt, *This I Remember*, 78.

"Now I was about to go there to live": Roosevelt, *This I Remember*, 76.

"I'll just have to go on being myself": Hickok, *Reluctant First Lady*, 85.

Chapter 39

"You can't do that" and "Oh yes I can": Hickok, *Reluctant First Lady*, 73.

"My dear": Hickok, *Reluctant First Lady*, 86.

"We were only separated by a few yards dear Hick": Faber, *The Life of Lorena Hickok*, 134.

"Is Mrs. Roosevelt really the natural, unaffected person" and "I think so": Hickok, *Reluctant First Lady*, 93.

"Well, it won't be long": Lorena Hickok to Bess Furman, undated (1933), Bess Furman Papers, box 27, Library of Congress.

"real, honest-to-gawd stories": Lorena Hickok to Bess Furman, June 27, 1930, Bess Furman Papers, box 27, Library of Congress.

"Gosh, won't I love being back": Lorena Hickok to Bess Furman, undated (1933), Bess Furman Papers, box 27, Library of Congress.

"Here was an outstanding woman reporter": Furman, *Washington By-Line*, 138.

"Would it be feasible" and "Instantly I saw vast news possibilities opening": Furman, *Washington By-Line*, 139.

"No newspaper woman could have asked for better luck": Furman, *Washington By-Line*, 153.

"Unless the women reporters could find something new to write about": Roosevelt, *This I Remember*, 102.

"There are possibly a great many things which are not purely political": "Women Poke Fun at Mrs. Roosevelt," *New York Times*, February 15, 1933.

Chapter 40

"No one except members of the family": Lorena A. Hickok memo to W. W. Chaplin, LHP, box 14, FDRL.

"the high spot of my newspaper career": Lorena A. Hickok to Malvina Thompson, July 23, 1947, LHP, box 17, FDRL (dated as 1949).

"Of all things, an exclusive to an outsider!": W. B. Ragsdale to Harold Faber, December 13, 1978, Doris Faber Papers, box 1, FDRL.

"As though I was a nice, tame little gal who was somebody's pet": Lorena A. Hickok to Malvina Thompson, July 23, 1947, LHP, box 17, FDRL (dated as 1949).

"last night out of captivity": Hickok, *Reluctant First Lady*, 88.

Chapter 41

"There's something I'd like to show you": Hickok, *Reluctant First Lady*, 90.

"armed truce": James Roosevelt, *My Parents*, 101.

"an understanding, a closeness, a bond": Douglas, *The Eleanor Roosevelt We Remember*, 29.

"I'd come out here, alone": Hickok, *Reluctant First Lady*, 92.

"All the sorrow humanity had ever had": Hickok, *Reluctant First Lady*, 91–92.

"my emancipation and my education": Lorena A. Hickok, "Mrs. Roosevelt Had Odd Sort of Childhood; Is Brought Up by Her Mother's Mother," *Schenectady Daily Gazette*, November 11, 1932.

Chapter 42

"the lowest ebb in the Great Depression" and "the clamor of a desperate, frightened public": Hickok, *Reluctant First Lady*, 93.

"It was very, very solemn" and "No woman entering the White House": Lorena A. Hickok, "Mrs. Roosevelt Impressed and a Little Terrified by Vivid Inaugural Ceremonies," *Canton Repository*, March 5, 1933.

"Least of all *this* woman": Hickok, *Reluctant First Lady*, 104.

"The important thing, it seems to me": Lorena A. Hickok, "Mrs. Roosevelt Impressed and a Little Terrified by Vivid Inaugural Ceremonies," *Canton Repository*, March 5, 1933.

Chapter 43

"Said good-bye to Hick": Faber, *The Life of Lorena Hickok*, 118.

"keep up a kind of intimacy which wipes out time and space": Roosevelt, *This Is My Story*, 72.

"Hick my dearest, I cannot go to bed to-night": ER to LAH, March 5, 1933, LHP, box 1, FDRL.

"often & about little things": Lash, *Love, Eleanor*, 384.

"Oh! darling, I hope on the whole" and "thought waves": ER to LAH, March 5, 1933, LHP, box 1, FDRL.

"Hick darling, Oh! how good it was to hear your voice": ER to LAH, March 6, 1933, LHP, box 1, FDRL.

"I can't kiss you so I kiss your picture": ER to LAH, March 9, 1933, LHP, box 1, FDRL.

"You have a stormier time than I do": ER to LAH, March 11, 1933, LHP, box 1, FDRL.

"Remember one thing always": ER to LAH, March 10, 1933, LHP, box 1, FDRL.

"All day I've thought of you" and "Your ring is a great comfort": ER to LAH, March 7, 1933, LHP, box 1, FDRL.

"My dear if you meet me" and "The one thing

which reconciles me": ER to LAH, March 9, 1933, LHP, box 1, FDRL.

Chapter 44

"I felt half choked" through "I wanted to tell her about a salmon colored schoolhouse": Lorena Hickok, untitled manuscript on the weekend of March 18, 1933, p. 1, Doris Faber Papers, box 3, FDRL.

Chapter 45

"He, more than any fifty men": "Business: Troubles of Mitchell," *Time*, November 18, 1929.

"A reporter should never get too close to the news source": Hickok, *Reluctant First Lady*, 96.

"I was given Hell": Lorena A. Hickok to Malvina Thompson, July 23, 1947, LHP, box 17, FDRL (dated as 1949).

"Trouble with this outfit is that they're spoiled": Lorena Hickok to Bess Furman, undated (1933), Bess Furman Papers, box 27, Library of Congress.

"I do understand your joy and pride": ER to LAH, April 6, 1933, LHP, box 1, FDRL.

"When you haven't the feeling of responsibility": ER to LAH, April 20, 1933, LHP, box 1, FDRL.

"I hate to hear you say": ER to LAH, April 3, 1933, LHP, box 1, FDRL.

"I hope that, whatever your decision": ER to LAH, April 20, 1933, LHP, box 1, FDRL.

"disgusted with myself" and "soiled": ER to LAH, May 27, 1933, LHP, box 1, FDRL.

"My zest in life is rather gone" through "You are my rock": ER to LAH, May 31, 1933, LHP, box 1, FDRL.

"I got sorer and sorer": Lorena A. Hickok to Malvina Thompson, July 23, 1947, LHP, box 17, FDRL (dated as 1949).

Chapter 46

"What I want you to do": Lorena A. Hickok, unpublished manuscript, introductory chapter, LHP, box 12, FDRL.

"I'm looking forward to the new job" and "It's such a darn complicated affair": Lorena A. Hickok to Harry L. Hopkins, June 7, 1933, Doris Faber Papers, box 3, FDRL.

"indoctrinated": Hickok, *Reluctant First Lady*, 143.

"I never knew anyone who had a more mischievous": Lorena A. Hickok interview, Robert Graff Papers, box 3, FDRL.

"Hick's rugwashing machine" and "It seems to

me that Washington": Hickok, *Reluctant First Lady*, 147.

Chapter 47

"Where would they hide us?": Hickok, *Reluctant First Lady*, 120.

"My dear, they're all Republicans up here": Hickok, *Reluctant First Lady*, 123.

"Well—you're the First Lady" and "I was so ticklish": Hickok, *Reluctant First Lady*, 122.

Chapter 48

"Damn!": Hickok, *Reluctant First Lady*, 128.

"unbecoming language": Roosevelt, *This I Remember*, 124.

"Oh spinach!": Hickok, *Reluctant First Lady*, 113.

"We've got to get out of this some way" through "respect and admiration": Hickok, *Reluctant First Lady*, 128.

"unearthly beauty": Hickok, *Reluctant First Lady*, 133.

Chapter 49

"the relief show": Lorena A. Hickok to Harry L. Hopkins, August 16–26, 1933, LHP, box 11, FDRL.

"a three-year Odyssey": Lorena A. Hickok, unpublished manuscript, introductory chapter, p. 2, LHP, box 12, FDRL.

"Harry Hopkins had one remarkable quality" and "When you're talking to somebody on relief": FDR, episode 5, "Forgotten Men," produced by Robert D. Graff, aired February 12, 1965, on ABC.

"Kickers" through "They'll never be any good any more": Lorena A. Hickok to Harry L. Hopkins, August 6, 1933, LHP, box 11, FDRL.

"they were not really people at all": Lorena A. Hickok, unpublished manuscript, introductory chapter, p. 1, LHP, box 12, FDRL.

"One by one, sometimes bold": Lorena A. Hickok, unpublished manuscript, introductory chapter, p. 3, LHP, box 12, FDRL.

"Suppose you were my wife": Lorena A. Hickok to Harry L. Hopkins, April 1934, LHP, box 11, FDRL.

"Tonight I feel like a great big sponge": LAH to ER, August 1933, LHP, box 12, FDRL.

Chapter 50

"I doubt if you'll ever find time": Lorena A. Hickok to Harry L. Hopkins, August 6, 1933, LHP, box 11, FDRL.

"I feel faint whenever I try to imagine": Lorena A.

Hickok to Mrs. Godwin, August 6, 1933, LHP, box 11, FDRL.

"I read parts of your letter to Franklin": ER to LAH, August 3, 1933, LHP, box 1, FDRL.

"You must be simply worn out": ER to LAH, August 5, 1933, LHP, box 1, FDRL.

"We're tired, too, lady": Lorena A. Hickok, August 7–12, LHP, box 11, FDRL.

"What a power you have to feel and to describe": ER to LAH, August 25, 1933, LHP, box 1, FDRL.

Chapter 51

"If you want to see just how bad things are" through "hadn't really hurt": Hickok, *Reluctant First Lady*, 136.

"obsolete" and "brick beehives falling into ruin": LAH to ER, August 1933, LHP, box 12, FDRL.

"The hills are still beautiful": LAH to ER, August 25, 1933, LHP, box 12, FDRL.

"Again tonight I have that sense": LAH to ER, August 1933, LHP, box 12, FDRL.

"instinctively liked and trusted": Lorena A. Hickok, unpublished manuscript, introductory chapter, p. 4, LHP, box 12, FDRL.

"the kind you or I might give to a dog": Roosevelt, *This I Remember*, 126–127.

"He thinks we are not going to eat it": Roosevelt, *This I Remember*, 127.

"We woke up one morning in hell": Cook, *Eleanor Roosevelt, Volume 2*, 143.

"Only a few of the resettlement projects": Roosevelt, *This I Remember*, 128.

Chapter 52

"Don't forget me, honey! Don't forget me!": Lorena A. Hickok, report on Kentucky, August 31—September 3, 1933, LHP, box 11, FDRL.

"Now, Franklin, you behave yourself": Hickok, *Reluctant First Lady*, 156.

Chapter 53

"in a daze" through "These plains are beautiful": LAH to ER, October 31, 1933, LHP, box 12, FDRL.

"Oh, my dear, I *do* get so hungry for letters!": LAH to ER, November 28, 1933, LHP, box 1, FDRL.

"Poor dear, what sad things": ER to LAH, November 2, 1933, LHP, box 1, FDRL.

"the desperate need for things": Lorena A. Hickok to Harry L. Hopkins, November 3, 1933, LHP, box 11, FDRL.

"Dammit, I don't WANT to write": Lorena A.

Hickok to Harry L. Hopkins, November 10, 1933, LHP, box 11, FDRL.

"There isn't—there can't be": LAH to ER, October 31, 1933, LHP, box 12, FDRL.

"I am prouder, dear, to know you": ER to LAH, November 11, 1933, LHP, box 1, FDRL.

"I thought I'd already seen about everything" through "It seemed like the end of the world": LAH to ER, November 11, 1933, LHP, box 12, FDRL.

"What a picture you can paint!" and "You feel too much": ER to LAH, November 14, 1933, LHP, box 1, FDRL.

"had a little longing (secretly)": ER to LAH, December 1, 1933, LHP, box 1, FDRL.

"I've been trying today to bring back your face": LAH to ER, December 5, 1933, LHP, box 1, FDRL.

"Funny everything I do my thoughts fly to you": ER to LAH, December 7, 1933, LHP, box 1, FDRL.

"We'll have tea in my room": ER to LAH, December 12, 1933, LHP, box 1, FDRL.

"I'd like to have you here that night": ER to LAH, November 24, 1933, LHP, box 1, FDRL.

Chapter 54

"Dear one it's getting nearer & nearer": ER to LAH, December 9, 1933, LHP, box 1, FDRL.

"Hick dearest": ER to LAH, December 23, 1933, LHP, box 1, FDRL.

"The greatest responsibility anyone can have": ER to LAH, April 14, 1933, LHP, box 1, FDRL.

"You shall dine in bed & sleep all you want": ER to LAH, December 25, 1933, LHP, box 1, FDRL.

"I think my real trouble is": LAH to ER, April 1, 1934, LHP, box 1, FDRL.

Chapter 55

"Dearest, it was a lovely weekend": LAH to ER, January 22, 1934, LHP, box 1, FDRL.

"I loved every minute": ER to LAH, January 23, 1934, LHP, box 1, FDRL.

"a lost feeling" and "the infinite succession of things": ER to LAH, January 24, 1934, LHP, box 1, FDRL.

"This *is* a fascinating job of mine!": LAH to ER, January 22, 1934, LHP, box 1, FDRL.

"Half-starved Whites and Blacks struggle in competition" and "I just can't describe to you": Lorena A. Hickok to Harry L. Hopkins, January 23, 1934, LHP, box 11, FDRL.

"Oh, dear one, it is all the little things": ER to LAH, January 27, 1934, LHP, box 1, FDRL.

"Strong relationships have to grow deep roots":
ER to LAH, February 4, 1934, LHP, box 1,
FDRL.

"Believe me, the next state administrator": Lorena
A. Hickok to Harry L. Hopkins, February 7,
1934, LHP, box 11, FDRL.

"half dead from fatigue" through "I read the thing
and wanted to curse": Lorena A. Hickok to
Kathryn Godwin, February 18, 1934, Doris
Faber Papers, box 3, FDRL.

"She is a rotund lady": "Relief: Professional Giver,"
Time, February 19, 1934.

"I'm so fed up with publicity": Lorena A. Hickok
to Kathryn Godwin, February 18, 1934, Doris
Faber Papers, box 3, FDRL.

"Miss Hickok would also go along": "Relief:
Professional Giver," Time, February 19, 1934.

"I don't suppose I ought to kick": Lorena A.
Hickok to Kathryn Godwin, February 18, 1934,
Doris Faber Papers, box 3, FDRL.

Chapter 56

"I believe it gets harder to let you go": ER to LAH,
March 26, 1934, LHP, box 1, FDRL.

"What a town for a glutton!": LAH to ER, April 9,
1934, LHP, box 1, FDRL.

"Mr. Hopkins, did you ever spend a couple of
hours": Lorena A. Hickok to Harry L. Hopkins,
April 13, 1934, LHP, box 11, FDRL.

"I'll give you more on New Orleans": Lorena A.
Hickok to Harry L. Hopkins, April 11, 1934,
LHP, box 11, FDRL.

"Oh, my dear, love me a lot! I need it!": LAH to
ER, April 11, 1934, LHP, box 1, FDRL.

"Dearest, I miss you & wish you were here": ER to
LAH, April 4, 1934, LHP, box 1, FDRL.

"I wonder if always I'm not going to feel": ER to
LAH, March 30, 1934, LHP, box 1, FDRL.

"I miss you very much": ER to LAH, March 29,
1934, LHP, box 1, FDRL.

"You give me so much more happiness than": ER
to LAH, March 27, 1934, LHP, box 1, FDRL.

"I've been thinking a lot tonight about Prinz":
LAH to ER, April 20, 1934, LHP, box 1, FDRL.

Chapter 57

"Oh! Lord, I'm getting to feel more like a
goldfish": ER to LAH, March 31, 1934, LHP,
box 1, FDRL.

"I've been very much 'Mrs. R.' all day!": ER to
LAH, April 6, 1934, LHP, box 1, FDRL.

"I love Mrs. Roosevelt dearly": Lorena A. Hickok
to Kathryn Godwin, February 18, 1934, Doris
Faber Papers, box 3, FDRL.

"would like a little privacy now & then": ER to
LAH, November 18, 1933, LHP, box 1,
FDRL.

"I'm glad you don't mind being Mrs. Doaks'":
ER to LAH, April 1, 1934, LHP, box 1, FDRL.

"Poor dear, I am so sorry I pursue you" and
"Ever so much love & think of me only as
Mrs. Doaks!": ER to LAH, April 5, 1934, LHP,
box 1, FDRL.

"I'd have died happy": LAH to ER, January 19,
1939, LHP, box 6, FDRL.

"Incidentally, sir": Lorena A. Hickok to Harry L.
Hopkins, May 4, 1934, LHP, box 11, FDRL.

"tizzy-whiz": Lorena Hickok to Bess Furman,
undated, Bess Furman Papers, box 27, Library
of Congress.

"Hick darling, I've just talked to you": ER to LAH,
April 29, 1934, LHP, box 1, FDRL.

"Oh! dear one I love you": ER to LAH, April 30,
1934, LHP, box 1, FDRL.

"Damn it, it's the same old story": Lorena A.
Hickok to Harry L. Hopkins, May 4, 1934, LHP,
box 11, FDRL.

"A stranded generation": LAH to ER, April 20,
1934, LHP, box 1, FDRL.

"Pardon me for getting personal": Lorena A.
Hickok to Harry L. Hopkins, April 25, 1934,
LHP, box 11, FDRL.

"Always in the background" and "With the possible
exception of the one on Puerto Rico": LAH to
ER, June 6, 1934, LHP, box 1, FDRL.

"You, Washington, the apartment in New York":
LAH to ER, July 3, 1934, LHP, box 2, FDRL.

"You cannot get so tired": ER to LAH, June 8,
1934, LHP, box 1, FDRL.

"One thing I'm sure about": ER to LAH, June 9,
1934, LHP, box 1, FDRL.

"I'd like to put my arms around you" and "We
must be careful this summer": ER to LAH,
April 16, 1934, LHP, box 1, FDRL.

Chapter 58

"I then proceeded to do the silliest thing": Hickok,
Reluctant First Lady, 158.

"I used to be a newspaperman myself": Hickok,
Reluctant First Lady, 159.

"This is my vacation": Hickok, Reluctant First Lady,
160.

"with Hick scowling": Lash, Love, Eleanor, 197.

"I know I've got to fit in gradually": ER to LAH,
February 8, 1934, LHP, box 1, FDRL.

"Miss Hickok will require a quiet, gentle horse"
and "How could you do this to me?": Hickok,
Reluctant First Lady, 161.

"Hick, your damned horse is asleep!": Hickok, *Reluctant First Lady*, 164.

Chapter 59

"more or less panted": Roosevelt, *This I Remember*, 142.

"We were never alone at all": Lorena A. Hickok interview, Robert Graff Papers, box 3, FDRL.

"I felt almost prayerful" through "And I said so, right out loud": Hickok, *Reluctant First Lady*, 170.

"blunt and peppery" through "I've been reading your reports": Hickok, *Reluctant First Lady*, 169.

Chapter 60

"a puzzled expression" through "I didn't tell anyone": Hickok, *Reluctant First Lady*, 172.

"No interviews": "Mrs. Roosevelt on Way to Portland," *New Castle News*, July 30, 1934.

"Really, I couldn't pose for any pictures" through "You won't mind if I don't talk to you": "First Lady Fails to Dodge Crowds," *Roanoke Times*, July 30, 1934.

"the plump, ruddy, and hatless Lorena Hickok" through "Please, please": Carolyn Anspaucher, "First Lady Tries in Vain for Privacy," *San Francisco Chronicle*, July 31, 1934.

"a pretty dreadful time": Lorena A. Hickok interview, Robert Graff Papers, box 3, FDRL.

"I was apt not to behave well" and "Franklin said I'd never get away with it": Hickok, *Reluctant First Lady*, 176.

"I hope you are having a happy, restful time": LAH to ER, August 15, 1934, LHP, box 2, FDRL.

Chapter 61

"for it is just a passing mood with me": ER to LAH, April 19, 1934, LHP, box 1, FDRL.

"Oh, I know you all think this is temperamental": LAH to ER, October 16, 1935, LHP, box 2, FDRL.

"I've been ready to chew everyone's head off!": ER to LAH, April 28, 1935, LHP, box 2, FDRL.

"I'm sorry I worried you so much": ER to LAH, May 2, 1935, LHP, box 2, FDRL.

"One thing I differ with you on": ER to LAH, May 7, 1935, LHP, box 2, FDRL.

"Over the years the type of love felt": ER to LAH, May 13, 1935, LHP, box 2, FDRL.

"I feel a good deal as though I were shouting into space": LAH to ER, September 26, 1935, LHP, box 2, FDRL.

"We ain't got nothin' to feed her" through "We may have the best intentions in the world": LAH to ER, October 19, 1935, LHP, box 2, FDRL.

"Lady, I can't push 'em": Lorena A. Hickok interview, Robert Graff Papers, box 3, FDRL.

"plodding along": LAH to ER, December 10, 1935, LHP, box 2, FDRL.

"I had had a big hot breakfast": Lorena A. Hickok interview, Robert Graff Papers, box 3, FDRL.

"Aw, hell, let's send some food out there": LAH to ER, December 10, 1935, LHP, box 2, FDRL.

"a wisp of a thing" through "to do something about Christmas for the old lady": LAH to ER, December 12, 1935, LHP, box 2, FDRL.

Chapter 62

"I have lived so much of my life": ER to LAH, January 26, 1935, LHP, box 2, FDRL.

"Darling, I wish I could give you emotional security": ER to LAH, April 29, 1935, LHP, box 2, FDRL.

"You will please not call my dear child names": Alicent Holt to Lorena A. Hickok, March 18, 1936, LHP, box 15, FDRL.

"When your letter was late this week": Alicent Holt to Lorena A. Hickok, February 25, 1936, LHP, box 15, FDRL.

"People naturally tell you their troubles, dear": Alicent Holt to Lorena A. Hickok, March 22, 1936, LHP, box 15, FDRL.

"If you were here": Alicent Holt to Lorena A. Hickok, April 27, 1936, LHP, box 15, FDRL.

"Dear, I'm so sorry about my tactless and selfish questions" through "Indeed I *do* need you": Alicent Holt to Lorena A. Hickok, March 18, 1936, LHP, box 15, FDRL.

Chapter 63

"If you steal a day or two away": ER to LAH, January 26, 1935, LHP, box 2, FDRL.

"I'm afraid you & I are always going to have times": ER to LAH, August 11, 1934, LHP, box 2, FDRL.

"Someday": ER to LAH, February 4, 1934, LHP, box 1, FDRL.

"lead a leisurely life": ER to LAH, April 9, 1934, LHP, box 1, FDRL.

"That's a tall order": ER to LAH, February 8, 1934, LHP, box 1, FDRL.

"I've thought of you so much": ER to LAH, April 18, 1934, LHP, box 1, FDRL.

"Oh, I know that, so far as your personal life is concerned" and "I'm holding on tight": LAH to ER, July 26, 1936, LHP, box 3, FDRL.

"I feel, as usual, completely objective": ER to LAH, July 27, 1936, LHP, box 3, FDRL.

"I'm wondering if you or I" through "a terrible calamity for millions of people in this country": LAH to ER, July 31, 1936, LHP, box 3, FDRL.

"I'm afraid my reasons" and "I truly don't think that what I do or say": ER to LAH, August 9, 1936, LHP, box 3, FDRL.

"I don't believe a soul": LAH to ER, July 31, 1936, LHP, box 3, FDRL.

Chapter 64

"And yet—as I'm about to give it up": LAH to ER, July 18, 1936, LHP, box 3, FDRL.

"I wonder if that Spanish business": LAH to ER, July 31, 1936, LHP, box 3, FDRL.

"would be the best history of the depression in future years": ER to LAH, September 1, 1934, LHP, box 2, FDRL.

"the color stuff": LAH to ER, November 20, 1936, LHP, box 3, FDRL.

"Most of them are *awful!*" through "I'll try not to gag": LAH to ER, November 19, 1936, LHP, box 3, FDRL.

"Dear, whatever may have happened since" and "You have been swell to me": LAH to ER, December 6, 1936, LHP, box 3, FDRL.

"in publicity or in some sort of 'contact' job" and "sell the fair": Lorena A. Hickok to Grover Whelan, November 11, 1936, LHP, box 17, FDRL.

"a kind of a survey of the whole organization": LAH to ER, January 4, 1937, LHP, box 4, FDRL.

"absolutely unfit" and "trying to control my impatience": LAH to ER, July 16, 1937, LHP, box 4, FDRL.

"I want to be interested in my job": LAH to ER, December 28, 1937, LHP, box 5, FDRL.

"ingrained newspaper habits" through "You know this as well as I": Thomas J. Dillon to Lorena A. Hickok, February 2, 1937, LHP, box 13, FDRL.

"It's the whispering that goes on about me": LAH to ER, January 6, 1938, LHP, box 5, FDRL.

"I doubt if the whisperings": ER to LAH, January 8, 1938, LHP, box 5, FDRL.

"No matter what you do": Roosevelt, *This Is My Story,* 115.

"perfectly joyous": LAH to ER, March 2, 1937, LHP, box 4, FDRL.

"Hicky's Hole": LAH to ER, January 23, 1937, LHP, box 4, FDRL.

"so sunburned that I looked like a half-skinned tomato": Lorena A. Hickok to Helen Gahagan Douglas, April 13, 1963, Helen Gahagan

Douglas Collection, box 180, folder 19, University of Oklahoma.

"This place has the most marvelous effect on me": LAH to ER, May 15, 1937, LHP, box 4, FDRL.

"Poor Prinz": LAH to ER, November 21, 1938, LHP, box 6, FDRL.

"You get so fond of things you plant": LAH to ER, May 5, 1945, LHP, box 9, FDRL.

Chapter 65

"I get so God damned tired": LAH to ER, January 14, 1938, LHP, box 5, FDRL.

"I'm all dried up inside, I guess": LAH to ER, August 27, 1937, LHP, box 4, FDRL.

"When you are together you can never forget" and "half-time": LAH to ER, January 22, 1937, LHP, box 4, FDRL.

"I'm glad we had a chance to talk": LAH to ER, September 8, 1937, LHP, box 4, FDRL.

"I didn't realize you felt we were drifting apart" and "no use in you coming here to be miserable": ER to LAH, September 9, 1937, LHP, box 4, FDRL.

"How you can even like me is beyond me": LAH to ER, November 11, 1936, LHP, box 3, FDRL.

"Perhaps I was right": LAH to ER, September 8, 1937, LHP, box 4, FDRL.

"It isn't worth the bother": LAH to ER, January 7, 1938, LHP, box 5, FDRL.

"This bores me to extinction": LAH to ER, April 15, 1938, LHP, box 5, FDRL.

Chapter 66

"God's gift to newspaper women": Black, *Eleanor Roosevelt,* 157.

"Those who read it and like it": Black, *Eleanor Roosevelt,* 114–115.

"I think I'm prouder of 'This Is My Story'" and "a hellish state of mind": LAH to ER, January 18, 1938, LHP, box 5, FDRL.

"to give as truthful a picture as possible": Roosevelt, *This Is My Story,* 357.

"Somehow it brings back and very near" through "As I look back over these last five years": LAH to ER, January 18, 1938, LHP, box 5, FDRL.

"Of course dear, I never meant to hurt you" and "Such cruelty & stupidity is unpardonable": ER to LAH, January 19, 1938, LHP, box 5, FDRL.

Chapter 67

"I'll be awfully glad to see you": LAH to ER, July 25, 1938, LHP, box 5, FDRL.

"inept fingers": Eleanor Roosevelt, My Day,

August 4, 1938, erpapers.columbian.gwu.edu/
browse-my-day-columns.

"This is a beautiful place": Eleanor Roosevelt, My
Day, August 1, 1938, erpapers.columbian.gwu
.edu/browse-my-day-columns.

"They are dark and mysterious at dusk": Eleanor
Roosevelt, My Day, August 3, 1938, erpapers
.columbian.gwu.edu/browse-my-day-columns.

"We hear only the drowsy insects" and "vegetate":
Eleanor Roosevelt, My Day, August 4, 1938,
erpapers.columbian.gwu.edu/browse-my-day
-columns.

"a grand week" and "The chief thing however":
ER to LAH, August 5, 1938, LHP, box 5,
FDRL.

"Long Island Express": pbs.org/wgbh/
americanexperience/features/hurricane-path.

"I can hardly describe to you my sensations"
through "The beauty of the place is just about
ruined": LAH to ER, September 26, 1938, LHP,
box 5, FDRL.

"Now of course it would be perfectly reasonable"
through "I'll wiggle through somehow": LAH
to ER, January 19, 1939, LHP, box 6, FDRL.

Chapter 68

"was a nightmare for me": LAH to ER, May 1,
1939, LHP, box 6, FDRL.

"the most disorganized mess I ever saw" and "This
job is getting to be simply impossible": LAH to
ER, May 4, 1939, LHP, box 6, FDRL.

"gobbled up": LAH to ER, March 16, 1939, LHP,
box 6, FDRL.

"I don't know—somehow, when I feel so low":
LAH to ER, May 26, 1939, LHP, box 6, FDRL.

"You know, of course, that I'm so thankful": ER to
LAH, May 23, 1939, LHP, box 6, FDRL.

"As for me—the only reason in God's world": LAH
to ER, April 26, 1939, LHP, box 6, FDRL.

"Most of the time Hick looks like a royal Bengal
tiger": LAH to ER, May 24, 1937, LHP, box 4,
FDRL.

Chapter 69

"I don't worry particularly about holding a job":
LAH to ER, November 14, 1939, LHP, box 7,
FDRL.

"You never do anything except" and "It was bad
because it brought": LAH to ER, December 31,
1939, LHP, box 7, FDRL.

"those huge, God-awful affairs": LAH to ER,
March 5, 1944, LHP, box 9, FDRL.

"But, oh, Lord, how does one": LAH to ER,
December 31, 1939, LHP, box 7, FDRL.

"I was so bitterly unhappy": LAH to ER, March 2,
1940, LHP, box 7, FDRL.

"It's a strenuous job alright": LAH to ER, March 8,
1940, LHP, box 7, FDRL.

"I'd like to very much": LAH to ER, January 29,
1940, LHP, box 7, FDRL.

"I roared over your letter": ER to LAH, January 31,
1940, LHP, box 7, FDRL.

"Whoever can convince the women": LAH to ER,
February 26, 1940, LHP, box 7, FDRL.

"The President is going to be under": LAH to
ER, March 2, 1940, LHP, box 7, FDRL.

"Darling, I'm sorry, but it's all Third-Term": LAH
to ER, March 8, 1940, LHP, box 7, FDRL.

"I groan": ER to LAH, February 11, 1940, LHP,
box 7, FDRL.

"And so how do you feel" and "I hope, dear, that
you won't mind": LAH to ER, November 7,
1940, LHP, box 8, FDRL.

"No, I don't look forward": ER to LAH,
November 8, 1940, LHP, box 8, FDRL.

"I don't know anyone in the world" through "I still
prefer the person": LAH to ER, November 11,
1940, LHP, box 8, FDRL.

Chapter 70

"[Molly] worries as to whether": ER to LAH,
November 15, 1940, LHP, box 8, FDRL.

"I honestly don't think you and Molly" through
"front woman to make most": LAH to ER,
November 16, 1940, LHP, box 8, FDRL.

"Oh, damn it—what have I ever done": LAH to
ER, December 27, 1940, LHP, box 8, FDRL.

"Democratic 'WIMMIN'": Nancy Elliott to Doris
Faber, January 29, 1979, Doris Faber Papers,
box 1, FDRL.

"the usual quarrels and jealousies": LAH to ER,
March 9, 1943, LHP, box 8, FDRL.

"I love the way all these women": LAH to ER,
May 4, 1941, LHP, box 8, FDRL.

"would get a big kick out of being invited": Lorena
A. Hickok memo to Mr. Mathews, December 1,
1941, Women's Division of the Democratic
National Committee Papers, 1933–1944,
box 115, FDRL.

"The trouble is that, when I sit in": LAH to ER,
April 26, 1941, LHP, box 8, FDRL.

"I doubt if anyone ever lived at the White House":
Lorena A. Hickok, unpublished autobiography,
ch. 13, p. 1, LHP, box 14, FDRL.

"In residence today? Or just a visitor?" and "Why,
how nice to see you!": Lorena A. Hickok,
unpublished autobiography, ch. 13, p. 4, LHP,
box 14, FDRL.

"Poor old fellow": LAH to ER, May 19, 1941, LHP, box 8, FDRL.

Chapter 71

"Turn on your radio!" and "I never saw a place change": Lorena A. Hickok, unpublished autobiography, ch. 13, p. 18, LHP, box 14, FDRL.

"In the early days when the President laughed": Lorena A. Hickok, unpublished autobiography, ch. 13, p. 6, LHP, box 14, FDRL.

"I could be the one person": Lorena A. Hickok, unpublished autobiography, ch. 13, pp. 7–8, LHP, box 14, FDRL.

"Franklin says he never knows": Lorena A. Hickok, unpublished autobiography, ch. 13, p. 8, LHP, box 14, FDRL.

"Mrs. Roosevelt would like you" through "I stared at her for a second": Lorena A. Hickok, unpublished autobiography, ch. 13, p. 9, LHP, box 14, FDRL.

"They told me in the usher's office" through "Darling, I hope you are comfortable": LAH to ER, October 22, 1942, LHP, box 8, FDRL.

"I'm awfully happy about it": LAH to ER, October 26, 1942, LHP, box 8, FDRL.

"I hope you will get a lot": LAH to ER, April 17, 1943, LHP, box 8, FDRL.

"I didn't take the trip for pleasure" and "My love to you dear": ER to LAH, September 12, 1943, LHP, box 9, FDRL.

"I talked to her": LAH to ER, September 24, 1943, LHP, box 9, FDRL.

Chapter 72

"hold[ing] the party together" through "And if our system is to survive": LAH to ER, October 30, 1942, LHP, box 8, FDRL.

"Fighting Mary": "Mrs. Norton Ends 26 Years in House," New York Times, January 2, 1951.

"I love her, too": LAH to ER, November 20, 1944, LHP, box 9, FDRL.

"Girls Assert Right to Yell Just Like Boys": "U.C. Women Conduct Campaign Without Men's Aid," San Francisco Chronicle, January 29, 1922.

"Dearest Madame Queene": Marion Harron to Lorena A. Hickok, November 22, 1943, LHP, box 13, FDRL.

"Hello my little Piccallilli": Marion Harron to Lorena A. Hickok, January 31, 1944, LHP, box 13, FDRL.

"You don't have a faint notion" through "more for others than for yourself": Marion Harron to Lorena A. Hickok, March 22, 1942, LHP, box 13, FDRL.

"My name is Butch": Marion Harron to Lorena A. Hickok, January 5, 1944, LHP, box 13, FDRL.

"an acre of peace": Marion Harron to Lorena A. Hickok, November 23, 1942, LHP, box 13, FDRL.

"You see, a day will come": Marion Harron to Lorena A. Hickok, August 30, 1944, LHP, box 13, FDRL.

"I thought often while I was there": Marion Harron to Lorena A. Hickok, January 5, 1944, LHP, box 13, FDRL.

"You ask—Do you make me happy?": Marion Harron to Lorena A. Hickok, November 14, 1944, LHP, box 14, FDRL.

"I don't care how much fussing": Marion Harron to Lorena A. Hickok, November 16, 1944, LHP, box 14, FDRL.

"All my love": Marion Harron to Lorena A. Hickok, October 5, 1944, LHP, box 14, FDRL.

"a place he loved above all others" through "Of course I knew it had to happen": LAH to ER, July 3, 1943, LHP, box 9, FDRL.

Chapter 73

"For your sake and his": LAH to ER, July 12, 1944, LHP, box 9, FDRL.

"the meanest campaign since 1928" and "Well—are you glad the darned old campaign": LAH to ER, November 10, 1944, LHP, box 9, FDRL.

"Six months, anyway": LAH to ER, September 14, 1944, LHP, box 9, FDRL.

"It isn't good for people to know": LAH to ER, November 20, 1944, LHP, box 9, FDRL.

"Were you ever right!" through "Darling—thanks for making me go to the doctor": LAH to ER, December 23, 1944, LHP, box 9, FDRL.

"The goodbyes have all been said": LAH to ER, March 21, 1945, LHP, box 9, FDRL.

"bewilderment and terror" and "I'll never forget his warm, fierce handclasp": LAH to ER, April 13, 1945, LHP, box 9, FDRL.

"Hick, I don't want you to come": Lorena A. Hickok to Molly Dewson, May 3, 1945, LHP, box 13, FDRL.

"I was terribly proud of her confidence in me": Lorena A. Hickok to Helen Gahagan Douglas, April 22, 1945, Helen Gahagan Douglas Collection, box 180, folder 18, University of Oklahoma.

"And from then on" and "For you and your future": LAH to ER, April 13, 1945, LHP, box 9, FDRL.

"It's one of the very few little things" and "It's 5 o'clock": LAH to ER, April 14, 1945, LHP, box 9, FDRL.

"too weary to do more than say I love you": ER to LAH, April 16, 1945, LHP, box 9, FDRL.

Chapter 74

"the foundation of freedom": Universal Declaration of Human Rights preamble, un .org/en/about-us/universal-declaration-of -human-rights.

"You must take as long as necessary": Mary Norton to Lorena A. Hickok, June 9, 1945, LHP, box 16, FDRL.

"if we ever get around to writing Mrs. R.'s biography": Lorena A. Hickok to Jeannette Brice, February 19, 1949, Doris Faber Papers, box 5, FDRL.

"Mrs. R. and I are co-authoring a book": Lorena A. Hickok to Helen Gahagan Douglas, September 24, 1952, Helen Gahagan Douglas Collection, box 180, folder 18, University of Oklahoma.

"I can't do it alone": ER to LAH, July 26, 1952, LHP, box 9, FDRL.

"It's fun": Lorena A. Hickok to Helen Gahagan Douglas, September 24, 1952, Helen Gahagan Douglas Collection, box 180, folder 18, University of Oklahoma.

"It's simply swell": ER to LAH, August 19, 1953, LHP, box 9, FDRL.

Chapter 75

"the usual mob": Lorena A. Hickok to Bess Furman, November 5, 1961, Bess Furman Papers, box 27, Library of Congress.

"Darling!": Faber, The Life of Lorena Hickok, 317.

"I have a special distaste for rich, arrogant old women": Lorena A. Hickok to Malvyn Douglas, July 26, 1966, Helen Gahagan Douglas Collection, box 180, folder 19, University of Oklahoma.

"a massive presence": Quinn, Eleanor and Hick, 341.

"No politics": Lorena A. Hickok to Helen Gahagan Douglas, September 21, 1957, Helen Gahagan Douglas Collection, box 180, folder 18, University of Oklahoma.

"the two bravest people I ever knew": Hickok, The Story of Franklin D. Roosevelt, v.

"very glad that this short book": Hickok, The Story of Franklin D. Roosevelt, vii.

"In my innocence I didn't think" through "I'm enjoying the writing of this book": Lorena A. Hickok to Helen Gahagan Douglas,

September 21, 1957, Helen Gahagan Douglas Collection, box 180, folder 18, University of Oklahoma.

"a hit, as much as juveniles ever are": Lorena A. Hickok to Jeannette Brice, July 25, 1960, Doris Faber Papers, box 5, FDRL.

"My books, bless 'em": Lorena A. Hickok to Jeannette Brice, April 3, 1963, Doris Faber Papers, box 5, FDRL.

Chapter 76

"She WAS a 'character'": Edith M. Dahowski to Doris Faber, March 8, 1980, Doris Faber Papers, box 1, FDRL.

"No author ever finished a book": Hickok, The Touch of Magic, vi.

"the way the ghouls are gathering round" and "Mrs. R. will be 73 next month": Lorena A. Hickok to Helen Gahagan Douglas, September 21, 1957, Helen Gahagan Douglas Collection, box 180, folder 18, University of Oklahoma.

"transition from a private individual to First Lady of the land": Hickok, Reluctant First Lady, flap copy.

"Of one thing I'm sure": Lorena A. Hickok to Helen Gahagan Douglas, May 14, 1962, Helen Gahagan Douglas Collection, box 180, folder 19, University of Oklahoma.

"The story in this book is a very personal one": Hickok, Reluctant First Lady, vii.

"never got off the ground in sales" and "I was horrified when I read it in print": Lorena A. Hickok to Anna Roosevelt Halsted, January 27, 1968, Anna Roosevelt Halsted Papers, box 30, FDRL.

Chapter 77

"How she garnered her strength": Gurewitsch, Kindred Souls, 274.

"I know how you hate to talk about being ill" through "little chatty, cheerful notes": Lorena A. Hickok to Esther Lape, November 21, 1962, Esther Lape Papers, box 1, FDRL.

"When you are feeling a little stronger": LAH to ER, September 25, 1962, Eleanor Roosevelt Papers, box 1820, FDRL.

"I loves yer very much, Missis Roosevelt!": LAH to ER, September 28, 1962, Eleanor Roosevelt Papers, box 1820, FDRL.

"I'm still horribly weak": Lorena A. Hickok to Anna Roosevelt Halsted, October 6, 1963, Anna Roosevelt Halsted Papers, box 30, FDRL.

"no use" and "I think you will know what that

means": Lorena A. Hickok to Esther Lape, November 21, 1962, Esther Lape Papers, box 1, FDRL.

"slipping away": Anna Eleanor Seagraves to Lorena A. Hickok, October 18, 1962, LHP, box 17, FDRL.

"All that show and fuss": Lorena A. Hickok to Esther Lape, November 21, 1962, Esther Lape Papers, box 1, FDRL.

"cruel to those who really love you & miss you" and "an obligation fulfilled": ER to LAH, December 19, 1935, LHP, box 2, FDRL.

"Anyway, I shall be nowhere around" through "Through it all": Lorena A. Hickok to Esther Lape, November 21, 1962, Esther Lape Papers, box 1, FDRL.

"spooky": Gordon Kidd interview with Doris Faber, Doris Faber Papers, box 9, FDRL.

Chapter 78

"Mrs. R. should have many more years": Lorena A. Hickok to Helen Gahagan Douglas, April 22, 1945, Helen Gahagan Douglas Collection, box 180, folder 18, University of Oklahoma.

"If you go before I do, my dear": Lorena A. Hickok to Esther Lape, November 21, 1962, Esther Lape Papers, box 1, FDRL.

"After your Mother left": Lorena A. Hickok to Anna Roosevelt Halsted, May 13, 1965, Anna Roosevelt Halsted Papers, box 30, FDRL.

"I never resented any of her friends": Lorena A. Hickok to Esther Lape, November 21, 1962, Esther Lape Papers, box 1, FDRL.

"She was outspoken, all right": Gordon Kidd interview with Doris Faber, Doris Faber Papers, box 9, FDRL.

"I can't help feeling terribly self-conscious": Lorena A. Hickok to Helen Gahagan Douglas, January 4, 1963, Helen Gahagan Douglas Collection, box 180, folder 19, University of Oklahoma.

"There was something very healing" and "The church was empty": Lorena A. Hickok to Helen Gahagan Douglas, November 18, 1963, Helen Gahagan Douglas Collection, box 180, folder 19, University of Oklahoma.

"It's the difference between the Chandor portrait": Lorena A. Hickok to Anna Roosevelt Halsted, June 9, 1966, Anna Roosevelt Halsted Papers, box 30, FDRL.

"a nice, shaggy wreath of the greens": Lorena A. Hickok to Anna Roosevelt Halsted, December 15, 1964, Anna Roosevelt Halsted Papers, box 30, FDRL.

"I made up my mind" and "Maybe there really is a God": Lorena A. Hickok to Helen Gahagan Douglas, December 27, 1961, Helen Gahagan Douglas Collection, box 180, folder 18, University of Oklahoma (dated 1945 in UO files).

"I'm inclined to be shy and ill-at-ease with little girls": Lorena A. Hickok to Anna Roosevelt Halsted, April 15, 1964, Anna Roosevelt Halsted Papers, box 30, FDRL.

"And do I love it?": Lorena A. Hickok to Helen Gahagan Douglas, December 27, 1961, Helen Gahagan Douglas Collection, box 180, folder 18, University of Oklahoma (dated 1945 in UO files).

"I love them of course": Lorena A. Hickok to Helen Gahagan Douglas, December 5, 1962, Helen Gahagan Douglas Collection, box 180, folder 19, University of Oklahoma.

"My life right now is pretty dull": Lorena A. Hickok to Anna Roosevelt Halsted, May 1, 1964, Anna Roosevelt Halsted Papers, box 30, FDRL.

"the long black evenings" and "great gulps": Lorena A. Hickok to Elizabeth Drewry, November 15, 1967, Doris Faber Papers, box 5, FDRL.

"I'll probably live for years and years": Lorena A. Hickok to Helen Gahagan Douglas, November 24, 1964, Helen Gahagan Douglas Collection, box 180, folder 19, University of Oklahoma.

"I hope there is no purgatory": LAH to ER, January 24, 1938, LHP, box 5, FDRL.

"disposed of as soon as possible" through "Although": "MEMORANDUM—(to be attached to Last Will and Testament of Lorena A. Hickok)," Henry T. and John Hackett Papers, box 54, FDRL.

Chapter 79

"stickler for clarity": LAH to ER, January 27, 1939, LHP, box 6, FDRL.

"a very great respect for the libel laws": LAH to ER, July 15, 1939, LHP, box 7, FDRL.

"because [your mother] thought I should": Lorena A. Hickok to Anna Roosevelt Halsted, June 9, 1966, Anna Roosevelt Halsted Papers, box 30, FDRL.

"I know that those letters were intended for my eyes only": Lorena A. Hickok to Anna Roosevelt Halsted, October 6, 1963, Anna Roosevelt Halsted Papers, box 30, FDRL.

"Your mother wasn't always so very discreet": Lorena A. Hickok to Anna Roosevelt Halsted,

June 9, 1966, Anna Roosevelt Halsted Papers, box 30, FDRL.

"The people at the Library are going to have conniptions" through "Esther will burn them": Lorena A. Hickok to Anna Roosevelt Halsted, October 6, 1963, Anna Roosevelt Halsted Papers, box 30, FDRL.

"I'll be damned": Lorena A. Hickok to Anna Roosevelt Halsted, June 9, 1966, Anna Roosevelt Halsted Papers, box 30, FDRL.

Chapter 80

"Probably about an hour later": Faber, *The Life of Lorena Hickok*, 330.

"the conniptions" and "fraught with an electrifying emotional impact": Doris Faber, rough draft of "The Life of Lorena Hickok," p. 2, Doris Faber Papers, box 7, FDRL.

"'Bury them!' I decreed": Doris Faber, rough draft of "The Life of Lorena Hickok," p. 5, Doris Faber Papers, box 7, FDRL.

"Eleanor Roosevelt was a great woman" and "could not believe that there were valid grounds": Faber, *The Life of Lorena Hickok*, 331.

"It's going to come out" and "very mixed emotions": Faber, *The Life of Lorena Hickok*, 332.

"I have chosen not to speculate": Faber, *The Life of Lorena Hickok*, 6.

"urged that my mother's letters be read": Lash, *Love, Eleanor*, vii.

"Just the thought of being forgotten" and "so we brought the tree to her": "Linda Boyd Kavars and Lorena Hickok," *The Hudson River Valley Review*, vol. 26, no. 1, Autumn 2009, 85.

INDEX